Thy Will

O Lord

3RD EDITION

My Imperfections & the Grace of God Revealed

Publisher's Name: Rabiu Elijah Omolaja

Email address: thywillolord2000@yahoo.com

Contact #: (214) 641-4577

ISBN: 978-1-962142-53-3

2 Books in 1

Kirkus Indie Review

A devoutly Christian Nigerian man's memoir of immigrating to the United States.

Omolaja's work covers the story of his life in two distinct sections, beginning with his birth in Ibadan, Nigeria... The author spent his early adulthood in the early 1970s, after a stint in the army, moving to different cities looking for work and usually finding it as a driver for wealthier residents, whom he came to see as "educated fools" for their materialist obsessions. Omolaja was raised as a Muslim but had a sudden revelation at the age of 21, when, he says, a disembodied voice whispered in his ear, saying, "Jesus is the Son of God, He is the Lord and the Savior of the world." His family members had him committed to a mental health institution, he says, but he remained determined to witness for Jesus. His spiritual path eventually led him to Selma University, a historically black Baptist Bible college in Alabama. However, Omolaja later experienced financial hardship as he moved around the American South, attempting to fulfill his calling to minister to the mentally ill and others struggling in society. The book's second half provides readers with chapters on a range of topics, including practical issues for Christians, such as the importance of water baptisms, and wider theological debates about prophecies, angels, and the might of God. Omolaja accompanies his thoughts on these subjects with ample biblical references and "Spiritual Exercises" in the style of a daily devotional... The book's autobiographical portion offers plenty of engaging and positive ideas, especially when dealing with the author's difficulty adapting to American life and his unflappably good intentions toward everyone he met. At the same time, readers may find some of his accounts of spiritual encounters difficult to believe...

- Kirkus Indie

Online Book Club Review

In his book, Thy Will O Lord, author Rabiu Elijah Omolaja details his conversion experience from the Muslim religion to Christianity. Part One consists of eleven chapters covering his life experiences, starting with his birth in Nigeria to eventually living in America. Not only did he spiritually struggle with a brand-new faith, but he also was introduced to a significant culture shock once in the United States as a college student. He doesn't hold back when explaining some of his downfalls, including divorces, but the message of God's love prevails. Answered prayers and open doors that led him to success are his testimony to attuning his hearing to heaven's voice. From out of his troubles, a ministry was born to serve the hurting and the afflicted in his community.

The second part, chapters twelve through twenty-two, is an in-depth look into the Bible with detailed questions and answers that revolve around scripture. It involves instruction regarding the basic principles of the Christian life, including topics such as baptism and speaking in tongues. Often, believers can get so wrapped up in spiritual things that they neglect the fact that one must attend to the natural side of life as well. It was nice to read his explanations on how to deal with both parts of ourselves. For example, he emphasizes the importance of being thankful for everything in one's life, and at the same, he offers advice on how to improve the immune system to keep it running at top speed. His blend of the two made the material feel authentic and applicable.

What I liked most about this was the author's honesty. He does not pretend to be perfect, but rather, he makes himself highly relatable to his audience by exposing his faults.

Through this sharing of past mistakes, he exemplifies the divine grace that is extended to cover our less than attractive choices that often land us into undesirable predicaments. His story depicts the redeeming love that is available to all.

- Onlinebookclub.org

The Moving Words Review

The book serves as a spiritual memoir, chronicling Omolaja's personal experiences, revelations, and struggles. At its core, "Thy Will O Lord" is an earnest quest for understanding one's place in the grand scheme of life and the universe, and reconciling that with the belief in an omnipotent, benevolent Creator. It is framed as a series of reflections and contemplations, each intended to shed light on different aspects of spirituality. While maintaining a respectful distance from divulging the specifics that could act as spoilers, it's safe to say that the narrative provides a roadmap for anyone interested in embarking on a similar spiritual quest.

Omolaja's writing is cerebral and inviting, encouraging the reader to not just skim the surface but to delve deep into the philosophical and theological aspects of spirituality. He raises questions that resonate universally, regardless of religious affiliation. One of the standout features of the book is its raw, unfiltered honesty. The author is not afraid to disclose his own imperfections, making the reader feel less alone in their spiritual struggles.

The book is well-written, with a clear structure and flow that makes it easy to follow yet challenging enough to stimulate intellectual and spiritual thought. The language is sophisticated, but not to the point where it becomes inaccessible. While the book clearly comes from a place of deep faith, it does not shy away from addressing the doubts and questions that naturally arise in the human mind. This balance makes it relatable to a broader audience. Although rooted in specific religious beliefs, the concepts explored have a universal quality. They touch on the human condition in a way that is meaningful to people from various backgrounds.

The book has an emotional depth that complements its intellectual rigor. Omolaja's journey is not just a cognitive exercise but a deeply felt experience, which he succeeds in conveying to the reader.

"Thy Will O Lord" is a potent work that manages to be both personal and universal. It is a compelling narrative, packed with insights that challenge and enlighten. For anyone grappling with the larger questions of human existence and the role of a higher power, this book serves as a thought-provoking guide. Its well-crafted prose and balanced viewpoints make it a worthwhile read for those interested in exploring the intricate relationship between human imperfection and divine grace.

The Moving Words Review, themovingwords.com

Dedication

This book is dedicated to all souls.

*I surrender all, I surrender all, Unto thee my blessed Savior
I surrender all.*

Contents

Book 1: MY LIFE STORY

Book 2: The Gospel

Book 1
MY LIFE STORY

Preface

It is a blessing that I have lived through many difficult life challenges and afflictions, survived every one of them, and now able to share my experience in writing to give hope and encouragement to others who may, at one point or the other in their lives, find themselves in similar situations. This book will make you laugh, it will make you cry, and I pray that it will grow your faith in the Lord. It is my true life's journey from my mother's womb to the present.

There are three threads that run through this book: 1) God's involvement in my life even before I was born, 2) my commitment to obey God even though I sometimes make a wrong turn, and 3) my uncompromising attitude to finish what I start even when quitting may seem more logical.

Many thanks to my beloved wife, Felisa Joy Omolaja, who is also my primary editor-in-chief, for recognizing the hands of God in my life and for her commitment to walk this journey with me. I am forever indebted.

Introduction

I t is not easy to admit that there is nothing perfect about any of us but I am not afraid to say that about me. Now 50 years in the Lord, I am still in the making, and He is not done with me, not yet!

If you are looking for a perfect person's story, please drop the book, it is not for you. If you believe however that there is no valley too deep to fill, and no mountain too high for God to level; if you believe that it is not impossible for God to take the foolish things of the world to confound the wise, and the weakest things of the world to shame the strong then, this book is for you. As I am led, so I am doing with this book: telling the story of my life.

There is a popular saying: "Without a test, there would be no testimony." I am a man of many afflictions and have experienced many victories amid the afflictions as well. It is written: "many are the afflictions of the righteous, but the Lord delivers him from them all" (Psalm 34:19). This Scripture has always amazed me. In fact, I preached on it on one Sunday at the One Victory Voice program on KNON Radio. This Scripture verse didn't say that "many are the afflictions of the wicked, the thieves, the whoremongers" but instead, it says "many are the afflictions of the righteous," the righteous. But, why the righteous?

I will be forever grateful for being able to witness God's faithfulness in my life. The more terrible the afflictions, the greater the victories. It is far from me, however, to think of the righteousness spoken of here as mine; no, it isn't. It was bestowed upon me, it was bestowed upon us by His grace, only by Grace and not of works, lest any man should boast (Ephesians 2:8-9). All human righteousness is as filthy rag. Glory and Honor to our God, Jesus exchanged His Righteousness for my unrighteousness on Calvary as He took ownership of my sins and nailed them to the Cross (2Corinthians 5:21). No one can adequately explain the exchange that took place on the Cross. Jesus paid my debt in full, once and for all. I am a debtor to Him who laid down His Life for me.

I am forever indebted to Him who took my place and died for the sins He never committed. He died for my sins. He went to hell for me. Hallelujah, the gates of hell cannot prevail against my Lord, Jesus cannot be detained, nor held in hell. He was too hot for demons, the devil, and hell to handle.

As you will read throughout this book, my imperfections are vividly depicted; they are portrayed in such a way as to expose my humanity and my interactions with the Divine as The Almighty God works His way through my life. Being born again, we are no longer living for ourselves but to do that which is pleasing to God. Jesus spoke of Himself, saying, "I came to do thy will O God." We are on earth to do His will. As followers of Christ, as Christians, we are to live as "a living sacrifice," a pleasant aroma unto God (Romans 12:1-2), not conforming to the ways of the world. We are to travel the narrow way, not the broad way. The narrow way is the way of holiness that leads to Heaven; the broad way is the way of sinners; it leads to hell. In Matthew 7: 13-14, Jesus said this:

"Enter ye in at the strait gate: for wide is the gate, and broad is the way, that leadeth to destruction, and many there be which go in there at: Because strait is the gate, and narrow is the way, which leadeth unto life, and few there be that find it."

As we walk by the Spirit, and not according to the lust of the flesh, we will witness God's purposes becoming a reality in our lives. God's desire is to dwell in us, be with us. God will show through us as we shine as lights in the world filled with darkness.

I have been crucified with Christ; it is no longer I who live, but Christ lives in me; and the life which I now live in the flesh I live by faith in the Son of God, who loved me and gave Himself for me -Galatians 2:20.

You need to know that God needs humans. He needs you; He needs me. God needs each of us more than we can ever imagine, but many of us are UNAVAILABLE. Many of us who are available are UNUSABLE. God needs you. There are some tasks He has designed to perform through you, here on earth, that only you can fulfill. Each of us is unique. Each believer is a unique vessel in God's hand. Each of us was designed to accomplish specific tasks working together to fulfill His Will.

What is baffling is that the last thing many of us want to think about is being used by God. It is like "Who cares?" especially when there are so many other things that are demanding our attention day by day. Well, God cares; but nevertheless, He will not force Himself on us. He can force Himself on us if He wants to, but He seldom does.

Why did the Scripture say that "many are called but few are chosen"? It is because only those few individuals who voluntarily and willingly answered the call, and played by the Constitution of the Kingdom, are chosen. Christians are citizens of Heaven, and the Bible is our Spiritual Constitution. Friends, you owe it to God. You are a debtor. Ask God, what He would have you to do while you are still living. Tomorrow may be too late. "The harvest truly is plenteous, but the laborers are few" - Matthew 9:37.

God needs us but He will not force Himself on us. He will not compromise His principles. If we, human beings, choose not to serve Him, He can raise up stones & rocks to worship Him (Luke 19:40; Matthew 3:9). I pray to God that I will not be replaced with a rock or stone. We have read in the Bible where God chose a donkey to speak in human language. We have read how God used a bird as a Chef in the wilderness to feed the prophet Elijah. With our God there is nothing impossible.

Yes, God needs us as His channels to witness His Son to the wayward and dying world, but He is not exclusively limited to using just us especially if we choose to reject His calling. He is God, and He can use anything He chooses.

Day after day, I have come to realize that God will not physically come down to earth to solve the world's problems; He has chosen us to be His channels through which He will reach the world. Isaiah says "Prepare ye the way (heart/soul/mind) of the Lord" – Isaiah 40:3. Jesus says, "I am the way, the truth, and the Life; no one comes to the Father but through me" -John 14:6. God was working through Jesus Christ &

Jesus Christ is working through us. He has chosen us to be the way by which He will continue to divulge His reconciliation message to the world. Let us not forget that we, human beings, are made of the same blood – Acts 17:26. We are so integral, so interconnected. Our survival depends on one another whether it is regarding our salvation, good health, peace or prosperity. None of us is a mountain unto himself or herself. It is my hope that you will see God's hand upon my life, my commitment to obey, my failures and successes, as you read through this book.

This book is 2 in 1. The first part of the book details the story of my life. The second part of the book is an appeal to the readers urging them to recognize the most important thing in this life. Do not be deceived; there is another life after death. Contrary to how we may think, the most important thing in this life is not our career or financial strength. It is not our good relationships with one another or political influences; it is our relationship with God. Humanity's definition of success is not the same as God's. What shall it profit a man if he shall gain the whole world and lose his soul? What will a man give in exchange for his soul? (Mark 8:36-37). The most important thing in this life is to submit our life to Him (James 4:7), which means to surrender our will to His will. Doing the will of God on planet Earth (Matthew 6:10) is the duty of all men but unfortunately no human being has adequately fulfilled this requirement. Romans 3:23 says that "For all have sinned and fall short of the Glory of God." Prophet Isaiah says, "But we are all as an unclean thing, and all our righteousness are as filthy rags..." (Isaiah 64:6).

Thanks to the Almighty God, what we cannot do for ourselves, God sent His Only Begotten Son to fulfill (John 3:16). Jesus came to die for the sins of the world. He died for your sins. He died for my sins. He went to Hell for us so that we don't have to go there. He is the Savior of the world. Would you accept Him into your life today? There is no other way (John 14:6). No other name under Heaven whereby we must be saved (Act 4:12). I have accepted Him. He is my Lord and Savior. It is the best decision I ever made. It will be the best decision you will ever make. I pray that this book will be a great help in your decision-making process. God loves us, and He doesn't want any of us to go to hell, but He will not force Himself, Jesus, or salvation on us. Each of us must have the desire to be saved.

I hope that you can see throughout the book that human failures can be an opportunity if we will simply surrender to Him, saying "Thy will O Lord. Father God, help me; I want to be usable."

Just a Recommendation

It is recommended that you read both the Preface and the Introduction to this book before you proceed if you haven't done so already. Reading the Preface and the Introduction first will set the stage for clarity as the book takes you through my life journey: from my mother's womb to the day the book makes it to print. I pray that the book will spark hope, inspire some courage, and help you to see God as He truly is, and see yourself as God truly sees you.

Chapter 1
FROM THE WOMB TO AGE 15

In the Womb: Before My Birth

According to my father, there was much family rancor during my conception: brothers fighting against brothers over the inheritances of their wealthy father, my paternal grandfather, who was married to many wives and had many children but left no will. After the death of their father, these children were unable to agree on who should take what or what should belong to whom. In those days the deceased mostly had no "Will." A simple "Will" could have prevented this hopeless family crisis.

There were litigations, after litigations and the family went back and forth, from court to court, hiring the best attorneys in town, and spending all their parents' fortune on legal fees and court costs. In addition to these court battles were senseless constant provocations, including physical fights among the brothers. In December 1952, during one of these fights, my father was held to the ground by some of his half- brothers while the rest of them were beating on him and villagers were spectating. My mother thought that, as a pregnant woman, if she got in the middle, she could break the fight and thereby save her husband. She thought they would be respectful of her pregnancy and stop beating on her husband. Well, she was wrong; she made a wrong calculation. When she got in between the fight, she got hit very hard in the stomach, started to bleed, and was rushed to the hospital. I was the unborn in her stomach. I could have been born dead but thanks to the Lord our God, He protected me; I didn't die. I was born a few weeks later. After hearing the story, I know for sure, and without any doubt that my life is purposeful.

My Birth

I was born in Adeoyo Hospital in Ibadan, in the then Western Region of Nigeria. Born into a family of 3: my father (whose birth name was "Yesufu," a.k.a. Daniel), my mother, Adeniun Ajini Odi, and my older brother: "Latifu" (who is now Lawrence). There were 13 children through our mother but only 6 of us—4 boys and 2 girls—made it through childhood. I am not sure how many children were deceased between me and my older brother, but I am the second oldest child today.

My journey started at Adeoyo Hospital at midnight between December 31st, 1952, and January 1st, 1953, and perhaps I was the first child born into the new year in Adeoyo Hospital that year. My older brother told me recently of the gifts bestowed upon me and my mother the day I was born including a headscarf with American flag prints on it. At delivery, my mother was almost at the point of death, and suffered many complications but I thank God, she made it through. She had me and lived long enough to see me grow into adulthood.

My Parents

My father was fairly educated. Nevertheless, he was a man with ability but deprived of opportunity. My mother was illiterate but a successful businesswoman. Speaking of my father, he was the only child in his family tree who was thought of as having what it takes to be successful on a college level. His parents sent him to college, and he was doing excellently until he was forced to drop out of college. The Bible teaches us that jealousy is a form of witchcraft. My father was envied and hated for his God-given ability.

My father dropped out of college due to the relentless pressure from the rest of the children and their mothers. My father was threatened, as he told me, that the rest of the children said to my father they would kill him and his mother if he thought he was better than the rest of them. "Do you love your mother? The best thing for you is to drop out of school and join the rest of us on the farm. But if you tell anybody about our plan, we will kill you first and then kill your mother (paraphrased)." That was what his half-brothers told him.

Well, the threat was so harsh and so real to my father that he decided to drop out of school. My father had to drop out of school knowing the lawlessness of the time and the determination of his brothers to cause him untimely grief over his mother or lose his own life in the process. He dropped out of school to join his siblings and his half- brothers at the farm.

Though tough on him, he had to tough it out. When the going gets tough, the tough get going. My father was not as successful in farming as his brothers were because farming was not his construct. Nothing he planted grew like those of his brothers. He tried but it seemed like his destiny had been altered by his half-brothers. I watched my father dabble in different occupations, but nothing seemed to work. He became a "self- made local bank" for Longe villagers, going from house to house daily to collect money from participants, any amount the individual wanted to save. He would collect a consented amount every day for 30 days. At the end of the 30 days, he would give the participants their money back minus 5%. The 5% was his portion for helping participants keep their money. He was good at bookkeeping and seemingly honest. My father was a disciplined man. He tried hard to put the pieces of his life together, but to no avail. The more he tried, the more it may have appeared that he failed. But I saw my father as he made a way out of no way and helped others in the process. I have watched my father become a basket maker. Baskets are basic must-have vessels. It is a common basic domestic need for housework and farmers. My father made different styles of baskets and sold them for reasonable prices, hoping to sustain himself financially. However, he found it difficult to make enough money to support the family.

After all of my father's efforts seemed to fall short, he decided to join my mother in her business, and my mother, who at this point, has become the primary breadwinner. That is the family dynamic in which I grew up.

My early memories: as you will discover in this book later, some of my childhood experiences are as clear as day, and some are foggy and elusive, especially after my eccentric experience during my call into the ministry in July of 1974. At the time of my calling which lasted for several days, it seemed many of my childhood experiences disappeared from memory and later resurfaced slowly, but gradually. I couldn't remember the actual date I was born nor the exact year I enrolled in the first grade. I remember throwing my right hand across my head hoping my fingers would touch my ear on the opposite side, the left side. In those days, that was how parents and teachers determined when a child was ready to start the 1st grade. No kindergarten or any other early education existed in my village at the time.

I am not sure of the year I enrolled in school, but I do remember that I completed the 6th grade in 1962. I remember also that I was a little advanced in my classes and was allowed to skip one or two grades during my elementary school years. If I was born on January 1st, 1953, according to my older brother, and graduated from elementary in 1962, that means I only spent 4 years in elementary. Nevertheless, I can only remember skipping one grade but maybe it was two. Around the time of my graduation, my older brother was also graduating from modern school as well. A modern school is a step above 6th-grade and a step below 12th-grade level education. I know I had a long way to go but how to get there was beyond my comprehension. In 1963, I asked my mother if I could go to live with her half-brother, Mr. Adelabu Adegbile who was a teacher at Eniosa village. I am not sure now how to get to Eniosa or if the village still exists. I lived with him for less than a year. It didn't work out, and I was forced to move back to Longe village with my parents.

My Childhood Stubbornness

Growing up, I was considered the most quiet and stubborn child. I was rightly labeled because I said very little and was not easily offended, but when I was offended or unjustly treated, I became noticeably quiet. In my quietness, however, I would still do my chores, follow my parents' directives, and maintain my due respect towards them even if they were the ones responsible for my protest. In my protest, however, I would not eat nor socialize; I stayed aloof until someone decided to reason with me. Not until the offender, whoever they may be, was ready to reason or justify their treatment of me, my protest would continue for as long as possible. Sometimes my form of protest was a hunger strike, and I was seldom able to talk myself out of it. Oftentimes, my mother would not watch me for too long without intervening. She would not allow my feelings to rule over me for too long before she found a way to make peace. She was truly a peacemaker in every way. In most cases, she would reason with me, not conceding, especially if I thought she was the culprit. She was always able to bring a smile out of me and get me to eat.

Today, my behavior would be labeled "manipulative," but I didn't know what that was at the time. I just wanted to be treated fairly. I thought, at the time, that I was an obedient child. I never argued with my parents. So, my thinking was, "If I can't argue with my parents when I feel offended by them, I have the right to remove myself from their presence and be alone."

Age 10 Through Teenage Years: Helping in the Family Business

Since I couldn't enroll in high school after I left Eniosa village in 1963 because of finance, the only option I had left was to learn a trade. To learn a trade, I must have a place to live in the city. I would have loved to live with my older brother who lives in Ibadan and recently graduated from modern school, but he couldn't find a sustainable job and was having difficulties financing himself. So, I decided to move back to the village before the end of 1963. At that time, my mother's business was at its highest. I saw that the harvest was plenty, but the laborers were few. I felt needed in the family business, but at the same time, it seemed also like I had no choice. Where else would I go? Surprisingly, what I thought to do for a year or so lasted for almost 5 years of my life and I did it with joy. I served my parents joyfully. I am so grateful that I did. It was labor-intensive, but I am thankful I was able to pay my parents back a little. They did so much for us. Dare to ask me about my parents, I will say they were the best. I share both of their qualities. I inherited both of my parents' intellectual strengths. I look like my dad, but I got my demeanor, compassion, and emotional strength from my mother. On my father's side, folks are more resilient, confident, and garrulous. On my mother's side, family members are more quiet, patient, and compassionate. Both sides of my family are kind and loving people.

My mother was a businesswoman. She would buy produce items and other commodities from farmers in our village and adjacent villages, then prepare the merchandise and finally transport the merchandise to open markets not far from the village. Throughout the week, we bought fresh produce, including palm oil, from different farmers. My mother's major purchases were palm oil, cocoa, and kola nuts. Then, we prepared these items to sell at an open market. There were many open markets in which we sold our goods. I can remember at least 2 of them even now: Mamu and Ajegunle, both averaging about 15 miles from the village. The buyers in these markets were mostly from the Ijebu and Hausa tribes.

On market day, we would get up as early as 5 am to be ready on time, load the produce on the bus, and head on to the open marketplace where the merchandise would be displayed. The market or consumption demand for certain products determines our loss or profit. Sometimes we sold at a gain, sometimes we simply broke even, and sometimes we sold at a loss. On some occasions, we opted to transport our merchandise to the marketplace the night before the market day and sleep over, hoping to gain an advantage over the rest of the merchants. Doing the sleepover sometimes helped us to be one among the first set of sellers that put merchandise on display and are ready to sell before the market gets crowded. I was a strong part of this routine, among doing some other chores, in serving my parents. I did this for 5 years and, to be exact, from 1963 through 1968 when I decided to move to the city of Ibadan which is around 20 miles from my village, Longe. Ibadan is the most populous city in what was then Western Africa. At 15 years of age, I was ready to navigate the world; I needed to discover myself, away from under the shadow of my parents.

Self Help Exercises

1. Briefly, how would you describe the environment in which you were born?

2. *How important is it to have a written "Will," regardless of whether one is rich, has a living spouse, children, siblings, or not?*

3. *The author, at about 10 years of age, completed his 6th-grade education but couldn't go any further because of his parents'*

financial situation. Can you relate to any of the author's childhood challenges?

Answers

All Personal

Chapter 2
BECOMING A PROFESSIONAL DRIVER AT AGE 16

L iving in Ibadan, within a year I learned professional driving. I obtained my professional driver's license in 1969. I was a professional driver for about 5 years (1969-1974) before my call into the ministry in 1974. During these years, I became acquainted with many rich and foolish individuals, people with material wealth, but who had almost zero consciousness of the true God. Their names may be Jacob, Joseph, Daniel, Isaiah, or any other notable Christian names, but they had no idea of the relevance of their names. They may be members of mainstream churches, but spiritually blind, with little or zero knowledge of the true God.

In my country, if you are wealthy, and have transportation but you don't want to drive yourself, you can hire a driver that may or may not live with you. I was one of those drivers driving these individuals to their destinations of choice. I thank God I didn't have to live with them except one, and it was only for about 3 months. For the most part, I was always able to go home at the end of the day. I remember vividly how I would drive 2 of these master's to their cult meetings during the day & at midnight. I could have been killed, used as a sacrifice in the middle of the night, and no one would have known anything or suspected that one of my masters was the murderer. But God refrained them from hurting me saying, in a way, "touch not mine anointed, and do my prophet no harm." -1 Chronicles 16:22. He has always protected me.

Devil or Idol worshippers have been around since the beginning. It started with Adam and his wife who chose to obey the serpent rather than obey God. We continue to see demonic activities running through the Bible: from the Garden of Eden to the building of the Tower of Babel in Genesis Chapter 11 and throughout the Bible. They may pick different names from one generation to another; it is still the devil working through all of them. Call it the Age of Enlightenment or any other less revealing name; it is the devil appearing as an angel of light (2 Corinthians 11:13-14).

Driving these educated fools, God was giving me a firsthand lesson. I call them educated fools because only the fool has said in his heart there is no God - Psalm 14:1. For people of such intelligence to think of man-made images as God's representatives is foolish.

I drove these individuals to church on Sunday morning and to their secret society meetings on Sunday night. I watched them changing from their suits or Church clothes into their cult worship uniforms, something that looked like rags and they themselves looked like lunatics in the outfit. I saw them gaiting and hopping like frogs in front of a mute stone or a statue. I saw them fall flat on their stomachs, prostrating before these deaf and dumb creatures. I have watched them performing rituals: giving offerings, eating, drinking, and dancing before these deaf and dumb gods. And then on Monday morning and throughout the week, I drove them to work. These men were elders at their churches, and they were all in positions of authority.

At the time, it didn't bother me at all because I, myself, had little concept of whether God exists or not, and, quite frankly, I didn't care. I thought these were educated individuals and they knew what they were doing. Now, looking back, I know I was wrong. I know they were wrong, blind, and foolish. The Bible is very clear on this:

Do not be unequally yoked together with unbelievers. For what fellowship has righteousness with lawlessness. And what communion has light with darkness? And what accord has Christ with Belial? Or what part has a believer with an unbeliever? And what agreement has the temple of God with idols? For you are the temple of the living God. As God has said: I will dwell in them and walk among them. I will be their God, and they shall be My people. Therefore, come out from among them and be separate, says the Lord. Do not touch what is unclean, and I will receive you. I will be a Father to you, and you shall be My sons and daughters, says the LORD Almighty. - 2 Corinthians 6:14- 18.

No one was so blind and so foolish as these men. I saw their objects of worship. Their images have hands that cannot move, eyes that cannot blink nor see, and their legs stuck to the base. At least they should remember that if human beings were created in God's image, He who created us should possess the ability to see, touch, and move around as we are. God is an Intelligent Being. –Psalm 94:9.

During the five years that I was functioning as a hired driver, I decided to join the army and drove in the military for about a year and a half. At the time, I didn't know the spiritual interpretation associated with my job as a driver, nor as a military person, but I would soon find out. Professionally, at the time, the people that I drove around were in total control of where they wanted to go. I drove the individuals to wherever they wanted me to take them. But what God was getting me ready for, later in life, on a spiritual level, was to prepare me to learn how to drive people's hearts toward Him, the Only true God, the Maker of Heaven and Earth. Jesus said that no one can come to the Father but through Him, Jesus Christ our Lord, and the Savior of the world. Jesus bridged the gap between God and humans with His own blood; no other blood will suffice, according to Acts of the Apostles 4:12.

1 Timothy 2: 5 "For there is one God and one mediator between God and mankind, the man Christ Jesus."

Joining the Military at Age 17

I love the military. No one asked me to join the army; I did it of my own accord. I love people in military uniforms, especially in camouflage. I love their uniform and mirror-like shoes. I wanted to be one of them, so I decided to join the army. I was about 17 years of age at the time. I was trained in Abeokuta, now part of Ogun State. After my training, I was sent to a military workshop as my base. My role was to drive the high-ranking officers. During my service there as a driver, I learned a lot of life skills, including self-discipline. Shortly before my 2nd year anniversary, it seemed I was hearing something telling me to quit the army. I tried to ignore the impression but the more I ignored it the stronger it became. It didn't make any sense to me to quit the army. Quitters never win, and winners never quit. I had only been in the army for less than 2 years and, to quit, "now?" "No," I said to the impression; I wanted to fulfill my term in the army.

Another reason why I thought it was insane to quit the army at the time was this: when I joined the army, there was a civil war (also known as the Biafra war) going on. It was at its most brutal stage. Soldiers were dying left and right. I knew that chances were I could go to war and possibly die at war but my heart was made up; I wanted to join. I wanted to serve my country. A few days after I joined the army, the war ended— no more war but—I continued to serve by driving the top-notch military personnel wherever they wanted me to take them. I also had a military jeep that I was able to drive home as permitted. That jeep was a character: I made it spin, jump, and bark like a dog. Anyhow, things were going very well. Many of my friends wanted a ride in the jeep, and so did the ladies. It was at this time that the impression kept coming to me that I should quit the military. I thought that was insane. I thought it was insane because being in the military commanded a lot of respect in my country. I loved the attention I was getting. I was a little corky, a little arrogant in uniform. I loved to be seen in that uniform. I thought smart, felt smart, and powerful, and everyone else I labeled "bloody civilian," whatever that means. The public accolade and respect were too surreal to walk away from. I struggled with the impression to quit the military, but I gave in eventually. How did I do it? I said to myself: "if I ask the military for a voluntary discharge, it wouldn't happen." I have never seen that type of request being honored under any circumstances. So, I started to brainstorm on how to get out.

I Quit the Military

I didn't know how I came to the conclusion, but one day I just simply stopped going to the barracks abruptly without thinking of the consequences. First, I told myself I will just take a couple of days off. Then a couple of days turned into 3 and 4, then 7 days. I stayed at home for over a week. I knew I was in trouble: I had been AWOL for over a week, I knew better. I knew that if I just showed up at the barracks and have no convincing excuse, my head would be shaved, I will be locked up, whipped mercilessly, and perhaps jailed or imprisoned. It didn't look good. And, if I didn't go back voluntarily, they would come and get me, and that is like a death sentence. So, I chose to show my face.

I got to the barracks in the military jeep, no questions asked. They told me to report to the sergeant major. Just as I already knew, I got my head shaved and was locked up for a few days, but there was no whipping. Then a trial date was set, which seemed like forever, but it did arrive eventually.

I had a very pretty girlfriend at the time. She came to the barracks, to see me in the cell where I was. Every soldier wanted a piece of my girl. She never came back. She was very afraid of what they would do to me. I thought I would be court-martialed and get prison time. I cried and cried and cried all the days I was waiting for a trial and hoped it would come sooner and be over with. When the day finally came, however, I wished it had never come. There were two of us. We were transported to a different office where there was a military judge who was assigned to hear our cases. I didn't know the name of the other soldier on trial with me. His case was heard first. He was sentenced to many years in prison. I wept very bitterly murmuring to myself, saying, "No one has ever been in prison in my family. God, please help me; I don't want to be the first one. God, please help me!"

It is my turn now to receive judgment. The officer read my case to the judge. I can't remember if I was asked any questions or if I tried to explain anything, but I knew I was guilty as charged. This military judge then looked at me, with his finger pointed at me and he said, "You know I can send you to prison, right?" I said, "Yes, sir." He then asked, "What do you think will happen to you?" I said, "I don't know, sir." He said, "Take the uniform off of him, and get him out of my office." I honestly thought it was a dream. I didn't tell this judge anything, but he read between the lines. I cried and cried, sweating profusely, and I remember pinching myself as I walked away from the judge's office. I thank God for being so merciful to me.

During her visit when I was locked up in that cell, my girlfriend brought me some civilian clothes to change into if, by chance, I got released. She didn't know the seriousness of my offense because I didn't tell her I was AWOL for almost 2 weeks. The soldiers walked me outside. I changed into my civilian clothes, and I still thought I was dreaming. I continued to pinch myself several times. Honestly, I was very ashamed but, at the same time, I felt relieved leaving the army, and not serving any prison time.

Now, the question is "now what?" The public respect when people see me in uniform was gone. Girls didn't see my jeep anymore. I have no job, no money, only my civilian clothes. I was 19 years old when I left the army.

Back to Civilian Life

When I left the army in the early 1970s, I reverted to driving the wealthy and foolish again, but now in Lagos, the capital of Nigeria at the time. I am no longer a military man, but a civilian. I remember driving one man in particular who received a death sentence by a court, for murdering innocent people and taking their land. This man had no mercy whatsoever. He coveted anything belonging to someone else, especially good land. He took what he wanted regardless of how many people died in the process. He was an unruly illiterate, no conscience whatsoever. He could not read nor write but he was filthy rich by stealing and robbing others for what they worked hard to have.

I also remember vividly a very young accountant with a very popular household surname. This was the only one I happened to live with temporarily. This man would drink all night long and have a hangover all day long on his accounting job. He stole from the company and customers. He got caught, litigated, and served some prison time. I remember driving him and his herbalist on the weekends to a remote jungle in Lagos area, to meet the gods for legal interventions. It didn't work. He was sentenced to many years in prison.

I drove many other notable people including a baker: Adegbindin, a police chief, a company CEO from India and many other business tycoons. Finally, I moved back to Ibadan. Until now, I was either a driver for a single person or the whole family but now I am about to start transporting a group of people, large group of people traveling together but heading to different destinations. There were 3 basic jobs that have being extensions of me: a driver, a military person and, later, a salesman. I have done some odd jobs as well, but these 3 jobs seem to express my purpose or purposes and they, seemingly, have some spiritual interpretations.

Self Help Exercises

1.   *Living in Ibadan, the author obtained his professional driver's license in 1969, driving different masters whom he describes as:*

a.   *rich and foolish individuals*

b.   *people with material wealth but who had almost zero consciousness of the true God*

c.   *people who may be members of mainstream traditional churches but have no idea of the true God*

d.   *all the above*

2.   *The author describes his life as constantly being at a risk driving wealthy masters. Though he himself didn't know the true God at the time, he believed he would be protected unhurt by these evil men. If he was a Christian at the time, which of the following Scriptures would have endorsed his belief?*

a.   *Psalm 23:4*

b.   *Matthew 7:1*

c.   *Genesis 1:1*

d.   *Exodus 15:26*

3.   *Which of the following statements is false? The worshipping of idols can be traced back to...*

a.   *Adam and his wife in the Garden of Eden when they obeyed the devil against God's instructions*

b.   *the people at the Tower of Babel*

c.   *Abraham's father and later the king Pharaoh in Egypt*

d.   *nowhere at all. Idols are myths. There are no idols in the world*

4. *Idol worshipping can mean any of the following:*

a. *worshipping the devil (Satan), his demons, and/or any of the fallen angels*

b. *worshipping anything that God created, whether in heaven or on Earth*

c. *exalting someone or something in one's life in such a way that it becomes more important than our God*

d. *all the above*

5. *Christians need to know that we cannot serve two masters. We need to know that...*

a. *we cannot partake in the temple of God, and of Satan. Christians are the temple of the living God.*

b. *God has commanded us to come out of idol worshipping, be separated, and He will be a Father to us*

c. *God is a jealous God. He will not share His children with deaf, mute, blind, lame, lifeless gods*

d. *all the above*

6. *The following statements are false except...*

a. *all roads lead to Heaven, including angel, star, moon, earth or sun worshipping*

b. *Jesus is the Only Way, the only Mediator between God and human beings*

c. *you can be a Christian and continue to live in sin. God doesn't mind, for He is gracious and merciful*

d. *none of the above*

7. *The author joined the military at age 17. he was...*

a. *trained in Abeokuta*

b. *trained in Lagos State*

c. *trained in Ibadan*

d. *not trained at all*

8. *In the army, after his training, the author was...*

a. *assigned to a military workshop as a driver*

b. *immediately sent to the warfront*

c. *assigned to fly a military helicopter*

d. *all the above*

9.   *Shortly before his second anniversary in the army, an impression came to him to quit the army. The following statements are true <u>except</u>...*

a. *the author first ignored the impression, but the impression just*

wouldn't go away

b. *the author believes in quitting*

c. *the author doesn't believe in quitting*

d. *the author believes that winners never quit, and quitters never win*

10. *The author enjoyed being in the military; the following statements are true <u>except</u> ...*

a. *things were going well for him in the army*

b. *there was no more civil war, what a better time to stay in the army and enjoy the benefits*

c. *the author is liked by friends and females who loved to ride in his popular jeep*

d. *the author was always in trouble with the authority figures in the military. He was mischievous*

11. *The author assumed that the army would not allow him to discharge voluntarily, so he wanted to provoke the military to force him into an early discharge. He must have...*

a. *believed that "obeying the impression" would be much more rewarding than the military benefits*

b. *believed that the One behind the "impression" is greater than him, the military personnel, and all the benefits combined*

c. *believed that though quitting the army could have resulted in a death sentence, he would rather obey the impression regardless of the possible adverse consequences.*

d. *all the above*

12. *After being on AWOL for about a week, the author showed up at the barracks. All the following occurred except...*

a. *he got his head shaved as predicted*

b. *he was locked up as predicted*

c. *he got his head shaved, was whipped as predicted, and was sent to prison*

d. *he was not whipped*

13. *Using your own judgment based on what you read about the author's case hearing and the judge's decision, the judge...*

a. *did not have enough evidence to sentence or discharge the author*

b. *knew the author and did show him some partiality*

c. *was somewhat confused about the case*

d. *was overtaken by the power greater than him. God was in charge and rendered the just judgment*

14. *After the judge discharged the author from the military, the author...*

a. *thought it was all a dream*

b. *was very ashamed that he had to leave the army*

c. *felt relieved at the same time that he was leaving the army*

d. *all the above*

15. *Leaving the army, the author forfeited a lot of benefits. He gave up...*

a. *the public accolade, the man in uniform, his popularity, the military power, and authority*

b. *his popular military jeep that spins and barks like a dog, the same one the ladies loved to ride in*

c. *his steady income and all other benefits that come with being in the military*

d. *all the above*

16. *Back to Civilian Life. After exiting the military, and back to civilian life, the author continues to work as a driver. The three basic jobs that have been the extensions of the author's life are the following except...*

a. *being a driver*

b. *being a military person*

c. *being a salesman*

d. *being a bartender*

17. *Looking back, the author believed that it was God telling him to quit the army, even though he had no knowledge of the true God at the time. That should indicate to us that there is God in each of us and that He cares for all of us regardless of our belief system. God is reaching out to each of us day by day. Circle True or False.*

18. *The Lord, our God Almighty, cares for all. He wants everyone to be saved and to come to the knowledge of the truth. Circle True or False?*

Answers

1d, 2a, 3d, 4d, 5d, 6b,7a, 8a, 9b,10d, 11d,12c, 13d, 14d, 15d, 16d, 17 True, 18 True

Chapter 3
JESUS FOUND ME: MY CONVERSION AND CALL TO THE MINISTRY AT AGE 21

I revealed myself to those who did not ask for me; I was found by those who did not seek me. To a nation that did not call on my name, I said, 'Here am I, here am I – Isaiah 65:1.'

Yes, the Lord found me when I was not seeking nor searching for Him. He preached Himself to me as He did with Paul on his way to Damascus – Acts 9. He is an Amazing God. I have never heard the gospel preached intentionally to me. In 1974, however, there was a census throughout the Nation, and I was hired to transport a group of people from Ibadan (in the South) to the northern part of the country. I did and came back safely, then decided to visit and spend the weekend with my parents in the village. It was on Friday, and I took one of my cousins (Gani, now dead) with me. Well, we did visit with them, but I wasn't feeling my best and I didn't know what was wrong with me. I thought it may have to do with the long trip to the North and back, and that I did not get any rest. Nevertheless, I was pressing through it as if everything was fine.

On Saturday however, on our way driving back from the village to the City of Ibadan, we got to the middle of the way, but I can't remember where exactly it was, I sensed that I needed to use the restroom very urgently. In my country, in those days there were no traveler's restrooms along the highway but maybe there are some now. So, I stopped the van to enter into the forest to use the restroom. And as most of us drivers do, I took a pack of cigarettes and matches in my hand. I also had a roll of weed in my pocket. I smoked weed only when I celebrated an occasion. I thought I had a good financially rewarding trip to the North and came back in peace, I went to visit with my parents, and everyone seemed to be doing well. To me, that was something to celebrate. So, I got into the forest, but I haven't squat as of yet. I put the dope in my mouth ready to light it up and couldn't but instead, I felt as if under arrest. I felt like someone in a catatonic state. It seemed like something suddenly just came over me and took over my mind. I felt somewhat intoxicated, but I wasn't drinking anything, and I hadn't smoked anything. Then, I heard a very clear unequivocal whispering in my ears. It started out very softly, then the impression became intensified saying: Jesus is the Son of God, He is the Lord and Savior of the world. The voice became so strongly registered and persuasive that I couldn't contain it any longer. I felt intoxicated and started to repeat what I heard: Jesus is the Son of God; He is the Lord and the Savior of the world. At that time, the sensation to use the restroom disappeared, and I stood there repeating what I heard for a very long time, but I wasn't exactly sure how long I was there. Nevertheless, the more I repeated what I was hearing, the more the sensation got stronger, and the more the sensation got stronger, the more I felt intoxicated and strange. I guess you can say that I was "high" on what I heard.

Eventually, I walked back to the road where I had parked the van. My cousin looked at me with a question mark on his face. He was an avowed Muslim; we were both Muslim at birth and growing up. He heard me repeating what I heard in the jungle, so he thought something went terribly wrong. He honestly thought that I was going crazy, knowing we were both Muslim. He never heard me saying anything about someone being a Savior prior to now, so my words did not make sense to him.

Well, I told him, it is over, and we can go home now. I got behind the wheel trying to start the engine, but it would not start. We drove the van there perfectly fine but now that it was time for us to leave, the van would not start. It wasn't the battery, all the lights were bright when we turned them on, and fluids were at the right level. What do we do next? There were no mechanics anywhere around and there was no Road Assistance as we have here in America. Even worse was that my cousin seemed to be afraid of me; he was listening to me talk about a Jesus who I claimed to be the Son of God in such an eccentric manner. Here was his argument: God never married; how could He have a child? The conception of Jesus Christ was difficult for him to understand - 1 Corinthians 2:14.

We sat there for a while, and it was getting dark. Then some villagers walked by us. We were city boys who must have looked like angels to these villagers. They have no help to render us. Finally, a guy (Kilanko) came, and he recognized me. He used to live in the same village as my parents when I was a child. He recognized me and I recognized him. He was not a mechanic, but he asked us if we wanted to spend the night at his house, and we said "Yes, but what about the van?" We left the van right there and followed him. He asked me a couple of questions, but my answers were not coherent enough for him. We got to his house, and I started prophesying to him and the ladies in the house. He ran to kill a goat to offer a sacrifice to the gods because he thought I was troubled by the evil spirit. Then I heard my Spirit telling me it was time to get out. So, I told him that we had to get back home right now. He tried to persuade us to stay and eat but I declined. He got dressed to accompany us because he was afraid someone might try to hurt us considering the way I was acting.

All three of us walked to the main road. It was dark at this time. We were standing by the highway but in less than 3 minutes, a van emerged from our far right, and we started waving the driver down for a ride. The driver pulled over and made a hand gesture to us to get in. There were 3 men in the van, all dressed in white robes: 2 of them sat in the front, and one person in the back. No questions were asked. The driver took us straight home. How he knew where I lived, I knew not. It was amazingly surprising. If you ask me who these people were, your guess is just as good as mine. I had no idea and still have no idea 50 years later. I know God sent someone to take us home, "that" I can say. Were they angels? I knew not. I tried not to read too much into it. When we got home, my cousin went back to his house, the guy (Mr. Kilanko) who escorted us also went back to a friend's house for the night, so I was left alone.

The house I was living in belonged to my deceased aunt, my father's older sister. People living in this house were tenants, and my father and his younger brother inherited the house. My father asked me to live in one of the bedrooms to keep an eye on the house. So, to the tenants, I am their landlord. As I was sitting in my room that night, with the light on, suddenly I started asking God for forgiveness of sins, and confessing that Jesus Christ is Lord and Savior. I asked Him to come into my life. Suddenly, the bedroom ceiling light blinked so violently that I thought the ceiling was on fire. At that time, I had no peace inside of me sitting in that room, and I had to get out. Without thinking I started yelling out "Bible, Bible, Bible." A guy called "Ilesanmi," one of the tenants who happened to be a Christian, and the person helping me to collect the rent from the tenants, heard me yelling for a Bible and rushed to give me his Bible. I took the Bible and went out preaching and singing: "Omo Jesu omo, omo Jesu tide, omo Jesu oseun." This song can literarily be translated as "Jesus' son is coming, Jesus' son is here, Jesus' son, thank you." It was past midnight at that time. So, I went out preaching to whoever I found along the way. The first place I stopped at was a cafeteria. I preached there. I was served some food, but I couldn't eat.

As I left the cafeteria, I sensed in my spirit that I needed to wear my shirt inside out and that was what I did and continued to walk. As I was walking around, I saw a Saturday night party in progress. I saw people eating, drinking, and dancing. I walked through the crowd preaching Jesus Christ, simply saying what I heard in the jungle. People looked at me funny. I looked different for real. I looked like I didn't belong in their circle. I had no shoes, my attire was not party-like, and my shirt was inside out. I looked like someone running for his life, except that I was preaching a Christ that they didn't really care to know or hear about. A lot of strange things happened that night. There were dogs barking at me but the closer I got to them with my right hand stretched out, they would keep silent till I passed by. That went on all night long, then I walked back home, maybe, around 6 a.m. By the time I got home on that Sunday morning with the Bible in my hand, the relatives have gathered waiting for me. One of my uncles came and tried to wrestle the Bible from my hand. He was a tall, big fellow, but I muscled up enough strength to slap him very hard, and the streetlights went out, came back on, thrice. Then, he turned me loose. He let me go.

For about 3 days, I would not eat, but I read the Bible, fasted, and prayed on my knees. Down the road, maybe 5 blocks from where I lived, was one of my paternal grandfather's homes. In that house, the occupants were uncles and distant cousins. I mostly go there when I choose to. So, one day before I was hospitalized, I decided to visit. I went there and started to prophesy to uncles and distant cousins that lived there. It was revealed to me that one of my uncles was an unapologetic thief who didn't know the Lord and needed to repent. I told him the revelation. I thought he would kill me but surprisingly he shook his head and walked off.

Another person I ministered to during this time was an older uncle. This is the man who almost killed my father on the farm (Erinwo), with a cutlass over an argument about a shifted landmark. Nevertheless, times have come and gone by since the fight. Now, their relationship has become somewhat civil, and my father wanted us to visit with him. So, we did. As he was about to get us something to drink, I started to prophesy to him. He looked at me strangely as if I was speaking in an unknown tongue. Well, maybe I was. None of them were sure of what was happening to me.

I Was Admitted into a Mental Hospital

A few days later, my father's younger brother came to see me and decided to take me to the mental hospital. I was taken to "Aro Mental Hospital," Abeokuta, in what is now "Ogun State," Nigeria.

I didn't argue with him at all. We took a cab but surprisingly there was a woman and her child in the back seat of the cab. The woman was holding the child. Someone was sitting at the front; I am not sure if they knew each other. I doubt it. So, both me and my uncle sat in the back seat with this woman and her child. My uncle wanted me to sit in the middle just to make sure I was secure. As we got in the taxi, the Spirit of God told me to tell the woman she was responsible for her child's suffering. There were so many other words God gave me for her. I told her she needed to repent. She cried bitterly. I obeyed God but what these people were doing with what they heard me saying I had no idea. Just like them wondering what was going on with me, I was wondering what was going on with me as well. I wasn't as desperate to lead any of these individuals to Christ but simply spoke the impressions that came to my mind. I watched people react differently. Some of them cried some laughed at me as if I was just crazy, and some showed no reactions at all.

Finally, we made it to the hospital. There were many doctors, nurses, and social workers standing by and looking at me as a new case. They were ready to go to work on me, and they did. I remember saying to these medical professionals that "I shouldn't be here. I don't know why I was brought here. There is nothing wrong with me, my head, or my mind. If you don't believe that there is nothing wrong with me, you will see a sign" (paraphrased). They looked at me crazy and strapped me down very fast. As they strapped me down, the hospital lights completely went off & on three times, just as it did in Ibadan when my uncle tried to wrestle the Bible from my hand. Seeing what happened, a staff yelled out "You are crazy for real. You think you are doing something, that is just coincidental." They put me to sleep, and I was kept for about a week, not as an inpatient but on observation. They put me in this apartment. It was a small building on a rock with a water canal under the building. I often sat outside the building and would be hearing my spirit telling me different things about Jesus, things like Jesus is the Rock of Ages. He is the Living Water. I saw many visions while in that building. I saw the Rock spread all over the earth, a type of Christ. I didn't know what all these things meant then. I was at that hospital for about a week, got discharged, and never went back; that was 50 years ago. I got back to Ibadan to face life again, but I didn't know how to. First, I must face the Brigadier.

Facing the Brigadier

At this time, I knew that the news had already gone to the Brigadier, the person who owned the van I was driving, the passenger van that quit on me on our way back from the village when visiting my parents. Now, I must go and explain to him in more detail what had happened, but I didn't want to go alone. My uncle, on my mother's side, my mother's younger brother (Adeyemi), who died in early 2019, agreed to go with me. We got to the Brigadier, and I was determined to tell him the truth, but he would not believe anything I was saying. I could see in his eyes, that if he knew he could get away with it he would have killed me and buried me in his backyard. He was overtly mad. He gnawed at me. He looked at me as one would look at his enemy at the battlefront but thank God, I was brave enough to have someone with me. He shook his fist at me and slapped his own head just to show how much emotional pain I had caused him. I pleaded, prostrating. I did everything I knew to show how sorry I was.

Before he employed me to drive his van, he demanded to keep my original driver's license while I drove around with a paper copy. So, he had my driver's license in his possession at the time, and that is the only leverage he had on me. He didn't shy away from using the leverage. He kept my driver's license to this day and probably has it if he is still alive. I was deeply sorry for how things turned out, but I knew it was a situation beyond my control. I told him where the van was, and I accompanied the tow truck to bring the van to the mechanic in the city. That was the end of that. Now, I am without a driver's license, no job, and no income. I don't know what else to do. So, I decided to go back to the village to stay with my parents, and to stay there until I can figure out which direction my life is heading.

Going Back to the Village to Live with My Parents

Going back to live with my parents wasn't that pleasant this time around. For one, I am now an adult and have been somewhat away from their shadow for about 5 years. This time, I am more of a liability than a helper. I was not asked to do any work because they automatically assumed I was having a mental breakdown. Within a year of staying with my parents, however, I was able to obtain another driver's license through a combination of help: my parents, older brother, and one of my uncles, a mechanic (Rasaki) who was residing in Oshogbo at that time. These individuals helped me to obtain a new driver's license, and I continued to stay with my parents for a few more weeks but no one knew that I had a secret plan.

One day my parents were away from home. I had been thinking about how I could get away but realized I couldn't do anything without money. My parents were still monitoring me trying to make sure I had no more episodes. Their eyes were on me, but I knew I had to get away and face life. I knew where my mother kept her money. So, I reluctantly went to her savings and took enough money to get me to another State in the Northern part of the country. When it comes to trust, my parents would lay down their lives trusting me.

I didn't want to steal from them, but I knew I had to leave the village. There was no hope for me living with my parents in the village. Every parent wants the best for their children, and that includes being able to live on your own.

Several months before, I had met a guy in Ibadan who had recently left Kano, not by choice. I have no clear details of why he left. He left Kano to live in Ibadan, but his wife and children continued to stay in Kano. He painted a picture of a prosperous city, and I wanted to give it a try. So, I took enough money from my mother's account and left the village. I left a note for my parents not to worry, I had gone to the North, Kano to be specific. I explained my rationale for leaving and specified the amount I took. My parents understood that when I made up my mind, I would follow through with whatever I set my mind to do. Remember, I am leaving the South for the Northern part of the country, looking for a neutral environment. I thought that leaving the South would help me to make some sense out of whatever it was that I was going through. I believed that God spoke to me in that jungle but at the same time, I can't deny the reasoning part of me that seemed to be questioning my calling into the ministry. It was a battle between faith and reasoning.

Even though the experiences I had with God on July 27, 1974, only lasted for a few days, the effects of His presence in my mind and body lasted for months. God seemed forever present with me. I was scared to do anything wrong, and when I did something wrong, I felt very sad and disappointed in myself. I continued to hear the soft gentle inner voice whispering to me about Jesus Christ. I can feel the constant presence of someone I believed was greater than I am, day by day. The more I tried to figure out what is next for me, the more confused I was. Then, I started smoking more cigarettes and drinking more alcohol. I was confused.

Running Away from God's Calling: I Moved to Kano City, Northern Nigeria

It was in 1975 when I decided to move to Kano in the northern part of the country, but I cannot remember the exact day or month. Getting to Kano, I searched for the person who I was recommended to stay with temporarily. I was surprised however at the reception I received. It felt like they were just waiting for my arrival. They seemed eager to see me. I felt honored. These were good people. I knew it was God's favor that went before me. God had touched their hearts before I got to them. He knew I needed that, and I was very thankful.

A few days later, I got a job at an iron or metal-making company. I lasted less than a week on the job. It wasn't for me. Then I got another driving job driving a company CEO. While functioning in a driver capacity, however, I was taking a salesmanship course concurrently, and somewhere during this time we lost the company's salesperson, and I was recommended for the position and accepted it. I became the company's salesperson, selling machine equipment and building materials. This position lasted for a couple of years and later I moved to another company that sold similar equipment and paid better. I was functioning in the same capacity at the new company and continued to work on my salesmanship correspondence courses. It was at this time I met the mother of my older children: Adijatu, now Maria. She was my first close relationship and convert, a Godly woman, and a great mother.

Transitioning Period: My Years in Kano

My life between July 27th, 1974, and January 9th, 1979, was a period of confusion and transition for me. In retrospect, it reminds me of the transition phase in Moses' life. Moses was 40 years old when he received God's call in Egypt, then in his transitioning phase, he ran away from Egypt and God's calling for 40 years. He eventually answered the call and then lived for another 40 years. Moses lived a total of 120 years, and he died. Do we all have to go through the transitioning period? I am not sure, but I went through it. I knew in my heart that I had a call, but I knew also that either I was not ready for it, or I was simply afraid of not knowing what to do next. I remember visiting different traditional churches, trying to get them to help me make sense of my divine experiences.

What troubled me the most was that few people believed me or recognized the call of God in my life. Hearing my testimony, some people looked at me like I was crazy; some nicely said to me, "God didn't have to do all that to call anybody, and that God isn't that dramatic." I almost began to believe that too, thinking maybe something was wrong with me. My parents were Muslim, and I was raised to be a Muslim. I didn't have a Bible nor had any prior knowledge of the Scripture. I was depending on the pastors, teachers, and Church folks to take me in and nurture me but, surprisingly, there was no one! I had no idea where else to look. It seemed at the time that I was in it all by myself until I met one evangelist in a small Celestial Church of Christ (CCC) in Kano. I felt like I had been looking for help at the wrong places.

The Significant Landmarks in Kano

There were many significant things in my life that originated in Kano City during my transition. These are landmarks and integral parts of my existence. It was in Kano that I met the mother of my older children. It was in Kano I taught myself further English, Mathematics, Physics, and Chemistry. It was in Kano that I stopped smoking cigarettes and drinking alcohol. It was in Kano that I discovered the Celestial Church of Christ, and it was the Pastor of this church who connected me with the Founder (Oshoffa) of the Celestial Church of Christ at their Headquarters in Lagos, Nigeria.

During my years in Kano, my mother came to visit, my father came to visit, my older brother came to visit and finally, one of my younger brothers, the one who is next to me, came to live with me temporarily, and decided to stay permanently, even after I had left the city to move back to the South.

Self Help Exercises

1. *The author, after his return from the census involvement, visited his parents in the village and took one of his cousins with him. On their way back from the village, all the following statements are true except...*

a. *it was on Saturday, on their way back from the village to the city of Ibadan, that he had to make a stop*

b. *he sensed the need to use the restroom, then stopped the van to use the restroom in the forest*

c. *he took a pack of cigarettes and matches and a roll of marijuana into the jungle with him*

d. *the author and his cousin had a good time, partying, coming back from their visit*

2. *The author, as he entered the jungle, and before he squatted or smoked anything, he started to experience the following except...*

a. *he felt as if under arrest*

b. *he felt like someone, or something, came over him and overtook his mind*

c. *he felt intoxicated but hadn't drunk nor smoked anything*

d. *all the above*

3. *The author heard a very clear, unequivocal whispering in his ears, saying that "Jesus is the Son of God, that He is the Lord and the Savior of the world." There are many Bible figures that had similar dramatic encounters with God, and these include but are not limited to...*

a. *Moses*

b. *Elijah*

c. *Paul*

d. *all the above and many more*

4. *Eventually, the author walked back to the road where he parked the van. His cousin looked at him with a question mark on his face because of what the author was saying about one Savior who died for the whole world. He thought...*

a. *the author was going crazy*

b. *the author was never a real Muslim*

c. *the author was no longer a member of his family*

d. the author was going through midlife crisis

5. When the author thought it was all over and it was time to go home, the engine (motor) would not crank or start, even though they drove it there in perfect working condition. Which of the following is true?

a. the author and his cousin were stranded in the middle of their journey

b. b. the cousin is now afraid to be around the author because of how eccentric he was, talking about Jesus.

c. the cousin was confused, saying God never married, and how can He have a child?

d. all the above

6. As the author and his cousin were waiting for whatever happened next, a man who knew the author's parents stopped and persuaded them to go home with him, and they agreed. Upon arriving at the man's house, the following statements were true except...

a. the author prophesied to the man and the ladies in the house

b. the man then sacrificed a goat to his gods, assuming that the author was disturbed by some spirits

c. The author refused to eat or spend a night. He told the man

"We have to get back home right now."

d. the author ate and drank, and did enjoy the goat sacrifices that the man made to the gods

7. The man escorted the author and his cousin to the highway to help them find a transportation to get home. Some of the surprises of the night were...

a. They waved down the first vehicle that emerged from the far right. The driver of the vehicle stopped, and willing to help

b. it was a white van, with three men inside the car, all in white robes. They stopped, waved at us, but no questions asked

c. the driver transported the author, his cousin, and the man that accompanied them straight to where the author lived without needing to ask for any directions

d. all the above

8. As soon as they got to the author's residence, the cousin and the man who escorted them home left, and the author was now alone. Not for very long, however, as the author stayed in his room and praying for forgiveness, and asking Jesus Christ to come into his life, his bedroom ceiling light started to blink violently as if the ceiling was on fire. The author experienced the following...

a. he had no peace sitting in that room

b. it was past midnight, and he stormed outside to preach the gospel to whoever he might find

c. he was given a song in his Yoruba language: "Omo Jesu mbo, Omo Jesu tide, Omo Jesu O seun."

d. all the above

9. Many strange things happened throughout the night; the author...

a. had no shoes and was inspired to wear his clothes inside out

b. ministered to the people he met that night. He looked so strange, like someone running for his life

c. dogs were barking at him, but as soon as he stretched out his hand in their direction, they stopped

d. all the above

10. *For about three days, the following statements are true* *except*...

a. the author would not eat but read his Bible, prayed and fasted for days

b. the author prophesied to many of his uncles, cousins, and one he described as an unapologetic thief

c. the author also prophesied to an older uncle who once almost killed his father over a landmark dispute

d. nothing like that ever happened

11. *Finally, a few days later, the author's uncle (who was his father's younger brother) came to take him to Aro Mental Hospital in Abeokuta, but the author continued to dream and see visions, prophesying to people including...*

a. a woman and her child in the taxicab that was taking the author to the mental hospital in Abeokuta

b. the doctors and the health providers at Aro Mental Hospital

c. the author seeing visions about Jesus Christ being the Rock of all Ages and the Water of Life

d. all the above

12. *Upon being discharged from the hospital, the author must now face the brigadier, the owner of the passenger van that the author was driving during his encounter with God. After explaining what happened to the brigadier, the author believes that...*

a. if the brigadier knew he could get away with it, he would have killed the author and buried him in his backyard

b. the brigadier was overtly mad. He gnawed at the author and looked at him as one would look at an enemy at the warfront

c. the brigadier intentionally seized the author's driver's license as leverage or revenge

d. all the above

13. Going back to the village to live with his parents, the author...

a. was more of a liability than a helper

b. was not asked to do anything because his parents assumed he was having a mental breakdown

c. was able to obtain another driver's license with the help of his parents, older brother, and uncle

d. all the above

14. One day, when the parents were away from home, the author carried out his secret plan. He...

a. reluctantly went to his mother's savings and took enough money to get him to another state in the Northern part of Nigeria

b. knew that when it came to trust, his parents would lay down their lives trusting him

c. confessed, saying, "I didn't want to steal from them, but I knew I had to leave the village."

d. all the above

15. Several months before the author went to live with his parents, he had met a man who had recently relocated from Kano to Ibadan, and...

a. the man painted a picture of a prosperous city (Kano) to the author, who was at the time looking for an opportunity

b. after the author had taken the money from his parents, he left them a note of how much money he took, explained the rationale behind his departure, and where he was going

c. the author believed that leaving the south would help him make sense of his experiences

d. all the above

16. Upon arriving in Kano, the author had the following experiences _except_...

a. he was well received by the people he was recommended to stay with

b. he got a job at a metal-making company, but the author lasted less than a week there

c. he later got a job as a driver, driving a company's CEO before he was recommended for a salesperson position

d. that once in Kano, everything about the voice following him around simply disappeared

17. The period between 1974 and 1979 was a period...

a. of confusion and transition for the author

b. that reminds the author of Moses' second 40 years of life when he was running away from Pharaoh and God's calling. Moses finally answered God's calling at 80 years of age.

c. of uncertainty

d. all the above

18. What troubled the author the most are the following _except_...

a. that very few people believed him or cared to recognize the call of God in his life at the time

b. that upon hearing his story, some people looked at him as if he were crazy and told him, "God is not that dramatic."

c. that the author himself began to believe that maybe something was wrong with him

d. *everyone was happy for him wherever and whenever he shared his story*

19. *Among the landmark experiences that the author cited in his book are the following: In Kano...*

a. *he met the mother of his older children*

b. *he taught himself further in English, Mathematics, Physics, and Chemistry*

c. *he stopped smoking cigarettes and drinking alcohol*

d. *all the above*

20. *During his almost five years of staying in Kano, the following statements are true except the author...*

a. *was first visited by his mother and later by his father*

b. *was visited by his older brother*

c. *was visited by one of his younger brothers who decided to live in Kano with him*

d. *had no one visited him because no one really cared as much about him.*

Answers

1d, 2d, 3d, 4a, 5d, 6d, 7d, 8d,9d, 10d, 11d, 12d, 13d, 14d, 15d, 16d, 17d, 18d, 19d, 20d.

Chapter 4

I ANSWERED GOD'S CALLING AT AGE 26 AFTER ALMOST 5 YEARS OF RUNNING

I moved from the North (Kano) back to the South (Lagos) on the 9th of January 1979. I reached and joined the Celestial Church of Christ in Lagos, then the capital of Nigeria. I met with the founder and told him of my call. He prayed with me. I felt warmly received. In a couple of days, I was provided housing and within a month my family joined me from Kano.

Regretfully, my Celestial Church's experiences left me with so many questions, even today. I asked many questions in my mind: why do we pray using candle/s? Why do we use green water? Why do we get the angels involved when we pray? Why do we walk around barefooted in white garments? I think all these practices are unnecessary for the followers of Christ.

God didn't send me to Celestial Church to fight her traditions. I found out later in the ministry that faith and tradition can co-exist in harmony. When traditions bump heads with the word of God, the word of God must win. Christians are commanded to pray in the name of Jesus. While praying with or without a candle may not be a sin Jesus says, "Whatsoever you ask in my name, I will do it" (paraphrased) – John 14: 13- 14. Christians walking around barefooted in white garments is very unnecessary, and not a New Testament practice. Jesus Himself wore Sandals, so did His disciples. If wearing a white garment is an indicator of one's holiness, everyone will get one, and that would be misleading. What did Jesus say?

Woe to you, scribes and Pharisees, hypocrites! For you are like whitewashed tombs which indeed appear beautiful outwardly, but inside are full of dead men's bones and all uncleanness. Even so you also outwardly appear righteous to men, but inside you are full of hypocrisy and lawlessness (Matthew 23:27-28).

I endured the Celestial Church of Christ's practices for two and half years and God told me to get out. The mother of my older children told me of a dream she had. She reported seeing me standing against the light. That was confirmation of an impression I have been having in my Spirit for a while. Out of the mouths of 2 or three witnesses, the truth is established. I must move out. Yes, I didn't have the money to relocate but I heard God told me to get out. I must get out and I did. But before then, my family and I were baptized by the parish Evangelist. That was nice. We got baptized in one river along Ikorodu Road, Lagos, Nigeria, according to Jesus' instructions in Matthew 28:19 and it is the only baptism I have to this day. I have nothing negative to say about the Celestial Church. I am a little disenchanted with some of her traditions that I observed at the time that were not in agreement with the New Testament teachings. Shortly before her dream, and the impression I was having to get out of Celestial Church, one of the elders of the church wanted to start a new branch at his own house and wanted me to oversee it, and I agreed. I guess he saw something of value in me. It didn't work out.

I Quit Celestial Church and Moved to Ibadan

In early 1981, I decided to move out of Celestial Church altogether. I moved to Ibadan with the help of my parents and my older brother who paid for a three-bedroom rental home for me in Ibadan. However, I had no money to pay for a mover, but I hired a mover anyway. On our way from Lagos to Ibadan, I finally told the mover we had to stop by my parents because I had no money. If I had told him that in Lagos before we took off, he wouldn't have moved me, I assumed. He grumbled a little, but he worked with me. He had no choice because we had made it past half-way. Many thanks to my mother, she helped me pay the mover. I moved into my new rented home, a new environment, waiting for my next steps to be. The home belongs to one self-made doctor who also claimed to be a Christian. He lived in the main portion of the building at the front with his 2 wives, and the tenants lived in the two rear wings of the building.

I Enrolled in Calvary Bible College

In about a month or so in the new environment, one of my co-tenants was sharing some of his Bible College experiences with me. This man worked during the day and attended Calvary Bible College in the evening. I was so excited that I just couldn't wait to enroll. I strongly believed that God did order my steps to dwell in this house because that was exactly what I needed. I felt in my Spirit that I needed to enroll in this college. The more we talked, the more my Spirit whispered in me, "you need to enroll." I enrolled at the college full-time: 8 a.m.-2 p.m., Monday through Friday. Now, the question is: how would I get the money to buy my books and pay tuition fees? Well, God made a way. Where He sends His servants, He provides for their necessities. I was able to pay a portion of my tuition fees and buy my books. The founder of the Bible College waived a significant portion of my school fees. God was and is Awesome. He is an on-time God. I completed the program and graduated with honors in 1983. I was one of the top 3 and, mind you, competing with students who had high school educational backgrounds; I was self-taught without a formal high school experience. With our God nothing is impossible.

My Invitation to Preach at Holy Ghost Apostolic Church

During my last year of Bible college, 2 things happened. The first thing is that I was invited to preach at the Holy Ghost Apostolic Church, and I accepted the invitation. The Church was founded by one of my distant uncles. It was a small size Church with many parishes all over Lagos and Oyo States at the time. My uncle was the Church Primate but worked full-time outside the ministry. I thought that was weird. I wondered "How could he be available for God or cater effectively for the ministry's needs if he is working full-time outside the ministry?" Well, now I can see why. I realized now that sometimes the options to do otherwise are not there. Paul was also a tentmaker. The difference with Paul is that he did not have to clock in or out making tents. Paul was available for God at any time.

Anyhow, the founder, my uncle whose official title was Primate, continued to work full time. He didn't know of my conversion to Christianity, however. It was one of the laymen or deacons (Ishola) who invited me to the Lagos parish, and I honored his invitation. I went to preach, and the Spirit of God moved in a very significant way. It was an exciting moment for me. God validated my ministry. After the first invitation, I was invited again and again and, eventually, the pastor and elders of the Church asked me to become a part of the ministry in sharing any Bible knowledge I may have with them. Then I started to hold revival meetings for the Church, both in Lagos and Ibadan as needed. I started a small Bible school class in Lagos, at Aguda branch location, on Saturday. I traveled from Ibadan to Lagos every week, back and forth. While in Lagos, I stayed in Brother Atundaolu's home. I worshipped with them on Sunday morning. I would then go back to Ibadan early in the week to hold a Bible Study on Wednesday evening, at one of Ibadan local parishes. I eventually became the Church's general evangelist.

During the first year of my minister in this church, people fell in love with me, and I was in love with them. Many of the ministers wanted the type of Bible knowledge I had, so I encouraged them to enroll in my Bible college. Three of the ministers (2 pastors and a teacher) subsequently enrolled in Calvary Bible College because of what they sensed in me, and they all graduated. They had pleasant experiences, and none was disappointed. On occasions, these brothers would join me in Ibadan where I was based, either as a group or as individuals. Every month there was a group prayer meeting on the mountain that lasted for days each time. They would come as time permitted, and we would go to the mountain of prayer together. Those are golden age days for me. I miss the physical mountain of prayer, but my closet has become my mountain of prayer in Amcrica.

Regretfully, I have lost contact with some of my old friends. I know that the thought of me is crossing their minds now and then, and their thoughts are on mine. These were good people, but it is true as one Yoruba proverb says, "childhood friends don't stay together forever." Life is a journey, not a destination. We may be absent in the body, but our spirits stay connected. Though life circumstances may have taken their toll on each of us, it is my hope that our paths will cross again.

My Invitation to Apply to Selma University, Alabama, USA

The second thing that occurred to me during my last year in Calvary Bible College was another invitation but this time it was to apply to a

University in the United States of America. As I explained earlier in the book, I was one of the top 3 students who graduated with honors at Calvary. Before my graduation, however, I had a dream. In that dream, I saw myself in a college setting with many white students and a few black students. I didn't think anything of it because I couldn't even imagine myself going overseas. I thought it would be impossible. When I received the invitation to apply overseas, I was shocked and dumbfounded. Then I remembered the dream and realized how wrong I could be. Glory to God, we can do all things through Christ which strengthens us. If God made a way through the red sea, rained down the manna in the wilderness, commanded a donkey to speak in human language, and turned a bird into a Chef in the wilderness to feed the Prophet Elijah, now tell me: What can He not do?

By reminding myself of the dreams I had, and some of the miracles God has performed, I was more confident than ever. I said to myself: if God says it is so, so it is. I took my invitation to apply to Selma University with me to the mountain of prayers. I was convinced that the dream I had and the invitation to apply to the university abroad seemed in agreement enough for me that I needed no more witnesses. So, I started to claim my dream, my next adventure into reality, calling those things that were not as if they were. I felt like God saw me as being obedient in a small thing and He is rewarding me in His own way. Coming to America was a big deal, especially being the first person in my family to step on an airplane. It was a possibility that never came to my mind until the opportunity presented itself. I asked the professor that gave me the invitation what would be the criteria. Of course, the first thing is money. The second thing is a high school diploma or its equivalent. Well, I have neither of the two. I told the professor "I had no money and had never attended a high school. So, now what?"

I Needed a GED

The professor said that I had to enroll in a correspondence study program for a GED. A GED is a high school alternative and if I completed the program and did well in specific subjects, the University would accept me. I did as he suggested. I studied, and studied, and studied. I did well in all subjects. God did crown my efforts. I completed the program and obtained my high school equivalency certificate. I still have the Certificate here with me in America. I thank God for the opportunity. Many of us have the potential but not the opportunity. I thank God for giving me the opportunity. An ability without the opportunity is a useless asset.

The Bible says that our gift will make room for us, but the gift must be d i s c o v e r e d a n d activated first. The question is "How may one's gift be discovered, activated, and even nurtured without being given the opportunity?" I saw people like me roaming the streets every day, people with curious brains, great skills, talents, and desires to excel, but the world refused to give them the opportunity. I see many gifts and talents wasting away on our streets. Some beautiful minds have been overrun by drugs because they are idle, and not stimulated. An idle mind is a devil's workshop. Let us remember that there is greatness in all of us. God does not make junk. We are perfectly, and wondrously made, and the devil knows that. He is a thief and a liar. The devil comes to steal, to kill, and to destroy.

For some of us who feel robbed of opportunity, I have something to say to you: don't be discouraged; keep on knocking on those doors of opportunity. I am convinced that God will touch someone's heart to give you the opportunity that you need and deserve. If we want something—anything—in life, we will have to put forth our best efforts to go get it and go get it lawfully. We may try and not succeed on the first try, maybe not on the second try either, but if we are persistent in our efforts, our dream will come to pass. Yes, persistence; nothing will fall in our lap. Go and make it happen, and make it happen lawfully.

A word of advice: we must watch the company we are keeping. We probably need to stay away from some of our friends, especially those friends with negative attitudes. God wants us to be successful in life. Success here is not limited to financial wealth. Success to me is when our ability is met with opportunity, to fulfill our God-given purposes on earth. One can be a trash collector and be successful. Are you happy with your job, or you are only doing it for money? Many people are miserable on the job. If you have a job and feel miserable doing it, maybe you are doing someone else's job. That may not be your calling. Our God-given gifts and talents are extensions of who we are to fulfill our purposes in life. Whether it comes with a lot of money or not, we have inner peace doing it. We have joy and inner fulfillment. Gifts and talents are not to be buried but to be activated and utilized. Those gifts or talents are extensions of who we are. God says that our gift will make room for us. By functioning in our God-given capacity, we can make a living doing what we enjoy. God is faithful. Our needs will be provided for and some of our wants as well.

Well, I got my high school equivalency diploma, but I had no money to finance my overseas University admission process, so I asked God "How do I proceed?" My attitude was this: it is better to try and fail than to fail to try. I believe also that no one can hold a strong man down without staying down with him. I will not allow anyone to tell me what I can and cannot do. I will not allow anything to prevent me from fulfilling my purpose.

Concurrently, I started to work on getting my high school equivalency diploma and seeking funds for my overseas education. I was doing all of this at the same time. I can tell you this: it was difficult. But, when the going gets tough, the tough get going. "I will not quit; I refused to quit," I told myself. I talked the talk, and I walked the walk. I asked the people whom I thought could help me financially; I sought help. I knocked on people's doors, people I knew, for help. I made my case to everyone I approached, and God crowned my efforts. Glory to God, I got the money for my overseas education and obtained my student visa.

Self Help Exercises

1. *The author moved from Kano to Lagos in early 1979 to join the Celestial Church. The following statements are true except...*

a. *the author met with the founder, and he felt warmly received*

b. *regretfully, the experiences the author had at the Celestial Church left him with many questions*

c. *the author stayed at the Celestial Church until God told him to get out of there, and he got out*

d. *none of the above*

2. *The author got out of the Celestial Church. The following are true <u>except</u>...*

a. *he became so wealthy before he left the Celestial Church*

b. *he moved to Ibadan broke and couldn't even pay the mover*

c. *he had to stop on the way at his mother's, who helped him pay the mover*

d. *he moved into a new environment, in a building owned by a self-proclaimed doctor*

3. *In his new environment, the author reported which of the following experiences?*

a. *he met another Christian who was already attending Calvary Bible College*

b. *he believed that God had ordered his steps and was excited about enrolling in Bible College*

c. *he was concerned about how he would pay for his books and tuition fees but believed that God would make a way*

d. *all the above*

4. *The author, sharing his "out of body" experiences, believes that a human being is, according to 1 Thessalonians 5:23,*

a. *a living soul. A soul is also a form of a spirit; it is invisible*

b. *a living soul, and he has the Spirit of God dwelling in him*

c. *a living soul. He has the Spirit of God dwelling in him, and he lives in a body*

d. *all the above*

5. *The Holy Ghost Apostolic Church was founded by one of the author's distant uncles. During his last year at Calvary Bible College, the author was invited to preach at the Holy*

Ghost Apostolic Church, and he accepted the invitation. The following statements were true except...

a. *that the author accepted the invitation*

b. *the Spirit of God moved in a very significant way as he ministered*

c. *as a result, three of the ministers decided to enroll in Calvary Bible College*

d. *none of the above*

6. *Before he was invited to apply to Selma University, the author...*

a. *saw himself in a dream, in a college setting with many white and a few black students*

b. *never thought he had any chance of studying in America or any European country*

c. *had no knowledge of any family member ever studying abroad*

d. *all the above*

7. *The author needed a GED or an equivalent to gain admission to Selma University. The following statements were true except...*

a. *he enrolled in a Correspondence Study program, completed the program, and received his high school diploma equivalency certificate while still in Nigeria*

b. *he did allow his lack of high school education to hinder him. He gave up too easily and would not even try*

c. *he still has the equivalent high school certificate he obtained*

d. *he believes that ability without opportunity is a useless asset*

8. *In his book, the author makes the following statements except...*

a. *I saw people like me roaming the streets every day, people with curious brains, great skills...*

b. *I see many gifts and talents wasting away on our streets*

c. *an idle mind is the devil's workshop... God doesn't make junk*

d. *we are victims of predestinations. Our lives are already mapped out regardless of our efforts.*

9. *Which of the following is false?*

a. *we will always succeed in everything that we do*

b. *sometimes we fail, sometimes we succeed... it is better to try and fail than to fail to try*

c. *one can be a trash collector and be successful*

d. *gifts and talents are not to be buried... the word of God says that our gifts will make room for us...*

10. *Which of the following statements is false?*

a. *When the going gets tough, the tough gets going. Quitters never win*

b. *we need one another; we ought to help one another because no single tree can make a forest*

c. *I need no help from anyone; as long as I have King Jesus, I need nobody else. Prayer is all I need, and everything will fall into place*

d. *God will use people, things, places, whatever He chooses to meet our needs.*

Answers

1d, 2a, 3a, 4d, 5d, 6d, 7b, 8d, 9a, 10c

Chapter 5
My Call to Minister to the Mentally Ill

I believe that God has been preparing me to minister to the mentally ill, the homeless, and people under demonic attacks. Here are some of my early experiences in dealing with Satan and his demonic forces.

My First Encounter with Demons' Activities: A Boy Was Delivered from Demonic Attack in 1983

A couple of years before my visa interview, I was in my living room and heard a shout for help. I rushed out, only to see a boy acting crazy. He was a nephew of my landlord. He was maybe ten years old. This boy was tearing up the clothes on his body, yelling and screaming. I had been living in this house for at least one year and had never seen the boy act like this. Brother Timothy was right there with me, and we looked at each other wondering what to do next. We both believed in the ministry of deliverance. I asked him if he would hold the boy, he agreed. This is my first time dealing with a demonic attack and, to be honest, I was just going by what I had learned about demonic operations, and how to deal with them by invoking the name and the blood of Jesus Christ. I commanded the demon to come out in the name of Jesus Christ. Suddenly, the boy was just as calm as ever. I was so happy as the 70 disciples that Jesus sent out in 2s in the Gospel of Luke. Glory! Demons obeyed me!

And the seventy returned with joy, saying, Lord, even the devils are subject unto us through thy name. Luke 10: 17.

Shortly after, in about an hour, this boy started acting up again. I was called to come out and pray for him again. I said to myself, "this demon obeyed us and left the boy but why did he come back?" And I heard a whisper in my Spirit saying, "You casted him out in my name, yes, but you didn't tell him where to go, and not to come back, ever."

Jesus in Matthew 12: 43-44 says "When an unclean spirit goes out of a man, he goes through dry places, seeking rest, and finds none. Then he says, 'I will return to my house from which I came...'"

I said to my friend, Timothy, "Now, I got it." I asked him to hold the boy down one more time, and I cast the demon out again, but this time I commanded him to go into the wilderness or as far as the Red Sea. No Red Sea in Nigeria, but this demon knew that I was trying to send him as far away as I possibly could, and there he went. The boy was set free instantaneously. He was set free completely from the demonic attacks forever. I saw him before I came to America in early 1986, and he was still free. No more demonic attacks. The experience did strengthen my faith.

God Raised a Dead Girl

In about 8 months after the boy's deliverance, around 7 a.m., there was a wailing or lamentation coming from the upstairs floor. This time it was about a 6-month-old female child who had just lost consciousness on her mother's lap. This was my landlord's daughter. Her mother decided that I might be able to help the child. She knocked violently on my door, forced the door open, and she just threw the child at me while she was crying in agony. I caught the child. She was heavy and seemed dead. I asked myself "Why did this woman bring her dead child to me?" Before I finished the thought, the Spirit prompted me. I realized that she had witnessed the miracle Jesus performed on the 10-year-old boy just 8 months ago. So, I held my peace.

Just as I didn't know what to do when the boy was acting up 8 months ago, I didn't know what to do with this girl either. I held her in my arms, knelt down, and was about to pray, when a man living across from me, in the same building, came out of his living room. He was a 2nd- grade teacher getting ready to go to class. He came in, asking if there is anything he can do to help. I asked if he could help me hold the baby. He agreed. I laid my hand on this little innocent girl. As I handed the girl to him, the girl was so heavy it felt like I was holding a log. There was no life in her. Then James 4:7 came to my mind, and I started

59

to praise the Lord for the opportunity to put James 4:7 into practice. I commanded the death demon to turn the child loose and come out of her in Jesus' name. I asked the Spirit of life to return and come back into her in Jesus' name. I repeated the command several times with my eyes closed. I was just exercising my faith hoping Jesus and His Father would Honor it, but I wasn't sure whether it would work or not. I was afraid to open my eyes to find out what was happening, but suddenly, the guy holding the child kneeling rose suddenly and pushed my hand away, saying, "She is warming up; she is breathing; she is opening her eyes." Her mother, who was standing 20 feet away from us heard that, and rushed toward us, snatched the girl from the man holding the girl and, saying "thank you, thank you, thank you." I said, "thank you, Jesus; thank you, Jesus." This woman didn't know the Lord at the time, but she knows Him now. Glory to our Faithful God!!!

These 2 experiences shaped my belief system regarding demonic roles in human lives and how to keep them at bay. John 10:10 tells us that the thief comes not, but to steal, to kill, and to destroy... The devil is the thief Jesus was talking about in the passage. Jesus has come so that we may have life and have it more abundantly.

Demons' Confessions

I have watched teenagers possessed by demons as demons confessed through them. A girl confessed to how different demons would use her to trouble her father. She showed us the jungle where she often held a meeting with many demons at night. She described the manner and methods she used to trouble her father. I have listened to a housewife confessing her roles in her husband's misfortune, and said she felt compelled to tell me. One of these housewives was married to a medical practitioner who was my first landlord in Ibadan.

In those days, I was a novice in spiritual matters. I was just listening, and watching their responses, but didn't know what to do with the information these people are voluntarily presenting. The devil was probably laughing at me then because these people were crying out for help, and I wasn't as helpful to them. Demons' involvements in human lives are real. They are here to destroy us, but thanks to our God, the believers have the victory. We have overcome the devil and his demons

60

by the blood of Jesus Christ, and by the word of our testimony - Revelation 12:11. Hallelujah!

Self Help Exercises

1. *The author described his first encounter with demons in a 10-year-old boy. He noticed...*

a. *that the boy was acting crazy... and tearing the clothes off his body*

b. *that the boy was a nephew of his landlord and maybe 10 years of age*

c. *that he never had seen the boy act like that before*

d. *all the above*

2. *To be able to cast demons out of people, one must, in addition to prayers and fasting...*

a. *believe in the ministry of deliverance*

b. *believe that the name of Jesus Christ is powerful enough to kick the devil out of people*

c. *tell the devil where to go after being cast out of his victims*

d. *all the above*

3. *Author described another miracle, and this time it was on a 6-month-old daughter, the daughter of his landlord. All the following were true except...*

a. *the author wondered, "Why did this woman bring her dead child to me?"*

b. *he commanded the death demon to come out of the child in Jesus' name and it came out*

c. *John 10:10 states that the thief comes to steal, to kill, and to destroy, but...*

d. *the child did die. No miracle took place at all.*

4. *The author reported more encounters with demon-possessed individuals, including the following except...*

a. *a girl the devil demonized to torment her father*

b. *a housewife that the devil demonized to persecute her husband*

c. *the devil has no boundaries; he can possess anyone that gives him access*

d. *the devil is afraid of anyone, holy or unholy, as long as one can quote Scriptures*

5. *The following statements are true except...*

a. *that when an evil spirit is cast out of a person, he is gone and never tries to come back*

b. *that when an evil spirit is cast out of a person, he will always try to come back*

c. *the demons' involvement in humans' lives are real, and their mission is to seduce us to sin against God*

d. *the Christians have overcome the devil by the blood of Jesus Christ and by the word of our testimony*

Answers

1d, 2d, 3d, 4d, 5a

Chapter 6
COMING TO THE UNITED STATES OF AMERICA

I am very thankful to God that my visa interview went favorably. About 13 of us went but only a few of us were approved. I happened to be the last one of those approved. I was very ecstatic that I received my visa but very sad for those who were not approved. These students have struggled to get the money, they paid the Professor, paid the tuition and went through a lot of red tape, just to get to the finish line and be told "sorry, not approved." That was devastating. I prayed for them and left the rest in God's hand.

I strongly believe that my experience with the immigration process from Nigeria to the United States of America was easy and painless because I was being obedient in following a vision that God had given me. My experience went quickly and appeared easy. Because of that, I believed that my migration was confirmed, and I was to follow my journey into my destiny in the United States. I knew He was the One sending me in this journey (Matthew 28:20).

Once I got my student visa, I started preparation. Then the day finally arrived for me to get on the airplane for the first time ever. A throng of people escorted me to the airport. These were my children, their mom, my mother, brothers and sisters, people from my church branches, and well-wishers. It was a bittersweet experience. Bitter because I was leaving my family, friends, and relatives, and who knows if we will ever see each other again. Sweet because it seemed an adventure to travel out of my only known country, to go to another country and see for myself how other people live. Our KLM airplane took off and before I knew it we were in Amsterdam. We transited at Amsterdam, spent a couple of hours at the airport, then took off to Atlanta, Georgia. From Atlanta, Georgia we flew a domestic flight to Montgomery, Alabama. Then, from Montgomery, Alabama we took a bus ride to Selma University in Selma, Alabama. Everything seemed like a dream. I had to pinch myself several times.

I did not know about Dr. Martin Luther King Jr. and the Civil Rights Movement in the United States at the time of my trip. Now I know that the first time I touched soil in the USA, I literally followed the footsteps of the American Civil Rights Movement. They are to be honored. Unto Jesus Christ, our Savior, and each of these giant freedom fighters, I am forever indebted.

The Surprises

There were many things I saw that took me by surprise when I got to Selma University's campus. I never thought I would see wooden houses, houses made of wood and sitting on pier and beam. I said to myself, "Our Nigerian buildings are stronger and better looking than this." I saw empty streets; it looked like a ghost town. It was January, and it was cold, so I said to myself maybe it was the cold weather that made people stay inside, and that turned out to be the case. I discovered later that Selma was a vibrant city. Anyhow, everywhere I looked seemed different from the America I had in mind, but I held my peace.

The Lack of Respect

Selma University is a Historically Black Baptist Bible College, and a member of Historically Black Colleges and Universities (HBCU).

On the first day of class I saw and heard some students calling their lecturers by their first names. I was surprised to see a lack of respect for older people. When I meet an older person, I would greet them by bowing down with my head approaching the ground and my palms touching the ground. Some people automatically reached out to grab or try to rescue me, perhaps thinking that I am having a heart attack. They thought "that" was strange. I always tell them I am not fainting, that is my culture. That is how we greet elders and show respect. The elder may respond by verbally showering their blessings upon us as one prostrates. Some may stretch out their right hand in our direction to show acceptance. Some may simply nod their head and smile. Some may show no emotion but still recognize obeisance. Contrariwise, here in America, it seems everybody shakes hands. What baffles me the most is seeing young people stretching out their hands to shake the elder's hand. At first, I was stunned but gradually retrained my brain, reminding myself that I am not in Nigeria but America, and when in Rome you do as the Romans do.

Food Challenges

Another challenge facing me was food but that wasn't a big deal because I am used to fasting, and I can survive with little food. The only thing I had to get used to doing here in America regarding food was to learn how to use utensils to eat with, rather than using just my fingers.

The Use of Profanity

Another challenge is the use of profanity. The "f" word, the "s" word, or any vulgarity were never part of my vocabulary. Here in America, I hear those kinds of words a lot and, even now, I am still trying to get used to hearing them.

Also, there are some words in America that I had to learn and understand quickly. For example, in my country, we called the storage area in the back of a car the "boot." Americans call it "trunk." The "bonnet" of a car they call a "hood." What we called trousers in Nigeria, Americans called pants, the driveways they called parkways, and parkways they called driveways. It took me a while to make sense of those words.

Jesus Visited Me on Selma University Campus in Alabama

This experience took place a few weeks after I landed at Selma University, in Selma Alabama. I was in a deep sleep, at night, and I saw Jesus with 2 angels, all in white robes. Jesus had a stern look on His face and I was wondering "why?" I questioned, in my dream, "why did He look so unhappy?" I saw His head as if it was spinning counterclockwise, with a stern look on His face. He didn't seem to be happy with whatever it was that He saw. In that dream, I didn't hear Him say anything, I can only assume that Jesus hated what He saw in that dream, not only within American society, but in the entire world. God hates sins, and if we love Him, we will keep His words. - John 14:23. Jesus wants us to be holy. He wants us to travel through the Narrow gate. The Narrow gate requires Holiness, and it leads to Heaven.

Broadway is the way of sinners, and it leads to hell. God wants us to be holy.

Enter by the narrow gate; for wide is the gate and broad is the way that leads to destruction, and there are many who go in by it. Because narrow is the gate and difficult is the way which leads to life, and there are few who find it. Beware of false prophets, who come to you in sheep's clothing, but inwardly they are ravenous wolves. You will know them by their fruits... Not everyone who says to Me, 'Lord, Lord,' shall enter the kingdom of heaven, but he who does the will of My Father in heaven. Many will say to Me in that day, 'Lord, Lord, have we not prophesied in Your name, cast out demons in Your name, and done many wonders in Your name, and then I will declare to them, 'I never knew you; depart from Me, you who practice lawlessness! Therefore, whoever hears these sayings of Mine, and does them, I will liken him to a wise man who built his house on the rock: and the rain descended, the floods came, and the winds blew and beat on that house; and it did not fall, for it was founded on the rock. But everyone who hears these sayings of Mine, and does not do them, will be like a foolish man who built his house on the sand: and the rain descended, the floods came, and the winds blew and beat on that house; and it fell. And great was its fall. – Matthew 7: 13-27.

Incompatible Roommates

In Selma University, I lived on the campus, I was assigned to a room with two other students. One of the students was another Nigerian, and we all came to together. His bed was straight up at the end of the room, far left at the corner against the wall, mine was in the middle on the left side also against the wall, and the third man, who was an African American guy occupied the first bed on the left against the wall. There were dividers in between the beds. The Nigerian guy was a Muslim, and when in the room he was either sleeping, studying for the class, or worshipping his Allah. I pretty much did the same. If I was not studying, I would be sleeping or praying. Our third roommate often traveled home on the weekend. During the week, however, he would invite his girlfriend over at night. The girl would quietly come in, and before we knew it, there were a lot of moaning sounds that got louder and louder until one or both climaxed. Believe me, it was annoying. This young man was very bright. He was a handsome individual who happened to love cigarettes, marijuana, and sex. We tried to talk him into stopping this midnight habit of his, but it didn't do us any good or make any difference. He told me I must be gay, and that I needed to ask the school to move me to another room. Mind you, I was the oldest person in the room. He told me "Man, what's up with you? You get you another room, man, you heard me, man?" I didn't want to make a report because of any possible revenge. I rubbed it in, and just continued to pray, and tried to be friendly with him just to show him there are no hurt feelings between us. To my surprise however, in about a week or so, I was asked to move to another room across the hall in the same building. This room already has one occupant, and I was asked to move in there. The man, the occupant, was a singer at his church, he was a handsome, light-skinned African American man. Not very long after he found out that I was a minister, he offered to travel with me to sing at my revival meetings.

Being Approached by a Gay Roommate

One Sunday, my new roommate decided to go to Sunday service with me to hear me preach. I said that would be great. I never read too much into any of his lewd behaviors, but my Spirit kept telling me to watch and to pray. On that Sunday morning, I got out of the shower with my chest out but everything else was covered. I was trying to get dressed for Church. Suddenly, this man started to make some "ishhhhh" noise at me. At first, I thought there was a snake in the room. I didn't know he was making sexual sounds about my chest or rib cage because I didn't know that much about gay men at the time. He said to me, "Elijah, I like good-looking men." I was like, "Why God, why me? I felt like I was going from a frying pan to fire—why me, Lord?" I sat him down and shared what I knew with him using the Scripture, not condemning him but condemning the sin I perceived of him. I told him, I like women, not men. I am not gay. I continued to share the Scriptures with him. At the same time, I was praying for him, for me, and for my former roommates. This man continued to go to church with me after our conversation. Then, people started to notice that we were friends. They started to talk about us as being lovers. I thought that my former roommate started the rumor, and he could be the one who recommended that the University paired me with a gay roommate, but I wasn't sure. Many of the students assumed that since my roommate and I are getting along so well we must be sexual lovers. Some students asked me if I was gay, I said no. "Do you all think I am gay because I have no girlfriend, and I am rooming with a gay man, and we seem to get along? Well, am I supposed to hate him because he is gay?" I asked them.

Evangelizing the Campus Students

About a month later, I felt in my spirit that God was instructing me to evangelize the campus students. I kept praying asking God to show me how I could do it because my English language skills weren't as good as I wanted, but I have always been able to write fairly well. I felt God was telling me to use what I have rather than thinking of my human deficit. So, I started to gather some Scriptures together: Scriptures on Salvation, Holiness, Sin and its Consequences, Forgiveness, Heaven and Hell, and the Devil and his demons. I purchased some cardboard and markers, and I started to inscribe the Scriptures on the cardboard. At the same time God opened a door for me to work in the campus Cafeteria through a work-study program. I became the dishwasher for the students after they finished eating and I had a fairly good relationship with the kitchen lady, Chef.

One day I asked the Chef if she would do me a favor. She said "sure, what is it?" Then I told her that God wants me to evangelize the campus students. She was a Christian herself. She said "Yes, I am not going to say no to that." So, I told her that I will need to borrow the cafeteria's 4 walls temporarily. I told her my plan to post every Scripture I had written on the cardboard, on the cafeteria walls. I took her by surprise because no one had ever made such a request. Though a little reluctant, she agreed. I posted the Scriptures on the wall. I did it early in the morning before breakfast. Not even an hour into breakfast, I saw students lining up to read the Scriptures, and I can hear them discussing it and saying, "Whoever put these words on the wall is right, and we need to change. We need to change our behaviors." This was going on every single day, after breakfast, lunch, and dinner for several months.

At first, the students were more interested in knowing who posted the Scriptures. As time progressed, the Scriptures became topics of group discussions among the students. It took them a while before they knew it was me who posted the Scriptures on the walls. I was excited to see that many of the students had started to go to church on Sundays, some of them were converted, many repented, and many students seemed to start taking their salvation seriously. Some of the teachers took an interest in the Scriptures as well.

Students would come to me for advice. I was happy to see some of those Scriptures still on the wall when I left the campus in the Summer of 1987. I made a difference. We are the light of the world. There is a song:

this little light of mine, I am going let it shine, this little light of mine, I am going let it shine, let it shine, let it shine, let it shine.

Evangelizing the City of Selma

In the Summer of 1987, before I left the Campus to go to Montgomery, God wanted me to evangelize the city. That seemed a little too tough to do, I said to myself. Then, I asked God how would I do it? Then He puts an idea on my mind, and in all honesty, it turned out to be the easiest thing I have ever done when it comes to evangelism. I designed a flyer on Salvation and walked the streets of Selma, Alabama, dropping the flyer in every church mailbox with instructions to the pastors on how to raise disciples in their congregations and encouraging them to set a soul-winning day—a day to get out of the 4 walls to reach the lost souls with the Gospel of our Lord, Jesus Christ. It worked. Our God is faithful. In less than 6 months, when I came back to visit Selma City on the weekend, I saw a couple of ministers in the streets, witnessing. All Glory and Honor belong to our God.

Social and Cultural Differences

The social differences were something that I had to learn quickly. I expected some social and cultural differences in every country but not as surprising as this: One day I was holding a conversation with my biology class professor, on the campus. We were members of the same Church. On that day however, after we ended our discussion and we were about to walk away, I said "I love you sir, and good night." He quickly yelled out saying "No, no, no, Elijah." Then he asked me to come here. I said, "Yes, sir." I walked closer to him, and then he warned me very nicely, but seriously, "Don't ever say that you love me in public anymore." He said it is okay to say that to him when we are in a church setting; otherwise, saying that to him in public carries a different meaning. He added that people who may have heard me saying "I love you" to him may be thinking we are sexual lovers. I was thinking in my head "What was he talking about?" Where I came from, we say "I love you" to one another at every opportunity we get. In Nigeria, brothers hug, holding hands, and girls do the same thing, and it doesn't raise any suspicion. It is a general expression of family closeness, and nothing more. Hearing my professor warned me as seriously as he did left my jaw dropping. I was scared and quickly apologized.

The Early Financial Struggle

There were undeniable financial challenges. All of the students who came from Nigeria at the time, including myself were facing possible deportation for non-payments. Our education tuition and fees were supposedly paid for in Nigeria before we stepped on the plane but unfortunately, the money didn't make it to Selma University. We were told before we left Nigeria (as I remembered it) that our tuition and fees were paid in full. The news of non- payment took all of us by surprise. Thank God, He intervened in time and on our behalf. With prayers, faith, our good behaviors on the Campus, and mostly the grace of God, we were allowed to complete our 2 years of education. Glory to God.

At the time, the financial struggle took a toll on me, but I refused to give up. I worked 2 jobs and enrolled in at least 15 college credit hours. Both of my jobs were kitchen jobs. One was on the campus and the second job was at a grocery store Deli, just for a few hours a day. I had to be financially responsible for my own basic needs. There was no one to help me in the United States of America. I was all I had with God on my side.

After graduation, I moved off campus to stay in a church building: Grace church, Selma Alabama. The lady pastor and her husband allowed me to stay in one of the rooms in the Church building while I cleaned and watched over the building. It was a moment of prayer for me. I had no gun for my personal protection or to protect the Church building, but I knew I had Christ. The Bible says, "...except the Lord keep the city the watchman wakes in vain." - Psalm 127:1. I had no guns, but I felt safe. After the summer, I got accepted into a graduate school in Montgomery, Alabama. It was Alabama Christian School of Religion. The founder, Dr. Turner, was a member of the Church of Christ. It was at this school that I met a pastor who introduced me to the woman who would soon become the mother of my twins. At Montgomery, I worked as an assistant janitor at the church where I worshiped and, later on, I worked at a grocery store to help collect and manage grocery carts.

The Inner Struggle and Guilt

Now we are at one of the landmarks in my life that I don't like to think or talk about: the Guilt. I felt guilty for leaving my children and their mother in Nigeria, not knowing the condition they were in, even though the church where I was ministering at, before I left Nigeria, was helping them financially. I missed seeing my children growing up. Of everyone and everything that I missed, I missed my children the most, and more than some fathers would. I missed my family very dearly. I missed my parents, my brothers, and my sisters. I missed my friends as well, but I was here facing situations beyond my control in the United States of America. I asked myself, "Why did I leave my children and their mother in Nigeria, while I am here, stuck, in America?" I have no money to travel home, no job, and I had no permanent resident status to access the government benefits that I needed so badly. If I had asked for a voluntary deportation, I may have gotten it, but I may never be allowed into the United States of America ever again. I was very depressed and confused.

In those days before I ever knew about calling cards, it would cost hundreds of dollars a month to make international calls to loved ones, and up to one hundred dollars or more to mail a couple of letters. I had no access to the internet or email as we do today. I felt stuck but, during all of it, I continued to sense the presence of God with me. Our God is a Promise Keeper. What did Jesus say in the Gospel of St. Matthew, Chapter 19, verse 29?

And everyone that hath forsaken houses, or brethren, or sisters, or father, or mother, or wife, or children, or lands, for my name's sake, shall receive a hundredfold, and shall inherit everlasting life.

The Disappointment

Up to this point, the education I obtained since I landed in America was only secular and that was not why I flew to America, all the way from Nigeria. I came to America to increase my Bible knowledge and better my relationship with God. I was hoping for a blockbuster, something that would ignite me from the inside out. I wanted more Holy Ghost Fire in my bones but, unfortunately, I experienced nothing like that at all. Nothing I learned increased my knowledge of God or made me a better Christian. God taught me many things I know about Him based on my own life experiences, Bible readings, and my personal daily devotions. The Calvary Bible College I attended in Nigeria had given me a solid foundation in the Lord. Yes, when it comes to Bible knowledge, I already had a very solid foundation before coming to the United States of America. So, to go back to Nigeria with a fragmentation of secular knowledge, and not sure whether I would be able to return would have put me back to square one. I didn't want to go back to square one. That would have defeated the purpose. I didn't want to shame myself. I didn't want to disappoint those people who believed so much in me. I asked myself: "if going back home emptyhanded would be my end-result then, why did I come to America in the first place?" So, I had to make a very tough decision, and I had to make it quickly. So, I did what I thought was best for me at the time. I stayed and was fully determined to tough it out. I didn't have many options. I let go of the relationship I had at home and started a new one. It hurts. It hurts me to the core that the relationship had to end that way. It was the most difficult decision I ever made. I will not wish my enemy, if I have one, to ever go through what I went through that led to the decision I made.

I must say this, however, there is nothing I can become in this country that will make up for the loss I suffered. Nothing can bring back those father-child childhood moments that I have missed. My children are grown now, raising their own families, and I am glad to live long enough to see that. Thanks to God Almighty, the 2 older children that I left in Nigeria are now here, in America and, a few years later, they brought their mother. God is a Promise Keeper.

Now, after I had been in America for about 2 years, I knew I had a decision to make, and I did. I started a new relationship in 1988. Being in a new relationship comes with its own set of challenges. There is more to read about my American Relationships later in this book.

The Rejection: Dallas Theological Seminary Rejected Me, and Reversed My Admission

I got married in 1988 to a lady who later gave birth to my baby twins. Shortly after my wedding in 1988, we left Montgomery Alabama and moved to Dallas Texas for my doctoral program at Dallas Theological Seminary. I was very excited when I received the acceptance letter from the school but unfortunately, my admission was terminated abruptly after a few weeks on campus and a few days of classes. I am not sure what prompted the termination.

Dallas Theological Seminary rejected me, and this is how I remembered it: we were given a questionnaire to express our doctrinal beliefs about some specific charismatic practices, including speaking in tongues, laying on of hands, and miracles among the lists. It seemed, at the time, that I was the only one who defended all of these practices, and confirmed they are acts of the Holy Ghost. Then, I knew I was in trouble because I was the only one with different views. A few days later, I received a letter from the administration; I said to myself "This may not be good," and I was right. The letter stated, in a sly technical way, that my admission was reversed. I felt persecuted. I have spoken in tongues in the past, not that I have the gift, but as evidence when I was baptized with the Holy Ghost. I cannot deny the reality. I have laid my hand on the sick in the name of Jesus and watched them fully recover. So, I cannot deny the reality. I was okay with their decision. I still have the rejection letter and will keep it for a long time.

Too Many Things Happening at the Same Time: I Lost My Parents

Unfortunately, it was during this time also that I lost both of my parents in Nigeria, in less than 5 years apart, but I couldn't raise enough money to go home to pay my parents' last respects. It is a scar so deeply embedded in my heart, but the Lord our God is my Comforter.

Between leaving Dallas Theological Seminary in 1988, and enrolling in East Texas State University, which is now Texas A & M-

Commerce, where I obtained my Master of Science Degree in 1996, I have studied in many other Texas colleges. I took a couple of correspondence and on-line courses as well before I obtained my doctoral degree in 2010. It has been a long journey to where I am today. All Glory and Honor go to our God.

My Health Issues: Demon Attacks & the Medical Community

I have a high respect for the medical community. They are ministers of God in their own right, but they are ministers only in a natural capacity. We know that all wisdom belongs to God. Nonetheless, many of the health issues we, Christians, are wrestling with today are demonic attacks in disguise and we cannot fight spiritual wars with natural means. It won't work. God is our Healer. He is the Doctor who operates without a scalpel.

We ought to recognize the contributions of doctors in our society. Doctors have helped deliver babies when mothers fall short of having them naturally. Doctors make alternative legs for Amputees, help replace failing hearts, lungs, kidneys etc. I, too, had a successful neck surgery in 2006 shortly after the release of the 1st Edition of my book, Thy Will O Lord, to correct a spinal cord injury. Physicians are God's messengers if their primary purpose is to save lives and/or make living more tolerable for human beings.

My Nerve Damage & Miraculous Healing

In the very early 90s, before my spinal cord injury in 2006, I had an accident on the job. I was newly hired at UPS and was there for a little less than 90 days when a heavy box of nails dropped off the shelf onto my shoulder. Immediately I felt a disconnection between my neck and my shoulder; it was very painful. I reported the accident and was sent home. The same week I was sent to a physical therapist for a few sessions of pain treatments. None of those things worked. Then I was told that UPS had rendered all the medical help they could render, and I am now on my own. I was told I was not yet fully employed, but on a probationary period when the accident occurred. That was correct. I have just started the job, and I could not argue their position. I had no money, and I was in pain. I went to Parkland Hospital a couple of times for assessments. I was in desperate need of relief. I don't like taking pills and I hate surgery. Finally, I was scheduled for surgery at Parkland. I couldn't wait because the pain was so severe. I couldn't hold my head nor raise my right hand. I felt mildly paralyzed on my right side, from my neck down. I wobbled when I walked. I felt like my life was over. My wife, at the time, suggested that I may need to go ahead and apply for disability. Well, I did not know how long that would take to be approved or even if I would be approved. I was incredibly sad, thinking my life could be over at an early age, and I have not accomplished anything that I came to America to accomplish.

Now, the day came to have the surgery. I went to Parkland Hospital and signed myself up. I went through the process all the way. They finally put me on the operation table. I was there staring at the ceiling, and the doctors, nurses, and interns, all started coming into the operation room. I started counting heads, and how many hands were ready to go to work on me. Suddenly, I heard a voice saying to me "Don't, don't let them do this surgery. If you allow this surgery, you are dead." I heard the voice only once, and that was enough for me. Something rose up in me. It was faith. And I yelled out "No, no, no, I changed my mind. I am healed. Jesus healed me." I was just talking faith, calling those things that are not, as if they are. Then the doctors, nurses, and all that were there for my operation thought I was just scared or a little anxious. So, they tried to convince me to go through it, but I made it clear that I changed my mind, and I had the right to do so.

Frankly, the only choice that they had left was to have me sign a release stating that I left against the doctor's order. I signed the release paper, got up and was getting ready to leave then one of the doctors came to me saying that he is a Christian too. He said to me "You have blessed me today." I wasn't sure what he meant. I know that getting out of there was what God wanted me to do and I did. With God, I know I can deal with the pain. I just believed that I would be healed and if not, that is ok too. As always however, God never fails. In less than 3 weeks of praying, confession of faith, slowly but gradually, I was miraculously healed without popping any pills or having surgery. God is Good all the time and, all the time God is Good. All of these experiences helped me to develop a keen interest in health education and, also, to learn more about the role of a person's spiritual life on his or her mental health and physical wellness.

Well, as you might have rightly assumed, I lost my job at UPS. I lost my job and couldn't find another. I couldn't find a job using my degree nor a decent odd job without a degree requirement.

One day I went around looking for a job at different business entities including gas stations. The girl at one of the gas stations looked at me strangely and said: "you have a master's degree and you're looking for work at a gas station, are you sure you are okay?" I said, "Yes, I am ok, and I am willing to do anything as long as it is legal to provide for my family." Prior to that I worked as a janitor.

Becoming A Taxicab Driver in America

I remember that I met a cab driver at Whole Foods Market in the late 80s, where I used to work for about 2 and a half years. I remember that the driver brought one of his regular customers to the store one day for grocery shopping, and that was about a year before I quit working at the market. It was at this Whole Food Market where I heard God asking me to quit my job and go full time into the ministry. And, as always, in those days if I am convinced it was God speaking to me, no question asked, I simply obeyed. So, I quit. Working at this store, the presence of God was so strong in my life that I just could not contain it. If I was taking a restroom break, I would pray quietly for as long as I was on that commode. When I had a lunch break, there were 2 employees who alternated to loan me their bedroom keys so I could go into their room to spend my lunch time in prayers. At home, there was no separate room where I could have privacy, so I prayed in the car or stopped at a parking lot with my driver seat lowered back. I would pray for 1 or 2 hours or longer. Now, to get back to my story, this driver would brag about how much money he was making driving a cab. He said he was making more money than people with a master's degree, and I believed him. Also, he said no one could fire him since he was using his own vehicle. Better yet, he said that income can be tax-free driving a cab. I remember all his words.

I know I had to find something dependable. The cab driver sounded good to me if it puts food on the table and help me to provide for my children. So, I applied to become a taxi driver. It was a natural profession for me because I made a living as a driver in Nigeria. So, I decided to start with the Royal Cab Company. It was a rental car. One year later I was able to buy my own vehicle and moved to another company. I drove a taxi from 1992 to around 1995.

Student at East Texas State University

In 1994, I was at DFW International Airport waiting in the taxi drivers' queue for passengers. Sometimes we spent 2 or 3 hours waiting in the queue, and I normally sat in my car reading the Bible or praying. This day I stepped out of the car and was holding a conversation with a guy. He told me he was attending East Texas State University with a major in counseling. I had never heard of that college before, I told him. At the end of our conversation, he suggested that I give the school a call. I did. I enrolled in their counseling program in 1994 before the school changed her name to Texas A & M University at Commerce. I was one of the first students to graduate under the name Texas A & M University.

My Employment at MHMR, Now Metrocare Services

In 1995, I was introduced to MHMR (Mental Health Mental Retardation) by one of my classmates for an internship. I have been with MHMR since even through the name changes. It was where I needed to be. I graduated from Texas A & M in 1996 with a Master of Science Degree and became a paid employee at MHMR as a caseworker. Later I obtained my professional license in 1998 and became one of the clinic's licensed professional counselors (LPC). I believed that God had me where He wanted me to be.

MHMR is a community support "Mental Health, Mental Retardation" clinic where mentally ill adults and/or children with mental retardation can go to see a psychiatrist, a nurse, and/or a counselor for mental challenges they may have. MHMR changed name to Dallas Metrocare in the 1990s and later Metrocare Services. I worked at MHMR, now Metrocare Services, from 1996 through 2008 with a brief intermission, and until I heard God told me to get out, and I did. I left the agency for good in 2008.

Self Help Exercises

1. *The author expressed his thankfulness to God for his visa approval at the American Embassy in Nigeria. All of the following statements are true except...*

   a. *about 13 of them went, but only a few were approved*

   b. *he received his visa but was very sad for those who were not approved*

   c. *the applicants, the students...went through a lot of red tapes in the process*

   d. *the author's visa approval is just a matter of "luck," and God has nothing to do with it*

2. *A throng of people that escorted the author to the airport on the day of his departure included...*

   a. *the author's children and their mom*

   b. *the author's brothers and sisters*

   c. *many well-wishers from the author's home church branches*

   d. *all the above*

3. *Coming to America, the author seemed to follow in the footsteps of the Civil Rights Movement's leaders. He journeyed through three of major historical cities in the United States of America, including...*

   a. *Atlanta, Georgia*

   b. *Montgomery, Alabama*

   c. *Selma, Alabama*

   d. *all the above*

4. Some of the surprises the author noticed when he got to

Selma in Alabama, were

a. *seeing houses built with wood, and appearing to be sitting on pier and beam*

b. *the empty streets*

c. *a and b*

d. *no surprises at all*

5. One of the cultural shocks that the author labeled as lack of respect is...

a. *that a young man would initiate a handshake when greeting an elderly man*

b. *not having African foods in the campus cafeteria*

c. *American students not speaking any African languages*

d. *American students not trying to dress like Africans*

6. The author, sharing his dream of when he was visited by the Lord and two angels, said...

a. *Jesus Christ had a stern look on His face*

b. *The Lord's head was spinning clockwise as He looked around*

c. *it didn't seem as if Jesus liked what He saw*

d. *all the above*

7. The author wrestled with "profanity" and some American vernaculars, including...

a. *using "f" and "s" words even in decent conversations*

b. *calling a "Boot" of a car a "Trunk," a "Bonnet" of a car a "Hood," the entrance of home garage, "a Driveway," and a high traffic road like the Toll Road is called a "Parkway"*

c. *calling Trousers "Pants"*

d. *all the above*

8. *According to the author, God still works miracles if we believe (Circle): True or False?*

9. *The health providers (though in the natural) are ministers of God as well (Circle): True or False?*

10. *All authority, including the political powers, are ministers of God according to Romans 13 (Circle): True or False?*

11. *After the author lost his job at UPS, and couldn't find a job, he...*

a. *became a cab driver to support his family*

b. *gave up on life and became a public liability*

c. *joined the military in America*

d. *none of the above*

12. *While driving a cab, the author...*

a. *went back to school for a more marketable degree*

b. *enrolled in a counseling program at ETSU which later became Texas A&M University.*

c. *graduated in 1996 with a Master of Science degree in Counseling from Texas A & M*

d. *all the above*

Answers

1d, 2d, 3d, 4c, 5a, 6d, 7d, 8True, 9True, 10True, 11a, 12d

Rabiu Elijah Omolaja

Chapter 7
MY BROKEN WEDDING RING FINGER: A WARNING OR PREDESTINATION?

I n the late sixties (1960s), and as a teenager, I was a soccer player. I could play any position and sometimes I played goalie. In one of our practices, I happened to be the goalie. A player from the opposing team hit the ball toward our goal net. The ball was flying in my direction ferociously with force and I intercepted it with both of my palms. Surprisingly, however, only one of my left fingers felt the full force, the full impact of the raging ball. The finger that felt the full impact of the ferociously flying raging ball was the one next to the pinky. It broke instantaneously and appears crooked to this day. Looking at the finger today, though healed, it is easy to notice its crookedness. It is depressing, for it serves as a constant reminder of my marital failures. It hurts deeply but, I must count it all joy according to James 1: 2.

...give thanks in all circumstances; for this is God's will for you in Christ Jesus. - 1 Thessalonians 5:18

Not until later in life, did I find out that the finger next to the pinky is traditionally a wedding ring finger. My broken wedding ring finger then became a significant metaphor or predictor of what some of my marriages or conjugal life would look like. In those days, I didn't think anything of the broken finger. I never knew there was a wedding ring finger until later in life. None of the married couples I knew in Nigeria wore wedding rings or desired to have one. It wasn't a big deal to me until now, not until I came to America and saw married couples with wedding rings. Even in my first marriage in America, neither of us wore a wedding ring or desired one. The broken finger accident had no meaning to me until now. I was 13 or 14 years old when the accident occurred. Now, in retrospect, it seems so metaphorical.

The Vision I Saw That Women Would Be My Downfall—Is It a Warning or a Predestination?

In 1975, shortly after my call into the ministry, and before I started any conjugal relationship, I had a troubling vision. In that vision, I was warned that women might be my downfall. I didn't think anything of it because I was so sure and said, "that would never happen to me." I said to myself, "that would be over my dead body." I then asked myself "how could I fall when I am not even up? No one knew me or knew anything about me or my ministry." At that time, the vision seemed so redundant. I saw also, in my dream, the first 2 ladies I would marry here in America, in a subsequence order, even before I left Nigeria. I saw each at separate times in my dream. The first lady I saw having my baby, the second lady I saw in bed with me. Both dreams came through, and both relationships ended up in divorce. Now I realize that many of the things I have experienced in America were revealed to me, ahead of time, either in dreams or through visions.

Sometimes, some things are just unavoidable in life. No matter how much we try to prevent them, they will show up. They are like an accident waiting to happen. They are an integral part of our existence. Without them, our life would be incomplete. I have, however, found a way to embrace all my life's experiences as patches that form the quilt of my life. Without any of these patches, my life would be incomplete. I embrace each of them rather than run away from them. They are part of me: the good, the bad, and ugly. They are what make me who I am today —stronger, wiser, and more forgiving. I know that God has

84

forgiven me. I have forgiven myself for any wrong I might have done, and I have forgiven all my abusers.

Disclaimer

I don't want to leave the readers with the impression that the hell I went through in life was predestined or ; that these experiences were programmed to show up at certain times in my life. Thinking that God chose those experiences for me would be very misleading. The wedding finger accident, the dreams about women being my downfall are not predestinations but warnings. I failed to heed those warnings.

Yes, nothing occurs to us without God's awareness. Whether it is a trial of faith, temptation, tribulation, or any type of affliction we may experience in life, God is not ignorant of them. And, to put it more bluntly, the devil can't touch any of us, the followers of Christ, without obtaining God's permission first. So, the questions are: since God wasn't ignorant of our predicaments, 1) what part does He play in them? 2) Why doesn't He prevent them anyway? And, if any, 3) what part do we play in them? I will attempt to answer these three questions to the best of my ability.

1) What part does God play in life's tragedies, trials, and challenges?

The only part I believe that God plays in our life's challenges is allowing them to take place. He is not the author of anything that makes our living miserable, but He allows them for reasons we may never know or understand. We know, however that God's thoughts towards us are not evil but good, according to the Scripture.

In Jeremiah 29: 11, God reveals what He thinks about us: *"For I know the thoughts that I think toward you, saith the LORD, thoughts of peace, and not of evil, to give you an expected end."* It is the devil who constantly condemning us before God and challenging our loyalty towards God at the same time. The devil always puts God on the defense when it comes to us, and God always asserts our loyalty to Him, and telling the devil that "no matter how many times you try to move me against my children, they will maintain their loyalty for me.

They are mine." So was the case with Job. Only with God's permission was Satan able to touch Job and any of us. Job proved the devil wrong. Yes, Job wished he was dead, cursed the day he was born, but he maintained his loyalty to God. There are not very many Jobs left on the planet Earth today (Job Chapters 1 & 2). As the case was with Job, so also it was with our Lord Jesus Christ. We must stay loyal to our God.

After His baptism, the Bible states that Jesus was led by the Spirit to be tempted by the devil after 40 days of fasting and hunger (Matthew 4). Satan launches his attacks on us, God's children, when we are most vulnerable. The devil, with his conditional two-letter word "If:" "If thou be the Son of God...", the devil tried to move Jesus to deny God as His Father, to worship hiṁ (the devil). Pay attention to Matthew 4: 8-10. The devil's attempt in all our trials and tribulations is to create enmity between us and God, using life's adverse events to negate God's love for us and, in the process, presenting himself as the best alternative.

The devil's tactics, as stated above, are not new. They are the same old Serpent's tactics that he was using before we were created. The devil started this rivalry war in Heaven. Whether you call him Devil, Satan, Lucifer, or the old Serpent, he was the first politician. He started his campaign against God in Heaven among the angels and he won the support of one-third of the angels, The devil campaigned against God saying he could rule better than God, and one-third of the angels followed him to depose God. Both Satan and the angels that followed him were thrown out of Heaven. Satan and these fallen angels are the evil spirits, the demons, that are tormenting us today. They are here to steal from us, to kill us, and to destroy us (John 10:10) but, Jesus has come to give us life, and to give us Life abundantly.

Isaiah 14: 12-14 states this about Satan, the devil called Lucifer:

How art thou fallen from heaven, O Lucifer, son of the morning! How art thou cut down to the ground, which didst weaken the nations! For thou hast said in thine heart, I will ascend into heaven, I will exalt my throne above the stars of God: I will sit also upon the mount of the congregation, in the sides of the north: I will ascend above the heights of the clouds; I will be like the Highest.

The angels who joined Lucifer to rebel against God are what we call evil spirits today, they are the demons working with the devil to make our lives miserable. It was the same Satan, called Lucifer in the beginning, and represented by the serpent in the Garden of Eden. The serpent deceived the first couple to disobey the first and one simple commandment. God had commanded Adam saying, "don't eat this one specific fruit". There were millions of other fruits to eat from, but don't eat from this one. How much easier can that be?

And the Lord God commanded the man, saying, Of every tree of the garden thou mayest freely eat: But of the tree of the knowledge of good and evil, thou shalt not eat of it: for in the day that thou eatest thereof thou shalt surely die - Genesis 2: 16-17.

Why doesn't God prevent life tragedies, trials, and challenges?

God is shielding us from a lot of evils every day (Psalm 125:2). We experience only the ones He allows to come our way. I believe that trials and tribulations are our schoolmasters to help us draw closer to God. Many of us probably won't pray or read the Bible until we are going through some adverse life challenges — I mean, until the devil throws something our way, and then we will seek God. It shouldn't be like that, but unfortunately, that is how some of us operate. When things are going well, we think we have it made, and we don't need God. But when we lose our job, someone is sick, or we are in some legal trouble, then we start hugging and kissing the Bible. For many of us, life problems may be a necessary evil to bring us closer to God.

2. Which part are we, humans, playing in our life tragedies, trials, and challenges?

There are different reasons why many of us go through unpleasant experiences in life, so many reasons that this book is not roomy enough to accommodate them all. Some of us are ignorant, doing things without knowing the dangers and chaos that they may bring into our lives. Ignorance can be deadly. Some of us are not paying enough attention to our lives and what is going on around us. We pray, but we are not watchful. The Bible says to pray and be watchful. So it was in my case. I was very prayerful, believing in everything and examining nothing.

The Bible encourages us to prove all things. Foolish faith can be deadly. An ungodly lifestyle is another culprit. We need to make sure we are not being chastised for our misdeeds or misconduct. Christians will overcome the devil if we learn to simply submit ourselves unto God, resist the devil, and he will flee from us as the Scripture had predicted. - James 4:7.

Self Help Exercises

1. *In the sixties (1960s), and as a teenager, the author…*

a. *was a soccer player who could also play any position, and sometimes he played a goalie*

b. *broke his finger when intercepting a ferociously raging flying ball flung in his direction*

c. *never played soccer*

d. *a & b*

2. *Later in life, the author learned that his broken finger was…*

a. *traditionally a wedding ring finger*

b. *was very uncommon experience for goalie*

c. *none of the above*

d. *all the above*

3. *In 1975, shortly after his call into the ministry, and before he started any conjugal relationship, he had a troubling vision.*

In that vision, the author…

a. *was warned in a vision that women may be his downfall*

b. *was self-assured that women would never be his downfall*

c. *was in the dark, didn't dream or see a vision about anything*

d. *a & b*

4. Sometimes some things are just unavoidable in life, and…

a. *no matter how much we try to prevent them, they will show up*

b. *they are like accidents waiting to happen; they will manifest*

c. *they are an integral part of our existence and unavoidable*

d. *all the above*

5. Life experiences, whether good, bad, or ugly, can be necessary experiences and…

a. *without them, our life would be incomplete*

b. *they are patches woven into our "Quilt of Life"*

c. *They are to be embraced as part of us. They function as our school masters. We are to learn from them, and not run away from them*

d. *all the above*

6. The author wants to leave the readers with the impression…

a. *that the hell he went through in life was his own making. He could have avoided all of them in flying colors*

b. *that the experiences were programmed, to show up sometimes in his life at certain times and places*

c. *that the dream he had about women causing his downfall, and the wedding finger ring accident were divine warnings.*

d. *none of the above*

7. The author recognized and confessed that though he was warned in so many ways...

a. *it was he who failed to heed those divine warnings*

b. *it was God who failed to protect him*

c. *it was God who failed to equip him to overcome those temptations*

d. *none of the above*

Note: Yes, nothing occurs to us without God's awareness. Whether it is a trial of faith, temptation, tribulation, or any type of affliction we may experience in life, God is not ignorant of any of them. And, to put it more bluntly, the devil cannot touch any of us, the followers of Christ, without obtaining God's permission first.

The devil is permitted to tempt the children of God to prove our loyalty to God. The best of us will be tempted – 1 Corinthians 10:13

8. Briefly, what does Jeremiah 29:11 mean to you?

9. After His baptism, the Bible states that Jesus was ...

a. *led by the Spirit to be tempted by the devil*

b. *led by pride to be tempted by Satan*

c. *simply telling a story, and there was no temptation at all*

d. *none of the above*

10. The devil's tactics in our day...

a. *are the same tactics he used in heaven to mobilize one-third of the angels to follow him in his treason*

b. *are still the same as that of the old Serpent in the Garden of Eden when he cornered Eve*

c. *are to present himself to us as the best alternative, claiming he loves us more than God would ever love us*

d. *all the above*

Note: The devil is a fallen Lucifer who also played an important role in Adam's and Eve's fall Isaiah 14: 12-14 states this about Satan, the devil, called Lucifer:

How art thou fallen from heaven, O Lucifer, son of the morning! How art thou cut down to the ground, which didst weaken the nations! For thou hast said in thine heart, I will ascend into heaven, I will exalt my throne above the stars of God: I will sit also upon the mount of the congregation, in the sides of the north: I will ascend above the heights of the clouds; I will be like the most High.

Group Discussion: How and why did the devil (Lucifer) fall according to Isaiah 14: 12-14?

Answers

1d, 2a, 3d, 4d, 5d, 6c, 7a, 8Personal, 9a, 10d

Chapter 8
MY MARITAL RELATIONSHIPS AND FAILURES

My life story would be incomplete without referencing my failures in relationships, both in Nigeria and here in the United States of America. Now, 50 years in the Lord, I am still in the making and not yet perfect.

I am very grateful to God that I am not oblivious or blind to my shortcomings, even though it is painful to admit. Being able to recognize my imperfections and doing something about them can only make me a better person and set me free. So, your judgment of me is irrelevant. I judge myself daily. The Bible says the truth shall set us free, and that is what I am doing here: telling it as it was without making excuses or trying to externalize my mistakes. I am coming to terms with the mistakes I have made and the people I may have hurt. It is not about being judged or seeking some sympathy because none of that is needed. I have accepted the consequences of the decisions I allowed myself to make, and those decisions that I have refused to make. Indecision is also a decision.

Unintentional Deception

My first relationship occurred shortly after my conversion and call into the ministry. It was during my running away from the Lord that I met the mother of my older children. I was deceptive; I didn't fall in love at all, and I am very ashamed of the part I played then. It started as a visit, and then the visit ended up as a permanent move-in. I could have prevented it, but I didn't — very regretfully.

I was wrong, very wrong. I knew in my heart that it was a one- way love. I remember telling myself that my love would eventually catch up with hers, but it didn't. When I realized what I had done, however, I tried very hard to pray God into it, but it didn't work. I have suffered so much in silence for the decision I made. I tried to tough things out in those years, even though I knew I was unhappy. This woman was my first and authentic supporter. She was the first person to tell me, during my running away from God, in Kano, to answer God's calling in my life. Even though at that time she was a Muslim, she saw something greater in me. Contrariwise, however, I didn't know who I was, except that I was experiencing all these strange impressions that wouldn't go away. This lady later converted to Christianity while we were still living together. We had four children together and lost two of them at an early age. It is truly a sad story to tell: VERY SAD. I stayed in the relationship through thick and thin until the separation came in 1986.

If I need to apologize to anyone in all of my conjugal relationships, she is the one. And I can only hope that she has forgiven me. She will always be a part of my life, regardless. I am forever indebted to her.

The Law of Sowing and Reaping

I believe in the law of sowing and reaping. Whatever a man sows, he shall reap. I have reaped what I sowed. What goes around, has come around in my life. I paid a heavy price for my deception and dishonesty to the mother of my older children. Would I have prevented it today if the same scenario presented itself? Yes, knowing what I know now, I would! I deceived my first lady, and I got deceived twice. I reaped what I sowed, and I can only trust God for His grace and mercy. Here are my imperfections and the grace of the Lord our God revealed. God's mercy triumphs over His judgment– James 2:13. Glory and honor to God for grace and mercy.

1st Payback

My first relationship in America was real to me until I was proven wrong. Except for the relationship I had in Nigeria with the mother of my older children, I went into all of my subsequent relationships with the hope to stay in them for the rest of my life. I love praying and fasting both in good and bad times. Prayers and fasting were, and still are, some of my trademarks. I was praying and fasting when I was introduced to this individual in Montgomery, Alabama. I strongly believed that the relationship was meant to be. It was unfortunate that it didn't turn out that way. The devil was too busy. It seemed the payback was so swift. The relationship lasted for 12 years. It could have ended in the very first year, but I wanted to tough it out. I sincerely thought the marriage would survive any storm that came its way if I tried harder but, not so, it didn't survive. The harder I tried, the more miserable we both were. We went to counseling, we talked to our pastor, but nothing seemed to work for us. We were both exhausted, and after 12 years of turbulence, we decided to go our separate ways and be available for our children. I remember my first ex-wife's suicide attempt and homicidal threats. I remember being almost run over, intentionally, by her car. I thought I could get killed if I continued to stay in this relationship but, still, none of us was willing to initiate a divorce. Finally, she served me divorce papers on the job on November 5th. To prevent unnecessary confrontation, however, I had to move out of our bedroom into the closet under the stairs. I slept in that closet for three months, then I finally moved out of the house. The Lord knows, it was an ugly experience, and I can't say that enough: it was UGLY.

2nd Payback

About two years or so after the divorce, I found myself in another relationship. To my surprise, however, this individual carried the same first name as my ex-wife. I ignored whatever that could mean. Looking back, however, there were red flags—a lot of red flags— that were ignored. The relationship lasted almost 14 years before she abruptly moved out of the house. I invested all of myself, everything I had, in this relationship. My financial situation was much better at the time, and I gave the relationship everything I got. After eight years in the relationship, things began to take a wrong turn slowly but gradually. I said to myself, this is just another cloud that will soon pass away. I was wrong. The last six years of our marriage were a nightmare. It was hell on earth, to say the least.

The relationship was so infested and chronically triangulated. It was not triangulated with another human competitor (not that I knew of), but with other things I dare not mention here in this book, but, nevertheless, I refused to divorce my wife. I had convinced myself there would be no more divorce. I told myself it wasn't fun the first time, and it wouldn't be fun now. I didn't want to have to start all over again, and I did not want to be celibate either; I needed a companion. Two heads are better than one, or so I concluded.

In my first marriage, I lost our house to my ex-wife because of the minors involved. She was awarded the custody of the children, and they would need a roof over their heads. I kept telling myself, I will not experience any more divorce, no more loss. God hates divorce and I hate divorce too. So, I asked myself, "Why is this happening to me?" Why me? Not again, I kept reminding myself. On September 3rd, 2016, after 14 years of marriage, my second wife decided to move out of the house abruptly, just like that. It was very hurtful. I thought it was just going to be a temporary thing. I waited for months and tried to persuade her to return. One month passed by, two months, three months, and six months went by; still, she refused to come back home. At that time, I figured, it takes two to tango. I had no choice but to file for divorce. I felt deceived, and betrayed, I reaped what I sowed. Six months later, the divorce became final and that was in June of 2017, to be exact. In September of the same year, God wiped away my tears. It is not good for a man to be alone. God provided me with a permanent mate. I met my final wife. Though my ex-wife was also a believer, she chose to leave me hanging; she chose to leave her home. Well, "life must move on," I reasoned.

I Corinthians 7:15, Paul states:

"But if the unbeliever departs, let him (or her) depart. A brother or a sister is not under bondage in such cases, but God hath called us to peace." Though she is a believer, she chose to depart. Our God is a God of peace, and not a God of confusion and chaos.

As they say, in my current marriage, "Three times is the Charm." So, help Me God!

The Thorn in My Flesh

It is a thorn in the flesh for me and my ministry that I am forever robbed of the testimony that many ministers have, are proud of, and enjoy giving whenever the opportunity presents itself. I wish I could be like one of those preachers who get up in the pulpit, in front of their congregation, speaking with such pride about how God has kept their marriages for over 40, 50, 60 or more years. My friends, I dream of that possibility every day, but I know it won't happen to me, not in my lifetime, unless God decides to double the length of my years on earth.

God hates divorce, and I hate divorce. I wish I could say that I have been married to one person all my life, but I can't. It is an undesirable part of me that I wish I could scrape away, but it is so indelible in my skin. I hold no grudge or resentment against myself or any other. And as often as I pray for myself, so also I pray for those individuals who have been in a relationship with me, whether they came into my life for better or for worse. At the end of the day, we are brothers and sisters in the Lord. If God is tracking every sin we commit, who among us can stand? One thread that seems to run through all of my marriages is my staunch commitment to give the relationship all I had. I held nothing back and stayed there for as long as humanly possible.

It would be fair to say that each of these women was good Christian lady in her own right, and she could have been a good match for someone else other than me, just as I could have been a good match for another woman, other than them. Nevertheless, our paths crossed for reasons none of us may ever understand. I did what I believe a husband should do in all of these relationships. Each relationship was different, and my financial situation was never the same, but I did as much as my circumstances allowed. I worked with what I had, and I think the same can be said of them. They gave me what they had. Unfortunately, our best was not good enough to keep the relationship together.

Common Mistakes Christians Make

Some of the common mistakes that we, Christians, make are the assumptions that if Christian couples are filled with unconditional love — the "Agape" kind of Love, enough Faith, and are quick to forgive, there should be no reason for Christian marriages not to work out. To make an absolute statement like that means our capacity to make choices is done away with. It would mean that any Christian man and/or any Christian woman can just pick any other Christian off the street for a spouse, and the relationship would be a match made in Heaven. While that is possible, it rarely happens. That kind of assumption can be misleading. There is a need for compatibility in other areas as well, including emotional, intellectual, financial, and personality compatibility. God created Eve specifically for Adam. Not every man is good for every woman, and not every woman is good for every man.

Love In Christian Marriages

To say that Christian couples divorcing simply don't have love can be very insulting. There are many kinds of love: Agape, Phileo, and Eros, and there may be many more. Agape, the God's kind of love, which we mostly talk about in the Christian community, is unconditional: for better or for worse. I have heard people say, "you don't have to marry who you love but you must love who you married." That is true, but it is also true that it takes two in the relationship to make the relationship work. Neither person in the relationship can hold the other person against his or her will. I am a living example. I gave all I had, and what I was giving was not good enough.

You can only give what you have and hope and pray it is sufficient. God hates divorce, and we should hate it too. Let us put out our best to keep our marriage together, and trusting God in the process. But, let everyone keep in mind that, even God, our loving God, who loves us so dearly and unconditionally; He, God, wants us to love Him back. Love is a two-way street; it must be mutual to work. One sided love will not do it. There is nothing any one person can do to protect the union, without the cooperation of the partner. It takes 2 to tango.

Faith In Christian Marriages

Another assumption is that Christians divorcing just don't have enough faith or trust in God to keep their marriage together. "That, too, can be misleading. Yes, we walk by faith, and not by sight, but, sometimes, being of the same faith does not necessarily mean we are good for one another. Even though there is spiritual compatibility, there are other needs that must be met as well including but not limited to physical attraction, physical fitness, emotional connectedness, mental wellness, intelligence, financial, and sexual compatibility. "He who finds a wife finds a good thing and obtains favor from the Lord." - Proverbs 18:22

Forgiveness In Christian Marriages

We must learn to forgive ourselves, and we must forgive one another if we are to make it to Heaven. There is no way around forgiveness. In Matthew 6: 14-15, Jesus says:

"For if ye forgive men their trespasses, your heavenly Father will also forgive you: But if ye forgive not men their trespasses, neither will your Father forgive your trespasses."

My prayer and hope is that we will learn to forgive ourselves for the ungodly parts we played. There is no perfection in any of us. If God is marking our iniquities in this life, none of us will escape. I thank God He is not dealing with us according to our transgressions. He is not judging any of us based on the mistakes we made yesterday or weeks ago, but He is more interested in what we are doing today, what we are doing now. Christianity is the life of the Son of God flowing through our body of dust. Shall we continue in sin that grace may abound? God forbid. Not forgiving oneself or others is a sin. We must confess our sins to one another (James 5:16) and forgive those who have sinned against us.

If we confess our sins, he is faithful and just to forgive us of our sins, and to cleanse us from all unrighteousness. - 1John 1:9

Proverbs 28:13 says: He that covers his sins shall not prosper: but whoso confesses and forsakes them shall have mercy.

For if you forgive men their trespasses, your heavenly Father will also forgive you. But if you do not forgive men their trespasses, neither will your father forgive your trespasses – Matthew 6: 14-15

I strongly believe that God has forgiven me, and He has forgiven them. It is good to know that God is not dealing with us according to our trespasses. Yes, God is not judging us; He wants us to repent.

Self Help Exercises

1. *The author, in self-reflection, says he…*

a. *is oblivious to his shortcomings*

b. *is not oblivious nor blind to his shortcomings, even though it is painful to admit*

c. *could not recognize his imperfections nor could he do anything about them*

d. *none of the above*

2. *The author believes that being able to recognize his shortcoming and being willing to correct them...*

a. *can only make him a better person in the Lord*

b. *is one more reason for anyone to pass judgment*

c. *is irrelevant*

d. *all the above*

3. *The author in his admission, say...*

a. *I judge myself daily*

b. *the truth shall set us free, and*

c. *that is what I am doing here: telling it as it was without making excuses*

d. *all the above*

4. *The author, in his admission, say...*

a. *I have accepted the consequences for the decisions I allowed myself to make, and for the ones that I refused to make*

b. *I should not reap what I sow, especially when it was done in ignorance*

c. *none of the above*

d. *all the above*

5. *The author, in his transparency, says...*

a. *My first relationship occurred shortly after my conversion and call into the ministry*

b. *It was during my running away from the Lord that I met the mother of my older children*

c. *I was deceptive; I didn't fall in love, and I am very ashamed now of the part I played then*

d. *all the above*

6. *The author admits his wrongdoing, saying ...*

a. *I was wrong, very wrong. I knew in my heart that it was a one-way love*

b. *I remember telling myself that my love would eventually catch-up with hers*

c. *When I realized what I had done, however, I tried very hard to pray God into it, but it didn't work*

d. *all of the above*

7. *Even though, the mother of my older children was a Muslim...*

a. *she was my first authentic supporter and who also encouraged me to answer the call of God in my life*

b. *she was able to see something greater in me*

c. *she later converted to Christianity*

d. *all of the above*

8. *The author recounts...*

a. *We had four children together and lost two of them at an early age. It is truly a very sad story that eats me up inside*

b. *I stayed in the relationship through thick and thin until the separation came in 1986*

c. *If I need forgiveness from anyone in all of my failed marital relationships, she is the only one*

d. *all the above*

9. *The author cried out...*

a. *I can only hope that she has forgiven me; She will always be a part of my life*

b. *I am forever indebted to her for the part she has played*

c. *I have paid a heavy price for my deception: I deceived once, and I got deceived twice*

d. *all the above*

10. *The author believes that he...*

a. *was ingenuous in his relationship with the mother of his older children*

b. *reaped a double portion of what he sowed: deceived once, and got deceived twice*

c. *suffered a great deal for his deception*

d. *all the above*

11. *The author states*

a. *God hates divorce, and I hate divorce*

b. *I wish I could say that I have been married to one person all my life, but I can't*

c. *It is an undesirable part of me that I wish I could scrape away, but it is so indelible in my existence*

d. *all of the above*

12. *The author speaks of some of the common erroneous judgments that many Christians make when a Christian marriage fails, and such statements include ...*

a. *if the Christian couples are filled with unconditional love, "Agape" kind of love, genuine faith, and are quick to forgive one another, there should be no reason for divorce*

b. *any Christian man can pick up any Christian woman off the street for a spouse (regardless of physical attraction or* mental status) and the relationship would be a match made in heaven

c. *that Christian couples divorcing simply don't have love, faith, and lack forgiveness*

d. *all the above*

13. *In Christian marriages, spiritual compatibility is #1, and also important in marriages are…*

a. *physical attraction, sexual compatibility*

b. *intelligence, emotional connection*

c. *finance, life purposes, and goals*

d. *all the above*

14. *The author advises married couples, saying: you can only give what you have…*

a. *Don't be afraid to give what you have, and hope and pray it is sufficient*

b. *Remember that God hates divorce, and we should hate it too.*

Put out your very best to save your marriage

c. *Don't quit. Don't give up. Don't give the enemy what he wants - John 10:10*

d. *all the above*

15. *The author is encouraging the married couples, saying that…*

a. *Christian couples must learn to forgive one another just as Christ forgives us*

b. *Christians must not seek revenge, and we must always find a way to make peace*

c. *a and b*

d. *none of the above*

16. Not forgiving one another is a sin, and sin will send us to hell. Forgive others, so that you can be forgiven...

a. Matthew 6:14-15

b. Matthew 5:23-24

c. all the above

d. none of the above

17. Though hell was not made for human beings, every unrepentant sinner will join the devil in hell...

a. Psalm 9:17

b. Matthew 25:41

c. Hebrews 9:27

d. all the above

Answer

1b, 2a, 3d, 4a, 5d, 6d, 7d, 8d, 9d, 10d, 11d, 12d, 13d, 14d, 15c, 16c, 17d

Chapter 9

DIVORCE & REMARRY IS ADULTERY: IS IT AN UNPARDONABLE SIN?

I want to start with the message I heard on a YouTube Channel on Adultery. It was late in the evening of October 8, 2024, I had just gotten into bed for the night, and I scrolled through a YouTube channel looking for something to watch before I dozed off. Then I came across a video about holiness, so I decided to watch some of it before I go to sleep. As I started to watch and listen to the video, and almost in the middle of it, the preacher said that divorce and remarriage is "unpardonable sin." He said that people who divorced for any reason other than infidelity, and remarried, have committed adultery, and that adultery is an unpardonable sin. He said that divorcees only have two choices: either they remain single until their ex dies and then remarry, or they can stay celibate for the rest of their lives. He spoke very passionately about it. "If you are divorced, for any reason other than infidelity, and you remarried, you are going to hell." According to the preacher, the only way to avoid hell is to stay single, die single, or, regardless of how long ago the divorce occurred, you must go looking for your ex-spouse and reunite. Even if your ex- spouse has remarried someone else or, perhaps, both of you have remarried and have children in your new relationships, you must end your new relationships and reunite. He said she is your wife, and you are her husband. The new relationship that you are both in must be ended. It is either you end that relationship and reunite with your ex- spouse or go to hell. He cited a Bible reference, the words from the Lord:

It hath been said, whosoever shall put away his wife, let him give her a writing of divorcement. But I say unto you, that whosoever shall put away his wife, saving for the cause of fornication, caused her to commit adultery: and whosoever shall marry her that is divorced committeth adultery. – Matthew 5:31- 32

Apostle Paul says this:

Now to the married I command, yet not I but the Lord: A wife is not to depart from her husband. ¹¹ But even if she does depart, let her remain unmarried or be reconciled to her husband. And a husband is not to divorce his wife. – 1 Corinthians 7:10-11.

My Question Is This: Is Adultery an Unpardonable Sin?

What God has joined together, let no man put asunder. Does that mean it was God who joined together every marriage that exists today, or do we sometimes join ourselves together for some other reasons without God's involvement?

Please, as you read my understanding of the Bible and belief system, hold fast to what you believe because your salvation is between you and your God. No one can send you to Heaven or Hell; only God can do that. So, please read this teaching with an open mind and allow the Holy Ghost to minister the WORD to you.

One of the thoughts that came to my mind is that most of us, married or unmarried, are going to hell if we stopped, after reading the preacher's message and supportive scriptures, and take the whole content literally. But then I started to look at some other Scriptures to interpret some of the teachings the Lord presented. Sometimes we need to do that. Out of the mouth of two or three witnesses, the truth is established. We know that marriage is the first institution that God established on earth, and the Scripture says, "what God has joined together, let no man put asunder". – Matthew 19:6. The foundation of our marriages should be God. It must be God that joined us together, or else it was the devil. But how do we know that it was God who has joined us together and not the lusts or some other underlined motives?

Many of our marriages are joined together by the lust of eyes: a beautiful face, handsomeness, unique appearance, career accomplishments, love of money, the desire to belong, and by many other personal reasons. Majority of our marriages are self-made decisions, and most of the times we think we can simply pray God into it, and He will honor our prayers. Some couples believe that if they are joined together before a judge or a pastor, that means their marriage met God's approval. That means it was God that joined them together.

A marriage joined together by God would have God at the center. Though a marriage with God at the center is not necessarily void of life challenges, just as Adam and Eve in the Garden of Eden, but none of those life challenges will be able to unseat the presence of God at the center. There would not be marital issues that cannot be resolved when God is at the center. God is peace, and a marriage without God at the center lacks peace. It would be hell on earth for such a couple because the devil is the one ruling over their marriage. It is the devil occupying the center, not God. God is peace.

Are we then doomed if we exit a relationship that lacks God at the center? Are we doomed if we dare to exit a toxic relationship where the devil is in control? Do you think we can pray God into a relationship He did not initiate, nor or approve? No, the Lord is not putting such a yoke on us. I strongly believe that Christians in toxic relationships have a way out. But if the unbeliever departs, let him depart; a brother or a sister is not under bondage in such cases. But God has called us to peace. – 1 Corinthians 7:15.

Art, thou bound unto a wife? seek not to be loosed. Art thou loosed from a wife? seek not a wife. But and if thou marry, thou hast not sinned; and if a virgin marries, she hath not sinned. Nevertheless, such shall have trouble in the flesh: but I spare you. 1 Corinthians 7:27-28.

Furthermore, the Lord here expands on His definition of adultery: But I say to you that everyone who looks at a woman with lustful intent has already committed adultery with her in his heart. – Matthew 5:28.

Just by reading the latter quotation above, the Lord's extended definition of adultery, one could deductively conclude that most of us, if not all of us, adult men and women, will go to hell without a doubt. Perhaps, there could be a few of us who have never committed a lustful look, and that is a big perhaps. The rest of us are doomed. But could that be true? Could it be true this is what the Lord is teaching His disciples? Many of the Lord's teachings could be subjected to "hermeneutical interpretations," when we use the scriptural verses to interpret the "not so easy to understand" scriptures. I will deal with some of those "not so easy to understand" scriptural verses later in this chapter. I know that we do not strive to understand in order that we may believe, but, rather, we do believe in order that we may understand. We must keep in mind, however, that our God is not a "god" of confusion and chaos. He is a God of peace and order.

Is Infidelity, Divorce & Remarry, and Other Sins Mentioned Below, Unforgiveable?

Do you not know that the unrighteous will not inherit the kingdom of God? Do not be deceived. Neither fornicators, nor idolaters, nor adulterers, nor homosexuals, nor sodomites, nor thieves, nor covetous, nor drunkards, nor revilers, nor extortioners will inherit the kingdom of God. And such were some of you. But you were washed, but you were sanctified, but you were justified in the name of the Lord Jesus and by the Spirit of our God. – 1 Corinthians 6:9.

Some Biblical Facts About Sexual Immorality, Divorce and Remarry in Christianity:

1. Fornication and adultery are not permissible in Christianity.

2. Divorce and remarriage are not permissible in Christianity if the ex-spouse is still alive. It is a sin but not unforgiveable sin.

3. Divorce is permissible in Christianity if it is based on infidelity.

4. Divorce and remarriage are permissible in Christianity if the spouse voluntarily departs.

5. A lustful look is a sin of "adultery of the heart" in Christianity.

6. Bestiality is a sin in Christianity. Sexual relationship between a beast and human being is an abomination.

7. Homosexuality is a sin. Marriage is between a man and a woman.

A marriage between a man and a woman is God's idea, and Sacred, from the beginning according to Genesis 2:21-24. Marriage is the first institution that God established on earth, and what God has joined together, let no man put asunder. – Matthew 19:6. Infidelity and Divorce in marriages should always be avoided, and…

- A Christian marriage should reflect the unconditional love between Jesus Christ and the church (Ephesians 5:25). Marriage is between a man and a woman according to God.

- A Christian marriage is expected to be peaceful because God is at the center of it.

- A Christian marriage without peace lacks God at the center because God is peace.

The litmus test:

If there is no peace in a marriage, if your relationship is toxic, then it is likely that God is absent. Either God is at the center and the foundation of our marriage, or it is the devil in charge. If you find yourself in a relationship where there are constant cutthroat arguments, physical and/or emotional abuse, that is not of God. Christian marriages should reflect the type of love that Jesus has for the church. Jesus is our Groom; and we, the Church, are His collective Bride. – Ephesians 5:25.

Many Christian marriages have become the devil's workshop. Rather than demonstrating the fruit of the Spirit: love, contentment, forgiveness, patience, mutual support, and respect, the couple's relationship is constantly in crisis mode, often in argument, dealing with suicide attempts, and homicide threats. One has a gambling problem, spending money set aside for utility bills on illegal substances, and both are having extramarital affairs. If that is you, if that is your relationship that I just described, you are living in hell already. It is the devil in charge of your relationship, not God. Well, can it be fixed? Yes, it can be fixed, but you cannot fix it alone. Both of you must want it fixed. It would take God, you and your partner to restore your broken relationship. Yes, both of you must want your marriage to survive for your efforts to pay off because it takes two to tango. God is peace, and He has called us to peace, not into foolishness or chaos. God is not the author of our chaos and foolishness.

Now, we should all agree that, without a doubt, that God hates divorce. I hate divorce with everything in me, and every born-again Christian should hate divorce and avoid it at all costs. Also, a lustful look is a sin and must be avoided. Divorce and remarriage are an abomination for the followers of Christ, and it they must be avoided.

However, none of the sins mentioned here are unpardonable sins. While lusting after a person with our eyes is adultery of the heart, it is NOT an unpardonable sin. While divorcing and remarrying is a sin, it is NOT an unpardonable sin.

For all have sinned and fall short of the glory of God. – Romans 3:23

All have sinned and fall short of the glory of God, and all our self-righteousness are as filthy rags according to the Scripture (Isaiah 64:6). We ought to thank God for His grace and mercy. If God is marking our iniquities, who among us could stand? – Psalm 130:3. I strongly believe that the Lord was showing us, in so many words, how our salvation depends largely on the sacrifice He would make, and He eventually made, on the cross for the sins of the world. John says…

Behold the Lamb of God, which taketh away the sin of the world. – John 1:29.

Greater love has no one than this, that someone lays down his life for his friends. John 15:13

For God made him who had no sin to be sin for us, so that in him we might become the righteousness of God. – 2 Corinthians 5:21

Who is he who condemns? It is Christ who died, and furthermore is also risen, who is even at the right hand of God, who also makes intercession for us. – Romans 8:34.

If we confess our sins, He is faithful and just to forgive us our sins and to cleanse us from all unrighteousness. – 1 John 1:9.

Once we confessed our sins and fully repented, the Lord has forgiven us. We are now a clean slate. The blood of Jesus Christ has washed us, cleansed us, of all of our sins. It is as if we have never divorced or committed any kind of adultery in our whole life. It is like a new beginning. Were you a murderer, a drunk, a thief, a homosexual, a liar? If you have genuinely confessed and repented of your sins, God has forgiven you. He is saying to you "I am not condemning you either;

go and sin no more." Let your past be past and forgive yourself for your wrong deeds.

Abraham & Adultery

Abraham listened to Sarah, his wife, had an affair with Hagar, Sarah's maid, and she gave birth to Ishmael. Ishmael is traditionally considered the Progenitor of the Arab people. God was intentionally silent towards Abraham for 13 years. At 99 years old, God finally spoke to Abraham, saying…

I am the Almighty God; walk before me and be thou perfect. – *Genesis 17:1.*

What did the Lord say to Abraham? "You have done it, Abraham, now you are going to hell!" Is that what the Lord said to Abraham? No, no, and no. The Lord didn't say that to Abraham but, instead, He told Abraham, "Walk before me and be perfect." God didn't ask Abraham to go and kill Ishmael or undo the adultery he has committed. He knew it was impossible to go into the past to correct our mistakes. Here Abraham had Ishmael, his first child, and a constant reminder of his sin of adultery.

Nevertheless, God forgave Abraham. Not only did He forgive Abraham, the Lord calls Abraham His friend. Abraham believed in the Lord, and it was counted unto him for righteousness.

And the Scripture was fulfilled which says, Abraham believed God, and it was accounted to him for righteousness. And he was called the friend of God. You see then that a man is justified by works, and not by faith only. – James 2: 23-24.

Can we really undo the sin of adultery or any sin for that matter? Must an adulterer undo the sin committed before she can be forgiven? Must a liar take back the lie he has told before he can be forgiven? Must a thief restore what he has stolen before he can be forgiven? The answer is a resounding "No." The Lord is merciful. Your sins are forgiven. He says, "Go and sin no more." If the adulterer, the homosexual, the murderer, the thief, and the liar would genuinely repent of their sins and confess it to God, He will forgive them as promised. The Lord, our God, cannot lie, and once forgiven, you now have a clean slate. It is as if you never committed adultery, murder or stole anything. You are 25 years of age and just went through a divorce, you can remarry, stay married, and divorce no more. The Lord, our God, cannot lie. It is impossible for God to lie.

If *we confess our sins, he is faithful and just to forgive us our sins and purify us from all unrighteousness – 1 John 1: 9 Paraphrased.*

Therefore, if anyone is in Christ, he is a new creation; old things have passed away; behold, all things have become new.

Now all things are of God, who has reconciled us to Himself through Jesus Christ, and has given us the ministry of reconciliation, that is, that God was in Christ reconciling the world to Himself, not imputing their trespasses to them, and has committed to us the word of reconciliation. Now then, we are ambassadors for Christ, as though God were pleading through us: we implore you on Christ's behalf, be reconciled to God. For He made Him who knew no sin to be sin for us, that we might become the righteousness of God in Him. - 2 Corinthians 5:17- 21.

Woman Caught in Adultery

And the scribes and Pharisees brought unto him a woman taken in adultery; and when they had set her in the midst, They said unto him, Master, this woman was taken in adultery, in the very act. Now Moses in the law commanded us, that such should be stoned: but what sayest thou? This they said, tempting him, that they might accuse him. But Jesus stooped down, and with his finger wrote on the ground, as though he heard them not. So, when they continued asking him, he lifted himself up, and said unto them, He that is without sin among you, let him first cast a stone at her. And again, he stooped down, and wrote on the ground, and they which heard it, being convicted by their own conscience, went out one by one, beginning at the eldest, even unto the last: and Jesus was left alone, and the woman standing in the midst. When Jesus had lifted himself, and saw none but the woman, he said unto her, Woman, where are those thine accusers? hath no man condemned thee? She said, No man, Lord. And Jesus said unto her, neither do I condemn thee: go, and sin no more. – John 8: 3-11.

Glory to the Lord, our God. He is just and merciful, and His thoughts are higher than ours. The Lord helped the self-righteous mob to recognize their own shortcomings before they cast their stones at the woman. Surprisingly, however, they all disappeared, of their own accord. They recognized their own shortcomings. It is easy-for us to be so quick to see the faults in one another and be so blinded to our own shortcomings. But God knows everything about each of us, including our secret sins. The Bible says the wicked will flee when no one is chasing him – Proverbs 28:1. The woman's accusers disappeared and very quietly. Then, Jesus asked the lady, "where are those thine accusers? hath no man condemned thee? She said, No man, Lord. And Jesus said unto her, neither do I condemn thee: go, and sin no more."

What a divine love. I am assuming here; Jesus probably told the lady: "go and get married and stay married."

Who is he who condemns? It is Christ who died, and furthermore is also risen, who is even at the right hand of God, who also makes intercession for us? – Romans 8:34.

When we find ourselves in sin, and we genuinely confess and repent of our sin, the Lord is bound by His promise to forgive us. If we genuinely repent and confess our sins, we are cleansed at once, through His Blood, the Blood of Atonement. It is as having a clean slate.

For I will be merciful to their unrighteousness and their sins and their iniquities I will remember no more. – Hebrews 8:12.

As far as the east is from the west, So far has He removed our transgressions from us. – Psalm 103:12.

God chose not to remember any of the sins we have confessed, and has forgiven us, because the Blood of Jesus Christ washed them away instantly. God sees them no more. Thanks to our God for His foresightfulness. He knew we would make errors on the way, and that is why Jesus is sitting on the right hand of Glory, even now, Interceding for us.

Who is he who condemns? It is Christ who died, and furthermore is also risen, who is even at the right hand of God, who also makes intercession for us. – Romans 8:34.

My word of encouragement: Let us do everything to keep our marriages, and if all efforts fail, and your life is in danger, or the individual deserted the marriage, divorcing is not an unpardonable sin. You are not going to hell. However, if you have the grace to remain celibate, that is the best option. I am one like you, a divorcee who would not remain celibate, and I am not going to hell. I have remarried and will stay married. Jesus told the woman, "Sin no more." He is saying the same thing to you, to me, and to whoever is reading this book: sin no more. "Divorce no more, lie no more, steal no more, murder no more, and practice no more sexual infidelity." Have you genuinely confessed and repented? God has forgiven you and washed away your sin. Now, you now have a clean slate. Go and sin no more.

Some of the "Not So Easy to Understand" Verses in the Book of Matthew, Chapters 5 and 10

Let us consider some other thought-provoking statements made by our Lord, Jesus Christ, in the Book of Matthew, Chapter 5, their interpretations using other Scriptures as guide:

Matthew 5:18-20: For verily I say unto you, till heaven and earth pass, one jot or one tittle shall in no wise pass from the law, till all be fulfilled. Whosoever therefore shall break one of these least commandments, and shall teach men so, he shall be called the least in the kingdom of heaven: but whosoever shall do and teach them, the same shall be called great in the kingdom of heaven. For I say unto you, that except your righteousness shall exceed the righteousness of the scribes and Pharisees, ye shall in no case enter into the kingdom of heaven.

Note: Obviously, an average reader could think that the Lord is bringing us back under the Law of Moses but that is not the Lord's intention, and here is why…

Interpretation: In Romans 3:20, the Scripture tells us that "By the deeds of the law, no one can be justified." Jesus came to fulfill the Law on our behalf. No one can keep the Law of Moses to the fullest, but Jesus did for us that, which we couldn't do for ourselves. He nailed the Laws to the Cross. – Romans 8:3. It is by Grace we are saved, not of works, lest any of us should boast. – Ephesians 2:8-9.

Matthew 5:21-22 :Ye have heard that it was said of them of old time, Thou shalt not kill; and whosoever shall kill shall be in danger of the judgment: But I say unto you, That whosoever is angry with his brother without a cause shall be in danger of the judgment: and whosoever shall say to his brother, Raca, shall be in danger of the council: but whosoever shall say, Thou fool, shall be in danger of hell fire.

Note: Just imagine where we could end up if we take this Scripture verse literally!

Interpretation: Jesus was just exposing our weaknesses. Just imagine: if getting angry at your brother without a cause or calling your brother or anyone a fool will send you to hell, then, that means Jesus died in vain, but we do know that He did not die in vain. The message here, for us, is to learn how to manage our emotions, and the words coming out of our mouths. Be angry, but don't allow the sun to set on your anger (Ephesians 4:26). Don't go to sleep on your anger. Learn to forgive quickly. In Matthew 6:14-15, Jesus says, if you forgive other people when they sin against you, your heavenly Father will also forgive you. But if you do not forgive others for their sins, your heavenly Father will not forgive your sins.

Matthew 5:23-24: Therefore, if thou bring thy gift to the altar, and there remembered that thy brother hath ought against thee; Leave there thy gift before the altar and go thy way; first be reconciled to thy brother, and then come and offer thy gift.

Note: How often do you see yourself making these kinds of trips to make peace with a brother?

Interpretation*: The Lord was simply emphasizing the importance of forgiveness. Christians shouldn't hold grudges, but many of us do. Yes, people do offend us, and we do offend people, but we are to forgive our offenders and ourselves just as Jesus forgives us. Now, assuming you are at a church service, and worshipping with what you have, and then you remember that a brother living seven hundred miles away is holding grudges against you. Though there were no telephones or email privileges in those days to reach and settle with your brother who lives* *far away from you but, nevertheless, the Lord says that you must leave your offerings an*

Ask yourself. do you honestly believe, literally, that this is the Lord's intent? No, I do not. However, I do believe that the Lord was simply emphasizing the necessity of being at peace with everyone in our lives, even those on the outside, and far away, no matter the cost. – Romans 12:18.

Matthew 5: 27-28: Ye have heard that it was said by them of old time, thou shalt not commit adultery: But I say unto you, that whosoever looks on a woman to lust after her hath committed adultery with her already in his heart.

Note: If the verse above can be taken at face value, many of us are going to hell.

Interpretation: We must learn to control our five senses. What we look at matters. Job says, I made a covenant with my eyes not to look lustfully at a young woman- Job 31:1. Any ungodly use of our 5 senses is a sin, however, any of these sins is not unpardonable.

Matthew 5: 29-30: And if thy right eye offends thee, pluck it out, and cast it from thee: for it is profitable for thee that one of thy members should perish, and not that thy whole body should be cast into hell. And if thy right hand offends thee, cut it off, and cast it from thee: for it is profitable for thee that one of thy members should perish, and not that thy whole body should be cast into hell.

Note: If this verse (above) can be taken at face value, many of us are going to hell or at the least, many of us would be amputees and have our eyes plucked out. Do we really believe that "that" is the Lord's teaching?

Interpretation: Can you imagine if every Christian that has looked lustfully at a woman or had stolen anything, either by circumstances, by necessity, or by just being carnal, should have their eyes plucked out, and their hands and legs cut off? Can you imagine that? Trust me, that is not the Lord's intention. Thanks to the Lord, His Blood cleanses us of all unrighteousness.

We need to know that our five senses are designed to connect and orient us to the universe. They are good God's investments (Genesis 1:31). However, they can become a trap for us if we are not smarter than the serpent or allow the serpent, the devil, to manipulate our minds. The 5 senses played a vital role in Adam's and his wife's disobedience in the Garden of Eden. They saw the fruit and the serpent (eyes were involved). They heard the serpent (ears were involved). They dialogued with the serpent and bit the fruit (mouths were involved). They touched the fruit (hands were involved) and, of course, their minds were involved. We must be very disciplined in how we use our senses. What we say matters. What we watch on our television sets matters. What we listen to matters. What we eat, say, and touch matters. More than our five senses, however, is our mind or heart. Our heart is the battlefield.

Also, we must understand that neither our eyes, mouth, ears, nose, legs nor hands can make decisions for us. Out of the heart proceeds evil thoughts, and those thoughts are carried out via some, or all our senses. For out of the heart proceed evil thoughts, murders, adultery, fornications, thefts, false witness, blasphemies. - Matthew 15:19.

Matthew 5: 31-32: It hath been said, whosoever shall put away his wife, let him give her a writing of divorcement. But I say unto you, that whosoever shall put away his wife, saving for the cause of fornication, caused her to commit adultery: and whosoever shall marry her that is divorced committeth adultery.

Note: If you were once married but divorced, and then remarried. You were in your twenties when this happened, do you believe that God wants you to celibate for the rest of your life, since you cannot make the other person stay in the relationship against his or her will?

Interpretation: Here, the Lord even went further on adultery, saying we cannot marry a woman who someone has divorced even if we are getting married for the first time. Though you may fall in love with the person; if the person you fell in love with is a divorcee, you can't marry her. Though she is 23 years old, and you are 23 years old and love one another, still, she cannot marry you. She must either stay celibate for the rest of her life or reconcile with her ex-husband. Here is the issue: the ex-husband doesn't want her. She couldn't compel her ex-husband to take her back, and even though you want her, she cannot marry you.

She must remain celibate for as long as her ex-husband lives, or until he dies.

Do we honestly believe that that is what the Lord is saying to us? Do I honestly believe that that is what the Lord is saying to me? No, I don't. I don't believe that the Lord is putting such a yoke on us. However, I strongly believe that the Lord is simply emphasizing the sanctity of a marriage. Marriage is sacred and should be treated with honor, and the bed undefiled.

Matthew 5: 33-48 - Again, you have heard that it was said to those of old, 'You shall not swear falsely, but shall perform your oaths to the Lord. But I say to you, do not swear at all: neither by heaven, for it is God's throne; nor by the earth, for it is His footstool; nor by Jerusalem, for it is the city of the great King. Nor shall you swear by your head, because you cannot make one hair white or black. But let [b]your 'Yes' be 'Yes,' and your 'No,' 'No.' For whatever is more than these is from the evil one.

Note: Though we cannot examine all the intricate verses in the Bible, but if we will give ourselves to studying the verses in the light of other Scripture verses, and allow the Holy Ghost to do the interpretation, we will find the Bible very harmonious. Our Bible is authentic, harmonious, and nothing contradictory.

Go the Second Mile *You have heard that it was said, an eye for an eye and a tooth for a tooth. But I tell you not to resist an evil person. But whoever slaps you on your right cheek, turn the other to him also. If anyone wants to sue you and take away your tunic, let him have your cloak also. And whoever compels you to go one mile, go with him two. Give to him who asks you, and from him who wants to borrow from you do not turn away.*

Love Your Enemies You have heard that it was said, you shall love your neighbor and hate your enemy. But, I say unto you, love your enemies, bless those who curse you, do good to those who hate you, and pray for those who spitefully use you and persecute you, that you may be sons of your Father in heaven; for He makes His sun rise on the evil and on the good, and sends rain on the just and on the unjust. For if you love those who love you, what reward have you? Do not even the tax collectors do the same? And if you greet your brethren only, what do you do more than others? Do not even the tax collectors do so? Therefore, you shall be perfect, just as your Father in heaven is perfect.

Interpretation: Who among us is sufficient and blameless in all of these things? The truth is this: our perfection is in the Lord. Only in Him our sins were judged and settled on the Cross, over two thousand years ago. Jesus paid the Price for our sins, in full, on the Cross by His Precious Blood according to the Scripture.

Yes, we cannot continue to live in sin that grace may abound. But, if we fumble, if we commit any sin, if we divorce and remarry, if we failed to protect the sanctity of marriage, if we lied, stole, or swear falsely, we must genuinely repent. We must genuinely confess our sins. We must make 180-degree turn from those sins, and the Lord will forgive us as promised. The Lord our God cannot lie – Pr. 28:13.

Matthew 10: 34-36: Do not suppose that I have come to bring peace to the earth. I did not come to bring peace, but a sword. For I have come to turn a man against his father, a daughter against her mother, daughter-in-law against her mother-in-last man's enemies will be the members of his own household.

Interpretation: Peace or Sword? One thing is certain: the Lord is not contradicting Himself. This Scripture must be interpreted. Jesus did not bring a sword but peace. Jesus didn't come so that we can go to war against one another. He is our Peace and hope.

Peace I leave with you, my peace I give unto you: not as the world giveth, give I unto you. Let not your heart be troubled, neither let it be afraid. - John 14:27.

Some Biblical, But Not Mandatory, Grounds for Divorce in Christianity

Note: Yes, there are biblical grounds for a divorce in Christianity, but you don't have to use any of them if both of you want to stay in your marriage, which is far better. God hates divorce.

Infidelity: Though infidelity can be a ground for divorce according to Jesus, but you don't have to divorce your wife or husband because of it, if you are willing to extend the grace and forgive your spouse. If you don't want to forgive, however, or if you have forgiven your spouse and still want a divorce, you have the option according to the Lord in Matthew 5:32.

Unequally Yoked: The Bible speaks also of being "unequally yoked" as another permittable ground for a divorce. Being unequally yoked is mostly characterized as partners belonging to different faiths. If there is genuine love, and the marriage is peaceful, belonging to different faiths is workable if the couple want to be together. – 1 Corinthians 7:13-15.

Being unequally yoked has many faces. If you are in a relationship with, perhaps, your first love and suddenly, he or she becomes a stranger. They turned 180 degrees on you. Now your partner stops seeking God but, instead, turns to worldly friends for advice. You are no longer happy to be around one another. What you like, they hate. What you hate, they like. You have become estranged towards one another. Tell me, where is the marriage? You are no longer a couple but 2 individuals living together. The Lord, our God, is God of peace, and He has called us to peace. Do you think that God wants you to stay in this kind of toxic environment, where there is no peace, where God is no longer in charge? Any relationship that lacks peace lacks God. We all need to remember that, in any relationship we are in, each of us has limitations. Remind yourself, that you can only control what you do in a relationship, and what the other person does is out of your control. God has called us to peace.

The Absence of Peace: Another justifiable reason for biblical divorce is lack of peace. God is peace. If you and your spouse cannot see eye to eye, physical and emotional abuse are a tradition in your household, you are sleeping in one room, and your partner sleeps in another. Money is constantly missing from the family account. The money set aside for utility bills is being spent on illegal habits, and the individual still doesn't think there is a problem or needs professional and/or spiritual interventions. That is like living in hell.

Do you think God wants both of you to be that miserable? Yes, marriage is work, and it is for better or for worse, but it will take the 2 people involved to make it work. God has called us to peace, not to chaos, confusion or foolishness.

A relationship void of peace is under the occupation of the devil and demonic activities. Those in that kind of relationship will experience hell on earth. It would be a hell on earth because God is no longer in it. You won't be any good for yourself, for your children, for your friends or family, and you won't be any good for God because you are not at peace. God has called us to peace.

Desertion: Another common reason for a divorce is desertion, and that is when your spouse suddenly departed, and exits the union. That happens more often than one can imagine. The Bible says, if the unbeliever departs, let him or her depart, and no one is longer in bondage. Marriage is "work," but you cannot make anyone stay in a relationship against their will. It takes 2 people in a relationship to work it out. In one of my own experiences, I went to work one day, and by the time I came back home, she was gone with more than 50% of my clothes packed along with hers, all gone. I pleaded for months for her to come back, but that never happened. It was a nightmare. I couldn't fully understand, but God does. All I could do was to trust in the Lord in the process, and not lean on my own understanding. It was beyond my control, but the Lord worked it out.

But if the unbeliever departs, let him depart; a brother or a sister is not under bondage in such cases. But God has called us to peace - 1 Corinthians 7:15.

Art thou bound unto a wife? seek not to be loosed. Art thou loosed from a wife? Do not seek a wife. But, if thou marry, thou has not sinned… – 1 Corinthians 7: 27-28.

My Conclusion

Marriage restitution is a Biblical principle and the best option when Christians couples are separated or contemplating a divorce. However, it takes the two in the marriage to make restitution work. But, when restitution failed and the couple divorced and remarried to someone else, they are not committing unpardonable sin according to many other scriptural verses. Here is our imperfection and the Grace of God revealed. God's mercy triumphs over judgment.

For judgment is without mercy to the one who has shown no mercy. Mercy triumphs over judgment. – James 2:13.

Unpardonable Sins

I know of only two unpardonable sins according to the Scripture: 1) Blasphemy against the Holy Spirit, and 2) Apostasy. Apostasy refers to those individuals who were once strong believers, filled with the Holy Ghost, but they come to a point in their lives, where they reject Christ, turn away from Grace and put Christ to open shame.

1. Blasphemy Against the Holy Ghost

In Matthew 12:31-32, Jesus says *Therefore, I say to you, every sin and blasphemy will be forgiven men, but the blasphemy against the Spirit will not be forgiven men.*

Blasphemy against the Holy Ghost is an unpardonable sin according to the Lord. Anyone who speaks a word against the Son of Man will be forgiven; but whoever speaks against the Holy Spirit will not be forgiven, either in this age or in the age to come.

2. Apostacy

Apostasy is falling away from Grace. It is like nailing the Lord to the Cross, all over again. It is an unpardonable sin.

For it is impossible for those who were once enlightened, and have tasted the heavenly gift, and have become partakers of the Holy Spirit, and have tasted the good word of God and the powers of the age to come, if they fall away, to renew them again to repentance, since they crucify again for themselves the Son of God, and put Him to an open shame – Hebrews 6:4-6.

Divorce and remarry is a sin of adultery but it is not an unpardonable sin. Stay with who you married to now and keep the Lord at the center.

He has not dealt with us according to our sins, nor punished us according to our iniquities. For as the heavens are high above the earth, so great is His mercy toward those who fear Him; As far as the east is from the west, so far has He removed our transgressions from us. – Psalm 103: 10-12.

"I, even I, am He who blots out your transgressions for My own sake; And I will not remember your sins. – Isaiah 43:25.

For some of us, with an exceptional grace as Paul, we can remain celibate which is better according to 1Corinthians 7: 7-9.

For I wish that all men were even as myself. But each one has his own gift from God, one in this manner and another in that. But I say to the unmarried and to the widows: It is good for them if they remain even as I am; but if they cannot exercise self-control, let them marry. For it is better to marry than to burn with passion.

The Lord Himself recognized this natural limitation for some of us.

He knew that not many of us could stay celibate as Paul did.

His disciples said to Him, if such is the case of the man with his wife, it is better not to marry. But He said to them, all cannot accept this saying, but only those to whom it has been given, for there are eunuchs who were born thus from their mother's womb, and there are eunuchs who were made eunuchs by men, and there are eunuchs who have made themselves eunuchs for the kingdom of heaven's sake. He who is able to accept it, let him accept it-Matthew 19:10-12.

Granted that none of us can undo the damage of infidelity, divorce, stealing, lie, murder, and other sins we may have committed, we can genuinely repent, and trust the Grace and Mercy of the Lord, our God. Yes, we cannot continue in sin that grace may abound, God forbid. However, we are saved by grace, not of works, lest any man should boast. All our righteous acts are like filthy rags –Isaiah 64:6.

My little children, these things I write to you, so that you may not sin. And if anyone sins, we have an Advocate with the Father, Jesus Christ the righteous – 1 John 2:1.

Who is he who condemns? It is Christ who died, and furthermore is also risen, a who is even at the right hand of God, b who also makes intercession for us. – Romans 8:34.

The Parable of the Pharisee and the Tax Collector

To some who were confident of their own righteousness and looked down on everyone else, Jesus told this parable: Two men went up to the temple to pray, one a Pharisee and the other a tax collector. The Pharisee stood by himself and prayed: 'God, I thank you that I am not like other people—robbers, evildoers, adulterers—or even like this tax collector. I fast twice a week and give a tenth of all I get. But the tax collector stood at a distance. He would not even look up to heaven, but beat his breast and said, God, have mercy on me, a sinner. I tell you that this man, rather than the other, went home justified before God. For all those who exalt themselves will be humbled, and those who humble themselves will be exalted. – Luke 18: 9-14.

As we can see, in this parable, the paleness of humans' self-righteousness (Isaiah 64:6), and how the Mercy of God triumphed over judgment. God deals with our hearts, not self-proclaimed righteousness. Those that worship the Lord will worship Him in Spirit and in truth. – John 4:24. God knows and recognizes a remorseful heart, and the one that is filled with self-righteousness and arrogance. Just as this tax collector, let us be honest with ourselves, and the Lord.

He has not dealt with us according to our sins, nor punished us according to our iniquities. For as the heavens are high above the earth, so great is His mercy toward those who fear Him; As far as the east is from the west, so far has He removed He our transgressions from us. As a father pities his children, so the LORD pities those who fear Him. For He knows our frame; He remembers that we are dust. – Psalm 103:10-14.

The Limitations of the Law

By the Deeds of the Law of Moses, No One Can Be Saved. For by grace, you have been saved through faith, and that not of yourselves; it is the gift of God, not of works, lest anyone should boast. - Ephesians 2: 8-9

But we are all as an unclean thing, and all our righteousness-es are as filthy rags; and we all do fade as a leaf; and our iniquities, like the wind, have taken us away. – Isaiah 64:6.

For what the law could not do in that it was weak through the flesh, God did by sending His own Son in the likeness of sinful flesh, on account of sin: He condemned sin in the flesh, that the righteous requirement of the law might be fulfilled in us who do not walk according to the flesh but according to the Spirit. – Romans 8: 3-4

...all have sinned and fall short of the glory of God – Romans 3:23.

Love Is the Fulfillment of the Law

Jesus says, A new commandment I give unto you, that ye love one another; as I have loved you, that ye also love one another. By this shall all men know that ye are my disciples, if ye have love one to another. John 13: 34-35.

For the commandments, you shall not commit adultery, you shall not murder, you shall not steal, you shall not bear false witness, you shall not covet, and if there is any other commandment, are all summed up in this saying, namely, you shall love your neighbor as yourself. Love does no harm to a neighbor; therefore, love is the fulfillment of the law. – Romans 13: 9-10.

If ye fulfil the royal law according to the scripture, thou shalt love thy neighbor as thyself, ye do well. But if ye have respect to persons, ye commit sin, and are convinced of the law as transgressors. For whosoever shall keep the whole law, and yet offend in one point, he is guilty of all. For he that said, do not commit adultery, said also, do not kill. Now if thou commit no adultery, yet if thou kill, thou art become a transgressor of the law – James 2: 8-11.

But when the Pharisees heard that He had silenced the Sadducees, they gathered together. Then one of them, a lawyer, asked Him a question, testing Him, and saying, Teacher, which is the great commandment in the law? Jesus said to him, you shall love the LORD your God with all your heart, with all your soul, and with all your mind. This is the first and great commandment. And the second is like it: You shall love your neighbor as yourself. On these two commandments hang all the Law and the Prophets – Matthew 22: 34-40.

Self Help Exercises

1.   *The author states that…*

a.   *Divorce and remarriage are a sin of adultery*

b.   *Divorce and remarriage are a sin of adultery, but it is not an unforgivable sin*

c.   *Jesus told the woman caught in adultery, "Neither do I condemn you. Go and sin no more."*

d.   *All the above*

2.   *When Jesus told the woman who was caught in adultery, "Neither do I condemn you. Go and sin no more," Jesus likely meant…*

a.   *You have done it, woman. You broke the law, and you are going to hell*

b.   *You must stay celibate for as long as you live, or you are going to hell*

c.   *You must look for your first husband, if you ever had one, and reunite with him no matter what it takes*

d.   *You can get married, stay married, and do not commit adultery anymore.*

3.   *Is it scriptural to use other scripture verses to interpret some difficult to understand Bible verses? True or False?*

4.   *Which of the following sins is unforgiveable?*

a.   *lustful look at a man or a woman*

b.   *getting drunk occasionally on the weekend*

c.   *stealing some foods because you are hungry*

d. blaspheming against the Holy Ghost

5. In the parable of the Pharisee and the tax collector, we learn that...

a. The Pharisee was counting on his own self-righteousness

b. The Tax collector depends solely on grace and mercy of God: the sacrifice the Lord made on the cross

c. Those who exalt themselves will be humble, and those who humbled themselves will be exalted

d. all the above

6. Christians must walk in holiness, but if we sin...

a. We have an advocate with the Father – 1 John 2:1

b. We are not condemned. Jesus is sitting on the right hand of Glory, interceding for us – Romans 8:34

c. We must repent, confess, and turn away from our sins – Proverbs 28:13; 1 John 1:9.

d. All the above

7. According to Jesus Christ, "Love" is the fulfillment of the Law. Which of the Scriptures below supports that?

a. James 2: 8-11; John13:35

b. Matthew 22:34-40

c. Romans 13:9-10

d. All the above

8. According to Romans 8:3-4, Jesus accomplish for us what we could not accomplished through the law of Moses. Circle True or False? _____

Answers

1d, 2d, 3True, 4d, 5d, 6d, 7d, 8True

Chapter 10
THE BIRTH OF SOUL FOR CHRIST MINISTRY, INC

In 1999, as my manner of life was, and still is, I loved to pray and fast. Praying was what I did during my lunch break. So, one day in September 1999, I was on lunch break and drove up the street to the intersection of Samuel Blvd and Jim Miller, where I found a shaded tree in a parking lot area, not too close to traffic. I parked the car, under the tree and began praying. In about an hour, however, I sensed in my spirit that the Lord was instructing me to register an entity where I can do Christian counseling, pray, and witness Jesus Christ to the homeless and mentally ill. Mind you, I tried to do those things even before then, at my clinic setting, but I was doing them at my peril because of the separation of church and state. If I got caught, I could be fired. When God told me that, I inquired the name to call the entity, and He gave me the acronym as SFC. I wondered, "what is that?" Anyhow, to make a long story short, the acronym became "Soul for Christ," and I added the "Ministry" in the singular. The entity was registered in 1999, incorporated in 2000, and became tax-exempt in 2001.

Ministering to the Mentally Ill and Homeless

I continued to work at Dallas Metrocare, and witness to the mentally ill and homeless in Downtown Dallas. In the year 2000, I opened the ministry's office in East Dallas on Gus Thomasson Road. I started a Bible study and prayer meeting for mentally ill and homeless individuals on Saturdays. I would pick up the individuals from the library in Downtown Dallas, bring them to the office, minister to them, feed them, and take them back to the library or their homeless shelter in Downtown. This went on for about a year.

About a year later, the desire to house some homeless individuals kept coming to me, but I did not have the money to provide the housing. I shared my impression with one of our board members, Kris. He was the first member on the board, and he is still a member emeritus. Kris was in real estate at the time, I think, and had a rental house. I spoke with him about the ministry's need, and he agreed to rent his house to us. I rented the house and had about seven homeless people living in it. We had Bible study on Wednesday nights, I took them to Christian World Church, where I worshipped on Sundays. Christian World Church was in Richardson at the time. Some of them gave their lives to the Lord. In those days, my second oldest daughter would go to church with us sometimes. We housed these homeless individuals for almost six months until I ran out of money.

With a divorce in process, attorney fees, child support, paying office rent, and paying for my own apartment, the only van I had frequently breaking down on me and, trying to take care of my two older children living with me, I almost had a breakdown, and maybe I did but didn't realize it. I told Kris I could not continue to rent the house any longer. He allowed me to stay there for a couple more months without any charge. It was a break that I needed at the time. May God reward him as He sees fit. Before the house was forced to close, three of the homeless individuals living in the house got financially rewarding jobs and moved out of the house without telling me. One of them has obtained a CDL and started driving for DART with good benefits. None of these individuals offered to volunteer or help the ministry financially or in any other capacity. I was happy, however that God used me as a vessel to give these individuals the motivation that they needed to move on with their lives. My assignment with them seemed completed.

We closed the house. Shortly before the house was closed, however, my only transportation, the Chevy passenger van that I was using to take the homeless to church and back, broke down. It would cost more than $2,000 to repair. It was the only transportation I had. I had never been on public transportation before, and I wouldn't mind learning, but there was no public transportation in Mesquite where I lived. All I could do was to pray and cry out to the Lord. I didn't have any other friends but the same guy, Kris, whom I invited to join our board a couple of years ago. I told him about the new problem I was facing, and he offered me his wife's old car, to use until I got back on my feet. I accepted his offer and, forever, I am grateful.

In less than three months, God gave me a 2-year-old SUV, a Nissan Xterra. I was surprised at the grace and mercy of God. The Psalmist says, "Surely goodness and mercy shall follow me all the days of my life: and I will dwell in the house of the Lord forever." Psalm 23:6. He is an on-time God. Through everything I went through, He always delivered me. He never left nor forsake me. The word of God says, "Many are the afflictions of the righteous, but the Lord delivers him out of them all." - Psalm 34:19. Glory to God, my righteousness is in His Son, Jesus Christ - 2 Corinthians 5:21. He exchanged His righteousness for my unrighteousness, and I am forever grateful.

Self Help Exercises

1. *In the author's account of the "Birth of Soul for Christ Ministry Inc.," the ministry was born...*

a. *when the author was having a lunch break*

b. *during a prayer at lunch break when the Holy Spirit spoke to him*

c. *at the intersection of Samuell Blvd. and Jim Miller, under a shaded tree*

d. *all the above*

2. *In the year 2000, the author opened his ministry's first office in East Dallas and...*

a. *started a Bible study and prayer meeting for the mentally ill and homeless individuals*

b. *would pick up the individuals from their homeless shelters and at the front of the Library in Downtown Dallas,*

c. *brought them to the office, ministered to them, fed them, and took them back to the library or their respective shelters in Downtown Dallas.*

d. *all the above*

3. *After about a year, the author had an impression that God wanted him to start housing the homeless, but he had no money to provide the housing. He opened a homeless shelter…*

a. *using one of his friend's homes. The shelter only lasted for about six months*

b. *but was forced to close the house due to going through the divorce, and having financial problems*

c. *many of the residents got good-paying jobs, and they started disappearing*

d. *all the above*

- -

Answers 1d, 2d, 3d,

_____

Chapter 11
THE PRIMARY MISSION OF SOUL FOR CHRIST MINISTRY INCORPORATED

Society calls them crazy; some religious congregations don't want them in their midst, many politicians think of them as parasites, irrelevant, and some family members are afraid to have them around. Where else will the homeless go? Who else will help the mentally ill?

Our Mission

The primary mission of Soul for Christ Ministry, Incorporated, is to help bridge the gap between individuals and their unmet basic needs, while at the same time educating them on how to work toward self-sufficiency.

Our History

Soul for Christ Ministry, Inc. was founded in 1999 by Brother Elijah as a community support organization primarily serving the mentally ill and homeless individuals. Since then, however, our services have extended to the elderly, single parents, low-income couples, troubled teenagers, those struggling with depression, anyone who is hurting, and reaching out for help. From 1999 to the present, Soul for Christ Ministry, Inc. has become a powerful force in eliminating hunger for many low-income neighbors in Dallas County and adjacent communities.

Our primary interest: the mentally ill

We may call them lazy, crazy, drug addicts, or use other damaging and degrading epithets, but let us not forget that these are also human beings. They are human beings first before they find themselves in the situations they are in. They are our neighbors, someone else's children, someone's parents, husbands, wives, sisters, brothers, nephews, nieces, cousins, uncles, and aunts. To our God, the restoration and well-being of the mentally ill and/or homeless individuals are just as important as yours and mine. Past and present experiences suggest that it is in our best interest and the best interest of our society that we reach out to the mentally ill and care for them as we would want to be cared for if we were in their position, if the roles were reversed. The mentally ill need you and me. They need all of us. They are our neighbors. There's nothing more worth rescuing on earth than a human soul. There is nothing worth our investments more than a human soul, and we need to understand also that not all mentally ill people are drug addicts but, to the contrary, many of the mentally ill and homeless individuals are truly victims.

God planted in me a comprehensive approach to help the mentally ill, a ministry that focuses on the whole person: body, soul, and spirit.

A Comprehensive Approach

In the early 2016, the Lord spoke to me about a facility where mentally ill people can come for a combination of interventions, including, but not limited to, nutritional foods, affordable housing, life skills training, health education, cognitive restructuring, job training and placement, behavioral counseling, GED preparation classes, adult literacy, computer classes, financial literacy, Bible study, and prayers for those desiring spiritual growth. The current traditional approach to help the mentally ill is too costly and less effective because it falls short of ministering to the whole person: the body, soul, and spirit. We are trusting God to provide for this mission.

Human beings are three in one. We are souls. Human souls are spirits, invisible, but not in the same class as the Spirit of God in us. We have a Spirit (the breath of God in all of us) and we all live in a body. With the Spirit of God in us, we know God; with our body we interact in the universe; and with our souls, we come to the knowledge of ourselves. These three are 1, and they must work together harmoniously, or else there would be schism or inner conflict, as it is written; no kingdom divided against itself can stand.

Mental Illnesses and Homelessness Are Not Just Government Problems

Mental health issues and homelessness are problems that affect not only the states, federal government, or the families of the mentally ill or the homeless. Mental health issues affect all of us directly or indirectly. The government may award disability checks, provide government housing, and food stamps to the homeless and those living with mental illnesses but, as good as all these supports may be, the mentally ill and homeless population need a more comprehensive approach than government benefits.

The government can incarcerate the mentally ill for acting crazy, but no government can incarcerate the demons responsible for human madness. The government may incarcerate the homeless for trespassing, but it cannot incarcerate the spirit behind the crime. The Christian community is obligated to fight these evils that are trying to take ownership of human souls.

The deliverance of the mind of the mentally ill is a noble call for Soul for Christ Ministry, Inc., and it should be a noble call for all of us if we are breathing, and our blood is red. We are our brothers' keepers.

We Can't Just Run Away from Them

There are family members who will do anything to keep a mentally ill relative away. Many religious congregations don't want the mentally ill around because they don't understand the illness or know how to deal with it. Many politicians think the mentally ill are irritants to society because they contribute very little to the economy and are known for putting excessive financial demands on the working society. As true as all of this may be, we can't run away from them or simply write them off as plagues or parasites.

The Homeless, The Mentally Ill Need Us

The homeless, and the mentally ill individuals need your help. Soul for Christ Ministry, Inc. needs your help. Together, we can assist the homeless and mentally ill individuals in regaining their dignity. Soul for Christ Ministry, Inc. is committed to making a difference in the lives and souls of individuals falling through the cracks. Please consider what part you may be able to play in this worthwhile endeavor. We brought nothing into the world, and when we die, we will take nothing out. May God keep you from all evil, bless you and your household is our prayers, Amen. Please help us continue to help those in need.

Please DONATE generously to this "helping ministry." We are passionate about helping the less privileged among us. You can make your donations on the Donation Page on our website at www.soulforchristministry.org or, you can mail your donations to our mailing address below:

Soul for Christ Ministry, Inc.

P.O. Box 570831

Dallas Texas 75357.

Your donations will help us continue to help those in need, and yes, together we can do more. May the Lord, our God, richly bless you and yours, materially, physically, emotionally and most importantly, in spiritual things.

Self Help Exercises

1. *The primary mission of Soul for Christ Ministry, Inc. is to…*

a. *bridge the gap between individuals and their unmet basic needs while at the same time educating individuals on how to work toward self-sufficiency*

b. *serve as a community support organization primarily helping the mentally ill, the elderly, and homeless individuals through nutritional foods, affordable housing, basic education, and counseling*

c. *serves whoever is hurting and reaching out for help*

d. *all the above*

Answer 1d.

StoryCorps Interview

My Recorded Interview with StoryCorps on November 9, 2019

For those of you who want to hear more about my journey through my voice, you can listen to my interview with StoryCorps by going to the website address below. The audio recording is easier to follow than the transcript. The transcript was defective and not properly transcribed. We recommend that you listen to the audio only. Thanks.

https://archive.storycorps.org/interviews/rabiu-omolaja-and-felisa-omolaja/#transcript

THE MAP OF NIGERIA

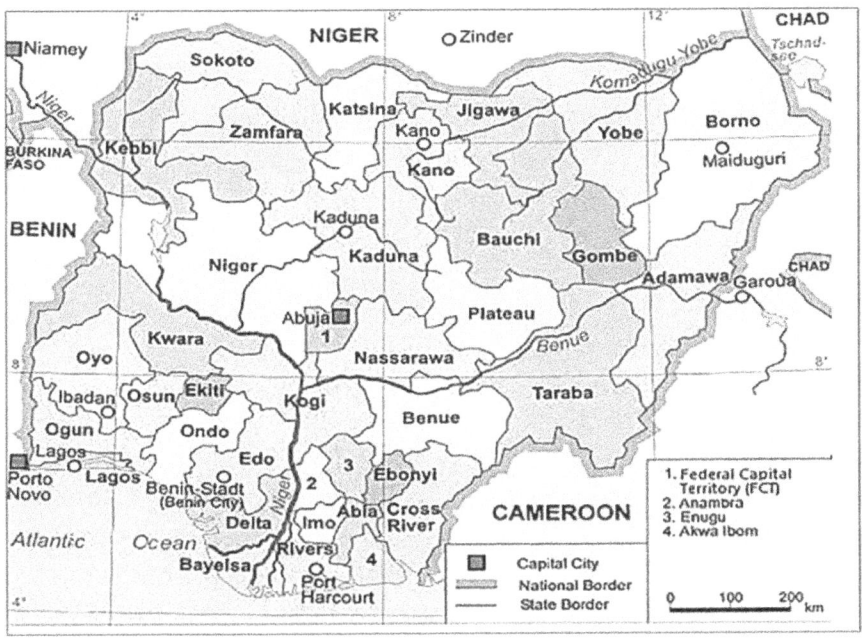

Book 2
The Gospel

Dedication

Unto Him who died, resurrected, and ascended into Heaven; unto the souls that He died to save, I am dedicating this book.

Preface

There is no quarrel between faith and reasoning. There should be no quarrel between faith and reasoning because God is the author of both. Where faith belongs, our reasoning is useless. Where reasoning belongs, our faith is ineffective. This is the principle, and the principle is this: whenever our reasoning is in conflict with faith, whenever our reasoning is in opposition to God's Word, our reasoning must yield.

Introduction

O ur success in life is not measured, should not be measured, by the size of our wallets. Life success is not measured by material wealth. We brought nothing into this world, and when we die, we will take nothing out, according to the Scripture (1 Timothy 6:7). Our lifetime possessions, the money in our bank accounts, our level of education, our looks, and popularity all become meaningless to us when we die. Society measures our success by our material wealth; God measures our success by who we are in Him. It is not our material wealth that determines our greatness in God's sight (Luke 12:16–20). Gold or silver cannot determine our destiny. Lazarus was a sickly beggar, a man of sorrow. He died and went to Heaven. The rich man died also, but he went to Hell (Luke 16:19–31). Even though God wants you and me to be blessed and prosper in material things, the salvation of our souls should come first. God wants you and me to have rewarding careers, intact families, be in good health, and have enough money to spend, but our relationship with Him should come first. "What shall it profit a man if he wins the whole world and loses his own soul? What will a man give in exchange for his soul?" (Matthew 16:26). John wrote, "Beloved, I wish above all things that thou mayest prosper and be in health, even as thy soul prospereth." Notice what John says, "as thy soul prospereth" (3 John 1:2). The prosperity and the salvation of your soul must come first. Are you one of those who still debate whether to be or not to be a Christian? It is my hope that after reading this book, you will be more enlightened and see the need to accept God's plan for the redemption of your soul. There are many also who have believed in Jesus Christ but continue to miss out on many of God's blessings and promises, either by genuine ignorance, lack of faith, self-neglect or ungodly lifestyles. Some Christians are fighting the

Goliaths of life that refuse to fall. They are struggling with mountains that refuse to move. Many believers are suffering in silence, cohabiting with thorns in the flesh, the messengers of evil that torment their bodies day after day, night after night. Some believers begin to question the veracity of the hope in them. They ask themselves in silence, "Will there be a light at the end of this dark tunnel?" To each and every one of us, I am dedicating this book. This book is written for believers and unbelievers alike. It is written to those who believe in Christ but are suffering in silence at the hands of the enemy. It is also written to those who still doubt the existence of God and the validity of the sacrifice of His Son on the Cross for the remission of the sins of those who believe. We Christians need to know that the devil, our enemy, is already defeated. We need to know that in Christ we are no longer victims but the victorious ones. You and I are not saved by the blood of the Righteous One to continue to suffer at the hands of the devil. We are not saved to stay sick, living miserably in pain and suffering. Physical pain and mental anguish are works of the enemy in disguise, according to the Scripture (see Luke 13:16; John 10:10). God is not the author of our pain or our suffering, and nor is He delighted in them. I trust the Holy Ghost to continue to minister to you as you read this book, in Jesus' Mighty name. Amen. Glory to God!

Spiritual Exercises:

1. *Since God is not measuring our success by our material wealth, how does He measure it?*

2. *What did you learn from the life and death of Lazarus and the rich man?*

3. *How will you convince yourself that God wants you to have the best in life have a good family, enough money to live on, and be in good health?*

4. *Why is it important to possess the salvation of your soul first rather than having much material wealth but losing your soul in the process?*

5. *This book is written for two categories of people. Describe the people in each category.*

Chapter 12
In the Soul

The plan of salvation is not to be understood by our brain. The human brain is a natural entity, trapped in and limited to the realm of the senses. That is why you and I are prone to believe only in what we can see, hear, smell, touch, or taste. We can educate our brain in secular knowledge such as mathematics, computer science, language, or philosophy, but, to the contrary, salvation is a spiritual experience. It goes beyond the realm of thinking and feelings. Salvation is Life, a flow of Life in the body of dust. God is that "Life." One of the reasons that many of us have difficulties accepting God's plan of salvation is that we are trying to understand its necessity and the process with our brain. Our need for salvation and God's provision for us to be saved is not understandable within the realm of senses. It is in the soul that conviction takes place, not in the head. It is in the soul where you and I develop a relationship with God.

Your soul is not your brain; it is not your heart.

The human soul is not observable. There are some professionals who are trained to monitor the activities of the brain, but no professional can monitor the soul. There are drugs capable of altering the activities of the brain, but no drug is capable of altering the soul. The human soul is not the heart. Our heart is a material organ designed to pump blood into the body. Some doctors are trained to replace failing hearts, but no doctor can replace the soul. I thank God for the doctors and their good work. We have doctors who mend broken legs, remove cancerous tumors, help mothers deliver their children, and prevent untimely death. These doctors have helped a lot of people to have another chance in life. By God's grace and through the work of these excellent doctors, we can witness many living miracles among us. There are people whom we come in contact with daily, individuals whom we never thought would be able to live for another day; we see them living fairly normal lives after successful heart transplants. We should thank God for the doctors, but there are limitations to what doctors can do. Glory to God, where doctors are limited, our God is unlimited. God is the Ultimate Doctor with the Capacity to operate both the body and the soul. God is the absolute authority in all things. Even more so, there is no human doctor capable of sending your soul to Heaven or Hell. God is the judge of all. Many Christians are healthy souls living in unhealthy bodies. A Christian may suffer heart problems, brain problems, diabetes, cancer, ulcers, tuberculosis, high blood pressure, physical pain, or any other poor health condition due to many reasons, such as self-neglect, dabbling in sin, poor lifestyles, or an ignorant or faulty belief system. We may be sick in the body, but we are still heavenly bound as long as we never stop believing in our Savior, Jesus Christ, as long as we hold fast to our salvation to the end. Lazarus was a godly man living in a sickly body. Lazarus died, and the angels took him to Heaven (Luke 16: 19–25).

Your soul is a mystery you may never understand.

The living soul is the product of a divine unity between God's breath and the earthly dust. "And the Lord God formed man of the dust of the ground and breathed into his nostrils the breath of life; and man became a living soul" (Genesis 2:7). This is a mystery that no human mind will fully understand. There is a body formed out of the dust of the earth by God's own fingers. The brain, the heart, kidneys, lungs, pancreas, all the internal organs, and outward features were present but only in a lifeless form. God breathed into the lifeless body of dust, and the lifeless body of dust became a "living soul," according to the Scriptures. Your soul is you. This is a mystery that we may never understand. Also, you need to know that there is nothing in Heaven, or on earth, or underneath the earth that is as precious to God as your soul. Human souls are the apples of God's eye. The human soul is a mystery, the most important among everything that God has created. That is why God gave you and me His very best to redeem our souls. God gave the world His only begotten Son, that whosoever believes in Him should not perish but have everlasting life (John 3:16).

Your soul is what needs to be restored, redeemed, born again

David wrote: "He restoreth my soul." It was not the Spirit that God restored. It was not David's body that God restored. It was David's soul. The Spirit, the breath of God in us, doesn't need to be restored. The Spirit is the presence of God, the Breath of God in us. When we die or are taken out of this body, if we believe in Him, the Spirit and human soul will spend eternity with God – (Ecclesiastes 12:7). The human body doesn't need to be restored.

Our body is a collective mass of earthly dust designed to connect us to the universe. It is also a form of transportation designed to shuttle us around while we are here on earth. When you and I reach the end of our journey on earth, our bodies will return to the dust where they belong (see Genesis 3:17–19). This body of dust will not inherit the kingdom of God (1 Corinthians 15:50). I am a soul, I have a Spirit, and I live in a body (1 Thessalonians 5:23). Some people may argue that human beings are spirits. This may be partly true because human souls, as well as spirits, are also invisible to the natural eye. The human soul, however, is not in the same class with the Spirit of God, the Breath of God in us. Human souls are vulnerable, unlike God's spirit. God's Spirit, the Breath of God in us, is God Himself. Angels are spirits (Hebrews 1: 13- 14), but they are not in the same class as God's Spirit. Angels are not God. Human souls are spirits but they are not in the same class with God's Spirit. The human soul is not God. God's Spirit, the Breath of God in us, is immutable and untouchable. When Adam and his wife sinned and fell from grace in the Garden of Eden, the Spirit of God in them, the breath of God in them, didn't sin or fall along with them. It was their souls that went wayward, separated from God, not the Spirit of God in them. God cannot separate from Himself. The Bible says that the soul that sins shall die (Ezekiel 18:4). It is the soul that will either go to Heaven or Hell, not the Spirit of God in us, nor our body of dust. On the other hand, however, and according to Jesus' statement in Matthew 10:28, we can deductively say that the unbeliever's body and soul will spend eternity in Hell.

Spiritual Exercises:

1. *The plan of salvation cannot be understood within the realm of our senses. Why?*

2. *Salvation is a flow of "Life" regenerating the soul. Who is this "Life"?*

3. *Describe the differences between your soul and your heart, between your soul and your mind, between your soul and your brain.*

4. *What are the mysteries involved in the creation of the living soul?*

5. *What in you must be saved and will either go to Heaven or Hell?*

Rabiu Elijah Omolaja

Chapter 13
WHAT HAPPENS WHEN A
PERSON BECOMES A CHRISTIAN?

There is tremendous joy in Heaven the moment a person becomes a Christian (Luke 15:7). God rejoices, Jesus rejoices, and the angels rejoice whenever a soul comes to the Lord. Each salvation that occurs on earth spells victory for God. The new child of God is moved from the death row into eternal life, from everlasting torment to everlasting joy. When a person is born again (John 3:3), the devil loses, and God gains. Our salvation, each salvation on earth, is an ultimate joy for God.

The person becomes God's temple, God's dwelling place.

Once a person has accepted Jesus Christ, he or she is no longer living life alone. Believers are not on this journey alone. We are in Christ, and Christ is in us. Our first and foremost responsibility after we have accepted Christ is to begin to learn who we really are in Him and who He really is in us. The more we know who we are in Him and who He is in us, the more Hell becomes uncomfortable, and the more the forces of evil will begin to tremble in our presence. The devil and his demonic forces are compelled to tremble in our presence. They are compelled to obey our commands. They must obey our commands not because of our strength or righteousness, but because Jesus paid the price. Jesus switched His place with us on the Cross. He took ownership of our sins, nailed them to the Cross, and gave us His righteousness. Jesus paid the price for my sin in full. Our Lord succumbed to torture as if He were powerless, but all the powers in Heaven and on earth were at His fingertips. He was bruised, scourged, and nailed to the Cross, hung between the thieves and murderers. Jesus died a humble, shameful death. He was buried, went to Hell because of our sins, but Hell was unable to hold Him. My Lord was too hot to handle, and He is still too hot to handle. Hell cannot detain my Lord. He rose on the third day.

Jesus rose from the dead and now dwells in us and among those who believe. The Scripture says that greater is He who is in us than he who is in the world (1 John 4:4). The devil knows the facts. He knows that Jesus dwells in believers. The devil knows that wherever Jesus is, there is God (1 John 4:15). He knows that wherever God is, there is the Holy Ghost (1 John 4:13). The devil knows that Christians are God's temple, Jesus' temple, and the Holy Ghost's temple. Our enemy knows that we are God's property and that he, the devil, has lost all rights, all privileges, and all authority over us. He has lost his authority over us because the glory that the first Adam and his wife forfeited because of their sin, the second Adam, Jesus Christ, has restored in obedience and righteousness (Romans 5:18–19, 1 Corinthians15:22).

The person's attitudes and lifestyle will begin to change from the inside out.

A genuine Christian will begin to experience some internal changes. Although he (or she) is still a human, he still has desires, and wants of life, but he lives not by bread alone but also by the Word of God. His main desire now is to do that which is pleasing in God's sight and, to be a living sacrifice, acceptable unto God (Romans 12:1). Jesus said that the fruit reveals the identity of a tree (Matthew 7:16– 23). By our conducts and the way we relate_to the world, you and I shall be recognized as the followers of Christ. Christians' lifestyles should reflect the characteristics of the Christ in them. Paul wrote, "Therefore if any man be in Christ, he is a new creature: old things are passed away; behold, all things are become new" (2 Corinthians 5:17). The believer's lifestyle and attitudes will begin to change from the inside out. Their life experiences will become more purposeful. The peace of God begins to conquer the soul, hope becomes alive, love for self and others abounds, godliness begins to show , faith increases, and impossibilities begin to fade away as the new Christian learns to trust God and put His Word first.

The person will begin to experience God's peace, God's presence.

Believers are protected from the wiles of the enemy. As the mountains surround Jerusalem, so also God surrounds His people

(Psalm 125:2). We know that if God is for us, no one can be against us. If the Lord is on our side, what can man do to us? (Psalm 118:6). With all the powers of Heaven on our side, how can we fail? We are of Christ and in Christ. In Christ, believers are made the children of the Most High God. Knowing that God is our Father and that He loves us, and that He will never leave us nor forsake us gives us absolute peace. It gives us confidence, joy, and hope that no one can measure. By thinking, believing, and confessing in this way, regardless of my circumstances, I ultimately changed the way I look at my existence, my life experiences, and all of their inconsistencies. God will keep him in perfect peace, he whose mind stays on God - Isaiah 26:3.

The person will begin to learn how to maintain a Christian identity, even in troubled times.

Becoming a Christian does not mean a life without trouble. In fact, the devil may throw obstacles our way to frustrate us. That is why we need to know who we truly are in Christ. Becoming a Christian does not mean that everything will always go well. We will encounter troubles and doubts from time to time. That is why we must learn to renew our minds in the Word of God daily (Joshua 1:8). Being a Christian does not mean that you can now win your enemy over. It doesn't mean that everybody will start loving you. In fact, there will be many who will hate you, including some in your own household (Matthew 10:21–22, 36). They did the same thing to our Lord. The Gospel of Jesus Christ and persecution are necessary enemies. It is not uncommon for those that strive to live a Christian l i f e to suffer persecution (2 Timothy 3:10– 12, 2 Corinthians 11:23–27).

The person will begin to learn how to overcome life's challenges through Jesus Christ.

There is no life without challenges, but as Christians, whatever the devil may throw our way, whatever the life presents us with, whether it is good or bad, we have the victory already. We are victorious not because of our own strengths, but because greater is He that is in us (1 John 4:4). We are victorious not because of our own righteousness, but because of the righteousness of His Son, whom He has made to be our righteousness. Informed believers have learned that all things work together for good for those who love the Lord and are called according to His purpose (Romans 8:28). Christians ought to look at life's challenges and see them as opportunities to show faith. Rather than telling God how big our problems are, we begin to tell our problems how big our God is. That is what puts our fear, our life's challenges, and all demonic forces on the run. In Christ, all our fears, life's challenges, and obstacles are defeated.

Spiritual Exercises:

1. There is joy in Heaven when one becomes a Christian. Why is that a big deal?

2. A Christian is God's temple, God's dwelling place. How can that be?

3. How can we suspect that someone is likely to be a Christian?

4. How can a Christian maintain their identity in troubled times?

5. How do believers overcome life's challenges?

Chapter 14
TO BE OR NOT TO BE?

On Becoming a Christian!

Becoming a Christian is a choice, not a must. God will not compel any of us to comply. Do you know that if God wanted to compel you or force the whole human race to become Christians, He could do it in a fraction of a second? Yes, He could, but He will not. It is true that God, indeed wants every one of us to be saved, according to Scripture (1 Timothy 2:4), but He will not force His salvation on us. God wants each one of us to exercise our free will to choose to be or not to be a Christian, either by accepting or by rejecting the provision He has made through the death and resurrection of His Son. There is only one way, only one mediator between God and man, according to Scripture (1 Timothy 2:5). "For there is none other name under heaven given among men whereby we must be saved" (Acts 4: 12). In Jesus Christ, you and I escaped the wrath of God that is coming upon the children of disobedience. Do not be deceived, my friend; though His wrath may tarry, it shall surely come. The Just God will inevitably judge the wicked world. There is Heaven, and there is Hell.

The first step to becoming a Christian is to acknowledge the existence of one God, the One who created the heavens and the earth (Genesis 1:1). But how can we possibly deny the Undeniable? Only the fool hath said in his heart that there is no God, according to Scripture (Psalm 14:1).

In the beginning, God created the heavens and the earth.

God created the heavens and the earth. He created us, human beings, in His image and He surrounded us with a host of innumerable evidence and wonders both on earth and in the atmosphere around and above us so that there would be no doubt that there is an Intelligent Being, a Power beyond this empirical reality. Consider the solar system:

On average, Mercury is about 37 million miles from the sun, Venus is about 67 million miles from the sun, Earth is about 93 million miles from the sun, Mars is about 142 million miles from the sun, Jupiter is about 483 million miles from the sun, Saturn is about 886 million miles from the sun, Uranus is about 1,780 million miles from the sun, Neptune is about 2,790 million miles from the sun, Pluto is about 3,670 million miles from the sun.

I want you to know that our planet and the universe are not a result of some big bangs and nor were they formed from a cloud of cosmic dust and gas, as some wayward minds are trying to convince us to believe. The creation of the heavens and the earth, and all that is within, upon, and underneath them, are the designs of an Intelligent Being called God. In His power and wisdom, He created them all. God created them all out of nothing. He stretched the heavens over the empty place and hung the earth upon nothing - Job 26:7

God created human beings in His image.

You and I are created in God's image (Genesis 1: 27). He formed us in such a unique way that there are no two individuals who look exactly alike, not even those we label as identical twins. With His providence, God formed each of us in our mothers' wombs (Psalm 139:14) as distinguished individuals. You should be proud that there is no other person in this world who looks exactly like you. Can you imagine the structure of your bones, your brain, your nervous system, reproductive system, digestive system, and respiratory system? Can you imagine the functions of your senses: your ability to see, think, feel, speak, smell, hear, sit, walk, or stay still? These are nothing less than the works of an Intelligent Being. His name is "Almighty," "Jehovah," "I am That I am" (Exodus 3:14; 6:3). I feel extremely honored. Human beings should feel honored, for there are no other creatures in Heaven or on Earth created in the likeness of the Almighty. The twenty-four elders in Heaven, the Seraphim, the Cherubim, all types of angels, including Michael, Gabriel, and Lucifer, with all his glory, were not created in the image of God. Do you understand now why the devil and his demons may be jealous of you?

Adam and Eve were created healthy, sinless, well-provided for, and clothed in God's glory in the Garden of Eden.

Adam and his wife were created healthy and holy unto God, without the concept of sin. They were innocent and lacked nothing. This first couple lived peacefully in the Garden of Eden, with God Himself visiting and fellowshipping with them in the cool of the day. Adam was given the dominion to rule over everything on earth. He gave every living creature on earth their names (see Genesis 2:18–23). He named his wife "Eve" (Genesis 3:20).

God established the first family in the Garden of Eden and gave them instructions.

God is Omnipotent: all-powerful; Omnipresent: ever-present; and Omniscient: all-knowing. Our God is a thinking Being, and He is perfect in all His ways. Before He put Adam and his wife in the Garden of Eden, He created everything they would need to survive and live happily in the Garden. He knew also that the enemy, Satan, would come into the garden to tempt the couple, and He warned Adam, "saying, 'Of every tree of the garden thou mayest freely eat: but of the tree of the knowledge of good and evil, thou shalt not eat of it: for in the day that thou eatest thereof thou shall surely die'" (Genesis 2:16–17). The instruction and the consequences for its violation were not ambiguous. God's instructions to Adam were understood, nothing esoteric. God didn't set Adam up to fail. God told him, "Thou shalt not eat." God informed Adam of the consequences if he chose to disobey. Obedience is better than sacrifice.

There were plenty of other fruit bearing trees in the Garden of Eden for Adam and his wife.

There were, perhaps, more than ten, hundreds, or thousands of other fruit-bearing trees that Adam and his wife could eat from in the Garden of Eden. That is why God told them, "Thou mayest freely eat" out of every fruit in the garden except one. God is a reasoning God (Isaiah 1:18–20). He told Adam why He didn't want them to eat it , "... for the day that thou eats thereof thou shall surely die" (Genesis 2:17). God didn't want Adam and his wife to eat from the tree of the knowledge of good and evil, because He knew that there was "evil" in it, just as its name implies. God was telling Adam something like this: "I am in you now, and my Glory is all over you for a garment, but the moment you put that evil in your mouth, I am out." God was telling Adam, "If you eat of that fruit, the devil will gain access to your soul, and I will not cohabit with the devil." God is a jealous God. He will not share his glory with the devil. Do you think that God was asking Adam to do something He hadn't equipped Adam and his wife to do? The answer is a resounding "no." Adam and Eve were created with the capacity to resist the devil, but at the same time, God trusted them with free will. God trusted them with the free will to obey or rebel His authority. God will not compel any of His creatures to comply. That was why Lucifer and one-third of the angels were able to revolt against God. They, too, were given free will. You and I, too, have the free will to obey or rebel against His authority. That is why some of us can be atheists, denying the existence of God, and still be alive. If God is a compeller, He could have stricken some of us into believing there is God.

Nevertheless, God will eventually judge the disobedience of men. Adam and his wife chose to betray and disobey God. They chose to rebel against the Hands that formed them. The couple chose not to submit themselves unto God as He desired. Adam and Eve chose not to resist the devil (James 4:7).

The first family yielded to the serpent and disobeyed God. God's glory departed from them.

The enemy came to Eve in disguise. The devil appeared in the form of a serpent and as a friend of the family. He won the friendship and interest of Eve first. I wonder why the devil didn't approach Adam but chose Eve. I wonder if that would have made any difference. Well, we will never know. The serpent started off the conversation with Eve. The more the conversation continued, the more his offer became appealing and made sense to Eve. The serpent was successful in whetting the first lady's appetite with words suitable to her hearing. The more Eve listened to the serpent talk, the more she became dissatisfied with God in her thinking. The Bible teaches that faith comes by hearing. If you listen to evil, chances are, you will begin to think evil. If you are thinking evil, you may begin to believe in evil, and eventually you will act evil. Our belief system is what shapes our thinking, and our thinking also can influence our belief system. These two will continue to impose on one another as long as we are in this body. What you believe and your subjective perception of reality are the main influences in your decision- making process. Upon these two, your feelings and behaviors are predicated.

After Eve's long and rambling conversation with the devil, she took a bite of the fruit that God had commanded them not to eat. Then she gave the fruit to Adam and he, too, took a bite of the fruit, according to the Genesis account. Consequently, and instantaneously, the devil gained access into their souls. Adam and his wife simultaneously lost their glorious, sinless nature. They lost their blissful state of innocence. Our first parents lost their beautiful fellowship with God. God's glory departed from Adam and Eve because He will not cohabit with evil. From that moment, Adam lost his authority and dominion over the earth for a bite of the fruit that God had commanded him not to eat.

He sold the human race under the authority of the devil. Adam and Eve gave the devil and his demonic forces what they wanted (see Genesis 3:1–24 account, and the devil's claim of the world ownership while he was tempting Jesus Christ - Luke 4: 5-7).

God's glory departed from Adam and Eve, but God did not forsake them completely.

Even though God was not pleased with what Adam and his wife had done, He nevertheless came down into the garden as usual to fellowship with them. It seemed like God was giving the couple the opportunity to repent (Proverbs 28:13). Instead of repenting, however, Adam and Eve ran off and hid (Genesis 3:8). A sinner will run when no one is chasing (Proverbs 28:1). God called Adam by name, but rather than answering God, Adam and his wife took off running and hiding. Can any man hide himself from the Most High God? Does He not fill Heaven and the earth, according to the scriptures? see Jeremiah 23:24; Psalm 139:7–8; and Amos 9: 2–4. When these two finally answered God's calling, Adam quickly shifted the blame on God, saying it was God's fault. He told God, "The woman whom thou gayest to be with me, she gave me of the tree, and I did eat" (Genesis 3:12). Then God turned to Eve, asking her why she did what she did. Eve, too, had someone else to blame. She told God, "The serpent beguiled me, and I did eat" (Genesis 3:13). Neither of them took responsibility for their actions. God didn't have time nor questions for the serpent, for He knew who was operating through it —the devil called Lucifer.

Obedience is better than sacrifice.

The children of God must keep in mind that whenever their reasoning conflicts with God's Word, their reasoning must yield. Adam and Eve failed to put God's Word first. A just God must render judgment (Genesis 3:14–19). God pronounced His judgment upon the serpent, Eve, Adam, and the Earth, but in His judgment, God also demonstrated His eternal love and mercy for human race. It could have been easier for God to destroy Adam and his wife instantaneously and eliminate human race once and for all, but He chose not to do that. Instead, God stepped down from His throne, came down from Heaven into the Garden of Eden, took one of the animals in the garden, killed it, and offered the first sacrifice on earth unto Himself for the remission of Adam's and Eve's Sin. God offered the blood of animal to atone for their sin, for it is written that without the shedding of blood, there will be no remission (of sin) (Hebrews 9:22; Leviticus 17:11). God sprinkled Adam and His wife with the blood of the animal before His anger could consume them. He clothed Adam and his wife with coats of skins and drove the couple out of the Garden of Eden (Genesis 3: 21–24).

We are the children of disobedience

Adam and Eve fell from grace and we, their descendants, fell along with them. You and I inherited the sin of Adam and Eve, their sinful nature, and all its adverse consequences. Do you know that you and I are sinners, not because we are sinning, but, to the contrary, we are sinning because by nature we are sinners? I will still be a sinner if I never committed a single sin since the day I was born. David wrote: "Behold, I was sharpening in iniquity and in sin did my mother conceive me" (Psalm 51:5). Paul wrote: "For all have sinned and come short of the glory of God" (Romans 3:23). Adam and his wife became estranged from God, who created them. You and I inherited their woes. Human beings have been estranged to God since the fall of Adam and Eve in the Garden of Eden. Human beings are estranged, wayward, and wicked from the womb (Psalm 58:3, Genesis 6:5)

The human race, the earth and all its wealth, were sold under the authority of the devil.

Since the fall of Adam and his wife, the earth and the humanity have been sold under the authority of the devil and his demons.

When the devil was tempting Jesus, he proposed to Him saying that if Jesus would worship him, he, the devil, would give Jesus all the kingdom of the world and all of their glory (Matthew 4:8–9). Though the devil is a liar according to Scripture, he wasn't lying at this particular time. Lucifer (Satan), the old serpent called the devil, is the prince of this present world. He became the prince of this world through the rebellion and the transgression of Adam and Eve. Jesus Himself referred to the devil as the prince of this present world (read Paul's comments in 2Corinthians 4:4, and Christ's comments in John 12: 31). Our Savior couldn't refute the devil on his claim of ownership, but instead Jesus used the Word of God to get the devil off His back. You need to know that the devil is present in the world and that he is reigning, but he doesn't have to reign over you if you are in Christ. The devil has no right to rule or reign over the children of God. Christians have only one Master and one Lord - Ephesians 4:5. His name is Jehovah, the God Almighty, the Everlasting Father, the Creator of the Heaven and the earth.

Though the devil is the prince of this world, he cannot rule over the children of God.

The devil is allowed to rule the world temporarily and with limitations. One of the limitations that God imposed on the devil is that he cannot rule the children of God. He has no authority over those who believe in Jesus Christ. Even though the devil is allowed to rule and reign over the unbelievers, he can only rule as far as God will let him so that God will remain the "All in All." It is true that the devil does not know everything, but he knows that his reign has some limitations. He knows also that his days on earth are numbered. The devil knows that he has a limited time to do whatever he sets himself up to do against humanity. That is why he is so restless, angry, and very impatient with us. When God asked him where he was coming from before He introduced Job to him, the devil responded, "From going to and for in the earth, and from walking up and down in it" (Job 1:7, 2:2). The devil is restless and very impatient with us. He wanders around, pacing the face of the planet earth like a roaring lion, looking for whom he may devour (1 Peter 5:8). He will not devour me. I have the real Lion in me. I have the Lion of Judah in me. Greater is He that is in me than legions of devils and all the demonic forces combined.

The animal that God killed in the Garden of Eden is a symbol of our Savior, Jesus Christ.

The animal that God sacrificed in the Garden of Eden is a symbol of Jesus Christ, who came to offer His body on the cross as the final sacrifice for human sins. Even though God offered the first sacrifice in the Garden of Eden to atone for the original Sin, He knew also that the blood of animals could only cover their sin; it cannot wipe it away (Hebrews 10:4). That is why God was able to keep account of the number of times the children of Israel had sinned against Him (Numbers 14:22). Yes, they offered animal sacrifices for their sins, but these sacrifices were only good enough to cover their sins; they could not wipe them away. Also, the animals' blood is not pure enough to redeem us fully to God. That is why we needed the pure Lamb of God. Jesus' death is the ultimate sacrifice and the end of all forms of sacrifices. Another reason we cannot be redeemed by the blood of an animal is that the Redeemer must be, as required by the Law of Moses, a human being. That is why angels cannot redeem us. That is why a tree, a stone, the sun, the moon, a river or any man-made religion cannot reconcile us to God.

In addition to being a human being, the Redeemer must be perfect in all ways. He must fulfill the Law of Moses and be holy, without sins of His own. Noah found favor in God's sight, but he was not holy enough to pay for Adam's disobedience. Abraham was a friend of God, but he was not perfect enough to save the human race (Genesis 17:1). Moses was the lawgiver, but he was not holy enough to reconcile us to God. David, the second king of Israel, was a man after God's own heart, according to Scripture, but he was not good enough to reconcile us to God. No human being was holy enough to redeem us to God except the only begotten Son (John 3:16), the Arm of God, who is the pure Lamb of God. His name is Jesus Christ, Wonderful, Counselor, the Almighty God, the Everlasting Father, and the Prince of Peace (Isaiah 9:6). The Holy Ghost called Him "Emmanuel" in Matthew 1:23.

Amazing God, Amazing Christ.

What is amazing here is that God offered the first sacrifice to cover Adam's and Eve's sin in the Garden of Eden and later in the Law of Moses. On the Cross, however, He offered the final sacrifice on the Cross to wipe away our sins once and for all, and forever. This time, glory to God, it was not with the blood of an animal. God atoned for our sins in full, with the blood of His only begotten Son, Jesus Christ, whom He sent to die for the sins of the world (John 1:29; 3:16; 1 John 4:14). The Bible says that He came unto His own, and His own received Him not, but those who believed in Him, He has given the power to become the children of God (John 1:11–12). The skin of the animal that God used to cover Adam and Eve's nakedness symbolizes God's righteousness, so that when God looks down on Adam and Eve, He doesn't see who they have become, but instead He sees His own righteousness, the coat of skin. All of these actions by God in the Garden of Eden point to Jesus Christ, our righteousness. In Jesus Christ, God chose not to remember our past failures. He chose to forgive us of our past, present, and future transgressions. When God looks at you and me, He sees nothing but Jesus Christ on us. God sees only Christ, whom He has made to be our cloak of righteousness. You and I put on Christ the moment we were saved. We are in Christ, and Christ is in us; His blood cleanses us daily from all unrighteousness (Ephesians 1:7 and 1 John 1:8–10).

Adam and his wife were chased out of the Garden of Eden to prevent them from eating the fruit of life and living forever.

Here again, we see the demonstration of God's love and mercy for the human race. God could have allowed Adam and his wife to remain in the garden, eat of the fruit of life and live as they were —estranged to God and miserable—forever. Can you imagine living as you are right now forever? Who would want to live under God's curse, in poverty, aches, and pains, wrestling with natural calamities, in conflicts and wars, with murderers, in sickness, at the mercy of pandemics such as Covid-19, other pestilences, earthquakes, hurricanes, among people of unclean lips, cohabiting with the children of the devil, and without any hope of escaping? Who would want that? I thank God for driven Adam and Eve out of the Garden of Eden and for preventing them from eating the fruit of life and living on earth forever in such a terrible state. (see Genesis 3:22–24). The human race should thank God always for His mercy, grace, foresight, and thoughtfulness.

God allowed Adam and his wife to retain their capacity to think, feel, and act.

There are three attributes that God allowed Adam and Eve to retain after their fall. These attributes, among others, are what separate human beings from robots and animals. First, Adam and His wife were allowed to retain their intelligence. Human beings can think. Second, Adam and his wife were allowed to retain their emotions. Human beings have the capacity to feel pain, sadness, and happiness. Third, Adam and his wife were allowed to retain their willpower. Human beings have the capacity to make choices among options. It is through the use of our willpower that God has assigned a divine tool to measure our obedience. Human beings are not like robots. Robots are mechanical, designed by humans, and programmed to do certain things at certain times. Human beings are not like animals. Animals live by instinct. We are not mechanical, nor do we live by instinct alone. Human beings are thinking beings. We have feelings and are endowed with the capacity to make choices among many life's options. Even when we refuse to make a decision, our indecisiveness is also a decision. These attributes, among others, are what give us the glorious classification of beings formed in the likeness and image of God (Genesis 1:26).

Your willpower is a divine gift, a formidable force in the decision-making process.

You possess special qualities that no one can take away from you. One of these special qualities is your "willpower." Our willpower is a precious gift and a divine measuring tool for obedience. You can give your willpower away, but no one can force you to surrender it. It is God's gift to you. God gave each of us the willpower to be able to choose as we please among life's many options. You cannot avoid making life decisions as long as you live. You must make decisions, whether it is a decision about career, a mate, physical needs, material and spiritual issues. Making life decisions is a must as long as we live. Choosing To be or not to be a Christian is one of the many life decisions we must make. It is a decision between an individual and God. Not deciding is also a decision and a function of your willpower.

With your willpower and freedom of choice comes responsibility.

God has given us the freedom to use our willpower whichever way we choose or see fit. With that freedom, however, comes responsibility. Each of us will be held accountable for how we use our freedom and the decisions we make or refuse to make. Look at the world around you; look at your friends, your relatives, co- workers, and all people in general. Everyone is doing their own thing in their own way. People worship what they want, eat what they want, go where they want, and do whatever seems fit in their own sight, and much of the time, their ways are not God's ways. But has God struck them yet? No, He hasn't, and He will not. The only time that God punishes unbelievers is when they interfere with His children or obstruct His plans. Do you know some people who are not in Christ and really don't care whether God exists or not? Do these people have jobs? I bet some of them do. Do they have families and enjoy the good things in life? I bet some of them do. Do they have roofs over their heads? Yes, many of them do. Do they enjoy God's natural blessings such as the rain, the sun, the moon, the stars, the air, and the earth's minerals? Yes, they do. God is merciful towards His creation. He is long-suffering toward us, but just as it was in the days of Noah when people were drinking and merry in their sins until the terrible flood overtook them by surprise, so shall it be for this generation (Luke 17:26–36). For the people in the days of Noah, tomorrow was too late. Today, God continues to ordain ministers and send them all over the world, even to the remote parts of the world, so that the Gospel of Jesus Christ is preached across the globe—to Jews and Gentiles, to the small and the great, to the poor and the rich, to the young and the old, to people of all colors and races, so there will be no excuse. My friend, this is your opportunity: you have your chance today, right now, as you are reading this book. Don't take your life and eternity for granted. Tomorrow may be too late, just as it was in the days of Noah. Please use your willpower and freedom responsibly.

Your belief system guides the decisions you make; it guides your thinking, feelings, and actions.

Regardless of whether you are a Christian or not, your willpower is a formidable force. This formidable force is guided, however, by your belief system. What you believe in has significant influence on how you live your life and the decisions you are making consciously or unconsciously. It is not the genes that you inherited from any of your parents that determine how you live. It is not the environment you were born in or live in that is responsible for what you choose to do or refuse to do. You and I choose to think the way we think, feel the way we feel, and act the way we act using our belief system as an invisible guide or a navigator. Imagine this—if you don't believe that a three-month-old fetus is a human being, would it be too difficult for you to vote "yes" on its abortion? No, it won't. But if you believe that a three-month-old fetus is a human being both potentially and actually, it is more likely you will vote "no" on its abortion. You will vote "no" even if you stand alone, and if your vote doesn't count, you may lament over its abortion. It is your belief system that guides and directs your life.

You cannot blame your senses for your decisions—your senses do not make decisions for you.

Our five senses are natural instruments created to help collect data from the environment, but they don't make decisions for us. You see the world with your eyes, but what you do with what you see depends on what you believe. Your ability to see, smell, hear, taste, and feel by touch are natural instruments designed only to orient you in the world. Eve saw and heard the serpent speak. She believed the serpent before she took a bite. Adam followed the same pattern. He listened to his wife and believed in her account of the devil's promises rather than believing in God. He, too, took a bite and henceforth handed the human race over to the authority of the devil.

You cannot blame your parents or your environment for your life experiences and the decisions you are making.

There are two strong natural influences in our lives. The first influence is DNA, the genetic blueprint we inherited from our parents— it is called "nature." The second influence is the environment, including all of our life's experiences—it is called "nurture." Upon these two natural influences, the psychology of personality is built. In the Christian community, however, these two formidable influences control us only as much as we would allow. It is true that we may not be able to change the body our parents gave us, but we don't have to think, feel, or act like our parents. You may be unfortunate to grow up in a dope house, but you don't have to be a dope addict. To succumb to the idea of a predestined personality or the thought that we are victims of heredity or environmental stimuli is what Sartre (1905–1980) called a "bad faith."3 Human behaviors are not exclusively contingent upon some inherited DNA or environmental stimuli. This is one of the errors of psychology and other schools of thought, or philosophical disciplines. Who knows the heart of a man? Read Jeremiah 17:9–10. Psychologists do not know us from the inside. Sociologists do not know us from the inside. Philosophers do not know us from the inside. Anthropologists do not know us from the inside. It is God, who created the heart that knows the heart of man. Human beings are not as irrational, mechanical, or robotic as the rebellious minds might suggest. We have the capacity to make choices among options. Cain and Abel were the first two children, born of the same parents. One chose to be evil; the other chose to love and fear God. Human beings can make Godly choices regardless of their genetic influences.

What was the devil's sin against God?

The devil was the first politician, and he started it in Heaven. He campaigned against God and managed to win the support of one- third of the angels. What was his motive? What did the devil want from God? The devil wanted to rule over God and God's creation.

How art thou fallen from heaven, O Lucifer, son of the morning! How art thou cut down to the ground, which didst weaken the nations! For thou hast said in thine heart, I will ascend into heaven, I will exalt my throne above the stars of God: I will sit also upon the mount of the congregation, in the sides of the north: I will ascend above the heights of the clouds: I will be like the most High. Yet thou shall be brought down to hell, to the sides of the pit. They that see thee shall narrowly look upon thee, and consider thee, saying, Is this the man that made the earth to tremble, that did shake kingdoms; That made the world as a wilderness, and destroyed the cities thereof; that opened not the house of his prisoners? (Isaiah 14: 12–17).

The devil wanted to be like the Most High God. Lucifer wanted to rule over God, who created him, He was thrown out of Heaven.

Some Bible scholars believe that the event took place between Genesis Chapter 1, verse one, and verse two. Some scholars dispute the timeframe of the account. To me, the exact timing of the event is not as important as the fact that it did take place.

Thou hast been in Eden the garden of God; every precious stone was thy covering, the sardius, the topaz, and the diamond, the beryl, the onyx, and the jasper, the sapphire, the emerald , and the carbuncle , and gold: the workmanship of thy tabrets and of thy pipes was prepared in thee in the day that thou was created. Thou art the anointed cherub that covereth; and I have set thee so: thou was upon the holy mountain of God; thou hast walked up and down in the midst of the stones of fire. Thou was perfect in thy ways from the day that thou was created till iniquity was found in thee. (Ezekiel 28: 13–15).

Lucifer was judged according to his treachery. He was cast out of the mountain of God. His fall was a downward spiral. Right now, the devil goes "to and fro" on the face of the earth and in between the Heaven and the earth. When the devil's time on earth expires, God will send him to Hell where he belongs. The devil, his angels, the nations, and the individuals who followed them will have their end in the lake of fire, in the endless abyss, in eternal burning, somewhere down, down below forever and ever, according to the Scripture (Psalm 9:17). Did you know that Hell was originally not made for human beings? Hell was made for the devil and his fallen angels, according to Matthew 25:41, but amazingly, Hell continues to enlarge itself daily because the multitude of people entering it increases day by day (Isaiah 5:14). Wide is the gate that leads to destruction (Hell), and many are they that go in (Matthew 7:13).

What was the devil doing in the Garden of Eden?

The devil hates God and everything that resembles God. He went into the Garden of Eden of his own accord. The devil's main desire and goal was to deceive Adam and Eve into sinning against God. The devil's mission is to do everything within his power to turn you and me against God. The devil will use lies, poverty, sickness, internal conflict, friends, family members, anything he can find to accomplish his mission. The devil is angry with us.

He is jealous of us, but do you know why the devil is jealous? He is jealous because we are created in God's image. I believe the devil thinks that God created us to provoke him to jealousy. Another reason why the devil probably hates human beings is that after he tricked Adam and Eve into sinning against God in the Garden of Eden, even though God judged Adam and Eve accordingly, He gave them a second chance. When the devil sinned against God, there was no second chance for him; just one strike and the devil was driven out of Heaven with no provision to repent.

The devil is mad at you, he is mad at me, and he will fight both of us to the end.

The Bible records an event when Jesus met face to face with a man possessed by a legion of demons—thousands of demons in one man. They bowed down before Jesus Christ, screaming:

And when he was come out of the ship, immediately there met him out of the tombs a man with an unclean spirit, who had his dwelling among the tombs; and no man could bind him, no, not with chains: Because that he had been often bound with fetters and chains, and the chains had been plucked asunder by him, and the fetters broken in pieces: neither could any man tame him. And always, night and day he was in the mountains, and in the tombs, crying, and cutting himself with stones. But when he saw Jesus afar off, he ran and worshipped him, and cried with a loud voice, and said, what have I to do with thee, Jesus, thou Son of the most high God? I adjure thee by God, that thou torment me not . . . and he asked him, what is thy name? And he answered saying, my name is legion: for we are many.

174

(Mark 5: 2–9)

The devil is mad, and he will fight you and me to the end; hoping he may take some of us to Hell with him. You need to be ready to fight the devil and his demons even after you have believed in Christ. Nonetheless, the weapons of our warfare are not carnal, but mighty through Christ for pulling down of stronghold (2 Corinthians 10:3–5). You need to know that the battle is won already through our Lord Jesus Christ. All you have to do is maintain your status in Jesus Christ and continue to profess your victory in His name. We claim our victory by knowing who we are in Christ and by confessing what God has done for us through Him, refusing to bow down to the enemy.

The devil knows that he is going to Hell, but he doesn't want to go there with his angels alone. The devil wants to take you there with him. He wants to take me there with him. If any of us end up in Hell, it is not because God wants us there. It is not because we are ignorant of God's plan to save our souls; rather, it is a choice that we made. Adam and his wife chose to sin against God. Both of them chose not to repent. Originally, Hell was not designed for us: human beings. It was designed for Satan and his angels.

The devil is a smart, ruthless politician. His political forces are present everywhere in the world.

The devil and some of his angels are on the loose. The most wicked ones among his angels are currently chained in the darkness until the Day of Judgment, according to Scriptures (Jude 1:6 and 2 Peter 2:4). The devil's angels that are on the loose in the world are called demons. They are the ones that are afflicting and tormenting our bodies, our souls, and the earth. They fill the world with sins, disease, poverty, and natural disasters. There are many demonic forces in the world. There are lying spirits, fever spirits, cerebral palsy spirits, depression spirits, foul spirits, deaf and dumb spirits, schizophrenia spirits, blindness spirits, filthy spirit, lust spirits, fornicator spirits, adultery spirits, envy spirits, hateful spirits, unforgiving spirits, etc. The devil even assigns different spirits to torment each individual, including you, based on your spiritual strengths and weaknesses. There are evil spirits assigned against each family, each city, each state, and each nation of the world. Question: How do we know which demonic spirits are assigned against a person, city, state, or nation? Answer: All you need to do is to observe the sins or ungodly activities of that person, city, state, or nation, and then you will know. Do you know that demonic forces are operating behind all ungodliness? The devil has arranged his ambassadors strategically all over the world to take over human domains. The devil has taken over human domains. He has taken over many individuals, many families, and even many Christian congregations. You can sense and feel the presence of demonic forces in many business settings, government entities, entertainment industries, and in many high places. The devil has arranged his garrisons strategically all over the world according to their ranks, strengths, and astute. Their main mission is to stage spiritual wars against God's creation and to torment, hoping he could take many of us to Hell with him.

How else could we, should we, or ought we explain what is going on in the world? You can see sex promotions on many of our television channels and the Internet. You can hear it on many of our radio stations and in our workplaces. There are fathers who get their daughters pregnant without any remorse for their diabolical behaviors. Children are raising children, and children are killing other children. Teenagers are losing their lives senselessly every day to gang violence. Movies that sell well in our society are laden with drugs and violent activities, promiscuity, evil communication, or all of the above. Many of us would do anything to heap up wealth, even though the Scripture warn us, saying, "The love of money is the root of all evil" (1 Timothy 6:10). Christians need to know that we are at war, but our war is not against flesh and blood. Our war is against spiritual powers, against the rulers of the darkness of this world, and against spiritual wickedness in high places (Ephesians 6:12).

Below are some of the behaviors of the devil, because we need to know how our enemy operates:

The devil is a Liar (John 8:44), and a Deceiver (Revelation 20:10). The devil is the Accuser of brethren (Revelation 12:10), the Dragon (Revelation 12:7), the old Serpent (Revelation 20:2), the Apollyon, the Destroyer, and the Abaddon, the Angel of the bottomless pit (Revelation 9:11). He is the Tempter (1 Thessalonians 3:5), a Murderer (John 8:44), the god of this world (2 Corinthians 4:4), the prince of the power of the air (Ephesians 2:2), and the only Enemy humans have (Matthew 13:39). The scripture describes him as the Wicked One (Matthew 13:19), the Ruler of darkness (Ephesians 6:12), and the Messenger of death (Hebrews 2:14). The devil comes to steal, to kill, and to destroy, but Jesus came to give Life and to give it more abundantly (John 10:10). You and I should know how the devil operates but, he is a defeated foe. The Son of God manifested to destroy the works of the devil.

Jesus came to redeem you and me from the sin of Adam and Eve through His death and resurrection.

The Scripture says that the wages of sin is death, but the gift of God is eternal life through Jesus Christ our Lord (Romans 6:23). It is appointed unto men once to die, but after this, the judgment (Hebrews 9:27). Jesus is the only mediator between God and men (1 Timothy 2:5). There is no other name under heaven given among men whereby we must be saved (Acts 4:12).

Wherefore God also hath highly exalted Him, and given Him a name which is above every name, that at the name of Jesus every knee should bow, of things in heaven, and things in earth, and things under the earth, and that every tongue should confess that Jesus Christ is Lord to the glory of God the Father. - (Philippians 2: 9–11)

My friend, you need to repent today. Repent and accept God's provision for your salvation. That is all God is asking you to do. God wants you to recognize that you are a sinner, that you are dead in sin, that you cannot save yourself, and that He has made provision in His Son to save your lost soul from everlasting torment, pain, and suffering. All you need to do is recognize your sinful state and accept His plan for your salvation. Jesus came and died for the sins of the world, and that includes you and me. He said on the cross, "It is finished" (John 19:30). Jesus atoned for my sins and for your sins. He paid the price in full. He is now sitting at the right hand of God, interceding for us. He is coming back to judge and to reign, according to the Scripture.

Salvation is a personal relationship with God.

You do not become a Christian just because your parents are, or were, Christians. That is like saying that you are a doctor just because your parents are, or were, doctors. You do not become a Christian just because you attend a Christian congregation. That is like saying that you are an attorney just because you go to the courtroom several days of the week. You don't become a Christian just because you are paying tithe and giving offerings, or because you are giving all your belongings to feed the poor. You cannot buy your salvation. You cannot buy the gift of God. Peter rebuked Simon who offered the apostles some money to obtain the gift of healing, saying: "Thy money perish with thee, because thou hast thought that the gift of God may be purchased with money" (Acts 8: 18–20). You don't become a Christian by simply wearing a long robe, just as you cannot become a nurse by simply wearing a nurse's scrub. Each of us must meet God's criteria to be saved, according to the Scripture. You don't become a Christian just because you speak in new or different tongues, or because you are a deacon or pastor of a Christian congregation. Judas Iscariot was one of the Twelve Disciples of Jesus Christ. He betrayed the Lord with a kiss and later committed suicide! You and I must meet God's criteria to be saved. God's only provision for you and me to be saved is by accepting Jesus Christ as our Lord and Savior (1 Timothy 2:5) and by living authentically as followers of Christ. Read Matthew 7: 21-23.

You can come to Jesus Christ just as you are, but you must come now, because tomorrow may be too late.

You can come to Jesus Christ just as you are but once you have accepted Him, you will not remain the same. It is not by your power or self-righteousness; it is by God's Spirit in you. It is the presence of Jesus and the Holy Ghost in your life that will begin to help your willing soul in the subsequent transformation, the character building, the new attitudes and Christlikeness of your soul. You must recognize your nothingness, that you are a dead man walking, a shadow of death, a vessel preserved for eternal torment and everlasting burning. You must confess that you were born in sin, that you are dead in sin, and that you can't save yourself and need a Savior. The fact that you are reading this book is one of the many ways God is appealing to you to escape the terrible judgment that is coming upon the children of disobedience. God cannot lie. He will judge the disobedience of men. Hell is real. The kingdom of God is real, and you have the opportunity to make a choice today, for tomorrow may be too late. It was too late for the people in the days of Noe or Noah (see Matthew 24:37–42).

When you come to Jesus Christ, you must come with one single motive—your salvation.

The main purpose of the birth, death, and resurrection of Jesus Christ was to redeem human souls. Our main purpose for believing in Christ must be the same: our redemption. Many of us want to come to Christ because of our illnesses, hoping that by accepting Christ, we will be healed. Others want to come to Jesus mostly for material blessings.

There is nothing wrong in seeking divine healing or material wealth in Christ. Divine healing and material blessings are all included in the package (3 John 1:2) of salvation, but they should not be our primary motive. Our primary motive must be for the salvation of our souls, and everything else should be secondary. We are not worthy, but He loves us so much that He exchanged his status for ours. He took ownership of our sins, nailed them to the Cross, and made us white as snow with His own blood. He took ownership of our unrighteousness, nailed it to the Cross, and gave us His righteousness. Your sins and my sins looked magnanimously awful on Jesus as He took responsibility for them on the Cross. God looked at human sin as they were piled up on His Son on the Cross; Jesus looked so repulsive under our sins that God could not behold His only begotten Son. For three hours, from the sixth to the ninth hour, there was darkness all over the earth. Jesus was condemned as if He were a sinner (Luke 23:44–46). He cried and cried, asking His Father: "My God, my God, why hast thou forsaken me?" (Mark 15:34). Jesus was punished for my sins and your sins. He took the punishment humbly and bowed his head under the crown of thorns. Jesus took our death and gave us His Life, His eternal Life (Hebrews 2:9–1). Jesus went to Hell for us so that we don't have to go there, but glory to God, Hell cannot detain Him. He rose just as He promised. My Lord rose on the third day. He rose. Jesus put the devil and his demonic forces to shame.

Escape the wrath of God. God's wrath is coming upon the children of disobedience.

I am asking you to accept God's love today. I am asking you to escape the wrath of God that is coming upon the children of disobedience by accepting Jesus Christ today, for tomorrow may be too late. God shall bring every work into judgment and every secret thing, whether it is good, or whether it is evil (Ecclesiastes 12:14).

He that believeth on the Son hath everlasting life; he that believeth not on the Son shall not see life but the wrath of God abides in him (John 3:36).

I call the Heaven and earth to record this day that I have set before your life and death, blessings and cursing: therefore, choose life. Please, choose "Life" today. Jesus is the Way, the Truth, and the Life. No one goes to the Father or to Heaven but through Him - John 14: 6.

Steps On Becoming a Christian!

To become a Christian, you must take the following simple steps: First, you must agree and confess that you are a sinner (Romans 3:23), and that you cannot save yourself. Second, you must repent of your sins (Acts 3:19). Third, you must believe in your heart (soul) and confess with your mouth, according to Romans 10:10. Jesus was born, suffered, and died on the Cross, in your place. Jesus took the ownership of humans' sins according to Scripture (John 1:29).

Invite Jesus Christ into your soul today, and He will come in as promised (Revelation 3:20). He is currently waiting on the outside, waiting for you to invite Him in. He is knocking on the door of your soul as you are reading this book, even right now. Let Jesus Christ in today. What will it profit a man if he is the richest man in the world, if he wins the whole world, but loses his own soul?

I want you to read the parable of Jesus Christ in the book of Luke 12:16–21. Heaven and Hell are real, my friend. God's coming judgment is real. Though it may tarry, it will surely come. The wrath of God is upon the children of disobedience (John 3:36).

Spiritual Exercises:

1. *What is the first step to become a Christian?*

2. *In the beginning, what did God do in Genesis 1:1?*

3. *Which creature did God create in His image?*

4. *What is unique about an individual?*

5. *Describe the condition of Adam and Eve before their transgression.*

6. *What instruction did God give to Adam?*

7. *How many fruit-bearing trees do you think may likely be in the garden?*

8. *What method did the serpent use to win Eve's trust?*

9. *How can we be considered sinners when we were not the ones who ate the fruit?*

10. *How did Adam surrender his authority to the devil?*

11. *Do you think that the devil is ruling you? Can he rule the children of God?*

12. *Describe the significance of the animal God sacrificed for Adam's sin.*

13. *How is it a blessing that God chased Adam and Eve out of the Garden of Eden?*

14. *What are the three attributes that Adam and his wife retained after their fall?*

15. *What is the function of your willpower?*

16. *What is important about human freedom and responsibility?*

17. *What is the function of your belief system?*

18. *What can you say about the functions and limitations of your senses?*

19. *Why can't you hold your parents or your environment responsible for your undesirable conditions or life challenges?*

20. *What was the devil's sin against God?*

21. *Why was the devil in the Garden of Eden?*

22. *Why is the devil mad at God, at you, and at me?*

23. *How is the devil a smart, ruthless politician?*

24. *Why was it necessary for Jesus to come and redeem us?*

25. *Describe how salvation is a personal relationship with God.*

26. *How do we come to Christ?*

27. *What will be your only motive to come to Christ?*

28. *Do you think you should wait another day to give your life to Jesus Christ?*

29. *Are you sure you have another day?*

30. *True or False? If you die today and haven't accepted Jesus Christ, you will certainly go to Hell. The door of repentance is firmly closed to you once you die, and you will be forced to spend your eternal life in hell with the devil and his demons.*

Chapter 15
NOW THAT I HAVE BECOME A CHRISTIAN, WHAT DO I DO?

If you have truthfully given your life to Christ and have accepted Him as your Lord and personal Savior, I congratulate you on becoming a Christian. You are now a rightful member of God's household. If you have confessed that you are a sinner, that you cannot save yourself, and you have repented and believe in your heart (soul) that Jesus came in the flesh and died for your sins on the cross, went to Hell for you, and that God has raised Him from the dead, there should be no doubt in your mind that you are saved; you are now a born-again child of God. And, God forbid, if you die today, even in a few seconds after your confession is made, you will be with our Lord Jesus Christ in the resurrection. Jesus told one of the malefactors that were hanged next to Him on the cross, upon his confession, that Jesus is the Lord: "Verily I say unto thee, today shalt thou be with me in paradise" (Luke 23:42–43).

As Christians, however, and as we start our walk with the Lord, there are certain things we must fulfill to walk in the footsteps of Christ. The following three elements are some of the requirements we must fulfill as we begin our walk with the Lord. The first thing we must fulfill is water baptism: to be baptized in water is a necessity for all Christians to fulfill all righteousness. The second thing we must fulfill is the Baptism of the Holy Ghost: to be Baptized of the Holy Ghost is a necessity for Christians who want to live in victory in a world filled with demonic forces. The presence of the Holy Ghost in a Christian's life is the power that is needed to overcome sin, the devil, and demonic forces. The Holy Ghost empowers us to stand against the devil, our only enemy. He equips us to love those who hate us. The Holy Ghost gives us the strength needed to overcome evil with good. He gives us spiritual gifts for the work of the ministry. The Holy Ghost secures and prepares us for the arrival of the Lord. The third thing we must observe and participate in, is the Lord's Supper.

None of the three requirements listed above must occur in the order that they are listed here after someone has given their life to Christ. Let us examine each of them briefly:

1. *Water Baptism*

Bear in mind as you read this section that water baptism is a necessity only after conversion has taken place; your salvation does not and will never depend on it. Water baptism was a necessity for Christ to fulfill all righteousness. Therefore, it does become a necessity for you and me as well, but here are a few exceptions however:

For example, today, in many of our congregations, new converts are not baptized instantly as they give their lives to Christ. Some new believers, depending on a particular denomination, are requested to attend instructional classes that may take up to twelve weeks or more to complete before they can be baptized. The truth is that if any of these believers died in between times—if they died between their conversion and water baptism—they will be with Jesus Christ at the resurrection. The thief who accepted Christ on the cross didn't have the opportunity to be baptized, but Jesus told him, "Today shalt thou be with me in paradise" (Luke 23:43). A. Jesus was baptized only to fulfill all righteousness.

Then cometh Jesus from Galilee to Jordan unto John to be baptized of him. But John forbad him, saying, I have need to be baptized of thee, and come thou to me? And Jesus answering said unto him, suffer it to be so now: for thus it becomes us to fulfill all righteousness (Matthew 3: 13–15).

Jesus was thirty years of age when He went to John to be baptized, according to Luke 3:23 and in accordance with the Jewish religion. According to the Jewish religion, a person must be at least thirty years of age before he can serve in the Levitical order or work in the tabernacle.

The soon-to-be priest is required to be washed in water, a form of consecration, before assuming his office.

From thirty years old and upward even until fifty years old, all that enter into the host, to do the work in the tabernacle of the congregation (Numbers 4: 3).

And Aaron and his sons thou shalt bring unto the door of the tabernacle of the congregation, and shalt wash them with water (Exodus 29: 4).

And Moses said unto the congregation, this is the thing which the Lord commanded to be done. And Moses brought Aaron and his sons, and washed them with water (Leviticus 8: 5–6).

John did baptize in the wilderness and preach the baptism of repentance for the remission of sins. And there went out unto him all the land of Judaea, and they of Jerusalem, and were all baptized of him in the river of Jordan, confessing their sins (Mark 1: 4-5).

Jesus is our High Priest according to the Scripture - Hebrews 7:17.

Without any sins of His own to confess, Jesus went to John the Baptist humbly to be baptized by him, to fulfill all righteousness (Matthew 3:16). What a marvelous example.

B. *Jesus Himself baptized some converts (John 3: 22–26).*

C. *Jesus commanded His Apostles to baptize those that believe with water.*

And Jesus came and spoke unto them, saying, All power is given unto me in heaven and in earth. Go ye therefore, and teach all nations, baptizing them in the name of the Father, and of the Son, and of the Holy Ghost: Teaching them to observe all things whatsoever I have commanded you: and, lo, I am with you always, even unto the end of the world. Amen(Matthew 28: 18–20).

And he said unto them, go ye into all the world, and preach the gospel to every creature. He that believeth and is baptized shall be saved; but he that believeth not shall be damned. (Mark 16: 15–16).

D. *The apostles fulfilled Jesus' commandment.*

I. *Peter baptized the believing Jews the day of Pentecost (Acts 2:38–41). ii. Phillip the Evangelist baptized the Samarians that believed (Acts 8:12).*

iii. *Phillip baptized the Eunuch of Ethiopian (Acts 8:35–38).*

iv. *Ananias baptized Saul, whose name later changed to Paul (Acts 9:17– 18).*

v. *Peter commanded the house of Cornelius to be baptized (Acts 10:47–48).*

vi. *Paul Baptized Lydia (Acts 16:14–15). vii. Paul baptized the jailers (Acts 16:30–33). viii. Paul baptized Corinthians' believers (Acts 18:8). ix. Paul baptized the household of Stephanas (1 Corinthians 1:16).*

In all of the examples cited above, baptism always followed after the conversion had taken place. Our baptism is simply a public testimony of the inner victory, which is the salvation of our souls. In baptism, we are saying to the world and reaffirming to ourselves that we are now dead, being buried with Christ (Romans 6:3–5). We are saying to the world and reaffirming to ourselves that we have buried the old self and are putting on the new (Galatians 3:27–28), that we were dead but now have risen with the Lord.

E. *Unnecessary confusion about Water Baptism*

Today, in our Christian community, there is too much confusion about water baptism. There are issues such as who is to be baptized, and at what age baptism is appropriate, the proper way to baptize, in whose name, the significance of baptism, and whether it is a necessity for the completion of our salvation? I don't have all the answers, but what I want you to learn here is that you and I need to follow in the footsteps of our Lord and Savior. We know that Jesus did not need to be baptized by John the Baptist, but He did it anyway in order to fulfill all righteousness. We know that Jesus had no sins to confess. We know that He had no need to repent of anything, but Jesus went to John to be baptized by him simply to fulfill all righteousness. After His death and resurrection, Jesus commanded His disciples to do the same, and that includes you and me, if we are of Christ.

i. Who is to be baptized?

Those who have repented of their sins and have accepted the Gospel are eligible for baptism. John preached repentance and baptism. Jesus preached repentance and baptism. The apostles preached repentance and baptism. There will be no other foundation laid except the one that is laid by Jesus Christ and His apostles.

ii. At what age is someone eligible for baptism?

If we take the position that baptism is to the Christians as circumcision is to the Jews, then everybody, including the babies should be baptized. If we take the position that a person must reach the age of accountability, then only those who are old enough to recognize their sins should be baptized. Personally, I see no harm in baptizing the children of Christian parents. I will say go ahead and baptize them; baptize your children if you are a believer, and make sure you encourage them to repeat their baptism when they reach the age of accountability, when they can distinguish between right and wrong.

iii. How do we baptize? Is it sprinkling or Immersion, or does it make any difference?

I read in the Bible where the apostles baptized some of their converts in the river, some were baptized in the house, perhaps in a pool of water. Many Christians don't think it matters whether one is immersed or sprinkled in water. I, myself, was baptized in the river, in 1979.

iv. In whose name do we baptize? Do we baptize in the name of the Father, and of the Son, and of the Holy Ghost, or in the name of Jesus Christ only?

We will need to find out what the name of the Father, the name of the Son, and the name of the Holy Ghost is first, in order to be able to baptize correctly. My personal opinion is that if we follow the footsteps of the apostles by simply baptizing in the name of the Lord, we are not sinning. But if someone wants to be baptized in the name of the Father, and of the Son, and of the Holy Ghost, such is not sinning either. This is nothing but a personal preference.

Baptizing in any of these two choices will not shut the door of Heaven to the new Christian. God, Jesus, and the Holy Ghost are One and inseparable. The body of Christ needs to stop this schism about water baptism.

The Father, the Son, and the Holy Ghost are One, and the same. Peter baptized the believing Jews on the day of Pentecost (Acts 2:38–41) in the name of Jesus Christ only. Phillip, the Evangelist, baptized the Samarians that believed (Acts 8:12-16) in the name of the Lord Jesus only. Peter commanded the house of Cornelius to be baptized (Acts 10:47–48) in the name of the Lord only.

v. What is the significance of Water Baptism?

Like I said earlier, Water Baptism is a public confession. When we go down in the water, we are saying to the world that we are now dead to sin, dead with Christ. When we come up out of the water, we are saying to the world that we are now alive, resurrected with the Lord into a newness of life.

2. *Baptism of the Holy Ghost*

As Christians, it is comforting for us to know that we are not alone in this journey. We need to know that God is with us, that Jesus Christ is with us, and that the Holy Ghost is with us. Their presence serves many purposes in our lives. The Holy Ghost resides in us to protect, to guide, to comfort, to remind, to preserve, to rebuke, and to chastise us when needed. The Holy Ghost empowers us, prunes us to be usable vessels, and strengthens us to be joyful in the presence of all life's challenges. The Holy Ghost will present us holy unto our Lord Jesus Christ upon His arrival. Being baptized with the Holy Ghost is a necessary component for believers.

A. *The Holy Ghost is the same as God.*

One truth we must learn is that wherever God is, there is Jesus Christ. Wherever Jesus is, there is the Holy Ghost. The Tri-Unity of God is not a concept but a divine truth. We Christians do not strive to understand in order that we may believe but, to the contrary, we do believe in order that we may understand. The doctrine of "Trinity" cannot be fully understood by our human minds. Imagine a triangle; it has three equal points, degrees, or angles. If you void one of the angles, the remaining shape will no longer be called a triangle; it has to be assigned another name. Think of the water that drops down from the atmosphere; it may come down as dew, rain, or heavy hail that beats everything into pieces. These three still maintain the same chemical contents. They are liquid water at the end with the same chemical property. God is God with no limitation. He can be everywhere, at any time, and concurrently with the same or completely different appearance. He can be the "Spirit of God descending like a dove." He can be the "Voice from Heaven," and He can be the "beloved Son," all three at once. He can be the Father, the Son, and the Holy Spirit, all at the same time (see Jesus' Baptism, Matthew 3:16–17). The Bible tells us that the Heaven and earth cannot contain God, which means that He is always present everywhere.

Isaiah introduced Jesus as Emmanuel (Isaiah 7:14, Matthew 1:23), which is interpreted as "God with us." In the book of Isaiah, Chapter 9, verse 6, Jesus is called "Wonderful, Counselor, The mighty God, The everlasting Father, The Prince of Peace." Jesus Himself said that He and His Father are one and inseparable (John 10:30). Jesus told His disciples, "Ye neither know me, nor my Father: if ye had known me, ye have known my Father also" (John 8:19). Jesus is God's Word. This same concept can be applied to the Holy Ghost. The Holy Ghost is God's Spirit and the third Person in God's Triangle, according to the Scripture. The Holy Ghost is just as equal with God, the same way as Christ is equal with God. Let me warn you here that the divine concept of the Trinity cannot be understood with our natural minds. What you and I need to do is believe. Again, you need to know that we Christians do not strive to understand in order that we may believe, but to the contrary, we do believe in order that we may understand that our God is an awesome God.

B. *The Holy Ghost and the gifts of the Holy Ghost are free gifts.*

Salvation is a gift, and so is the Holy Ghost and His gifts. We don't beg God for our salvation. We simply honor God's provision to be saved by believing and accepting Jesus Christ, the Lamb of God, who came in the flesh into the world of sins, died on the cross, and took away the sins of the world. Once we are in Christ, receiving of the Holy Ghost and His gifts becomes our legitimate rights. We don't beg God for it just as we didn't beg God for our salvation. We simply accept and receive the Holy Ghost by faith. The Holy Ghost then distributes His own gifts to us, as He wills or desires (1 Corinthians 12:4–11), for the work of the ministry. Remember, as He desires. Since His arrival on the Day of Pentecost, the Holy Ghost has never left the earth. He is here with us and will stay permanently until our Lord, Jesus Christ, arrives.

We receive the Holy Ghost by faith; there are no rituals to perform other than accepting Him by faith. No Christian receives the Holy Ghost or any of His gifts by personal power or at will. We receive the Holy Ghost and His gifts by faith. Not as I choose—no, no—but as He chooses. If it depended on my choice, I will probably choose to be an apostle, a prophet, an evangelist, a pastor, and a teacher all at the same time. If I could pick and choose, I would choose to be a miracle healer, performing miracles whenever I want— raising up the physically and spiritually dead, casting my shadow upon all that are sick and healing them all. I would choose to be able to save the murderer before he kills another person. I would be doing all at my will. My friends, that was never the case, and never would it be. Our sufficiency is in Christ. There are several biblical accounts of how converts received the Holy Ghost. I want you to read up on the following passages:

1. *The believing Jews in Jerusalem on the day of Pentecost (Acts 2:1–4).*

2. *The Samaritans and Judea (Acts 8: 14–17). Acts 9: 1-18*

3. *The Gentiles (Acts 10: 44–48).*

4. *The Disciples of John (Acts 19: 1–7).*

C. *What signs do you need to know that you are filled with the Holy Ghost?*

Christians walk by faith and not by sight. Many believers are looking for a sign or signs before they are convinced that they are filled with the Holy Ghost. The only evidence I know to look for is the Fruit of the Spirit as described in Galatians 5:16–25. The fruit will reveal the identity of a tree.

How else can we know that we are Spirit-filled if not by our lifestyle? We may speak in different tongues or in the languages of angels, but that doesn't tell our audience anything. A person's lifestyle will speak louder and more convincingly than all manner of tongues combined. The apostles were able to overturn the world (Acts 17:6), not only because 1) they were filled with the Holy Ghost and speaking in different tongues, but also because 2) their lifestyles convicted their audience. The lives of the apostles were in harmony with what they preached, and it supported their claims. Their dedication (Acts 6:4), love, and compassion (Acts 2:44–47) were what set off the unquenchable spiritual fire, a conviction, in the hearts of their audience. The apostles did not convict the world simply because they were speaking in tongues. Not so, my friend. They were able to convict their world because Jesus Christ was able to live through them. These were living sacrifices for Christ. How many people do you know today or in the past who are speaking in tongues? You are not to judge them, but what do you know about their lifestyles? How would you describe their lifestyles? My friend, if you are looking for a genuine sign to know whether, or not, you are filled with the Holy Ghost, all you need to do is look at yourself in the mirror. The Word of God is our mirror. Look and compare your lifestyle with the Word of God. Begin to ask yourself, "How am I doing? How do I look in this spiritual mirror? Am I living for God biblically as Jesus commanded? Am I living biblically as the apostles recommended? Are there any changes in my drives, desires, and attitudes or am I still craving, and yielding to, the old lusts? Let us examine what the Scripture says:

This I say then, Walk in the Spirit, and ye shall not fulfill the lust of the flesh. For the flesh lusteth against the Spirit, and the Spirit against the flesh: and these are contrary the one to the other: so that ye cannot do the things that you would. But if ye be led of the Spirit, ye are not under the law. Now the works of the flesh are manifest, which are these; adultery, fornication, uncleanness, lasciviousness, idolatry, witchcraft, hatred, variance, emulations, wrath, strife, seditions, heresies, envying, murders, drunkenness . . . which I tell you before, as I have also told you in time past, that they which do such things shall not inherit the kingdom of God. But, the fruit of the Spirit is love, joy, peace, longsuffering, gentleness, goodness, faith, meekness, against such there is no law. And they that are Christ's have crucified the flesh with the affections and lusts. If we live in the Spirit, let us also walk in the Spirit. (Galatians 5:16–25).

D. *How does the new Christian receive the Baptism of the Holy Ghost?*

First, I want you to know that the Holy Ghost is present in you the same moment you accept Christ (1 Corinthians 6:19). Don't be deceived; wherever Jesus is, there is God. Wherever God is, there is the Holy Ghost. Nonetheless, the Baptism of the Holy Ghost is a necessary step after conversion has taken place. This means that you must be saved first before you can be filled with the Holy Ghost. You cannot put new wine in a ragged bottle. Warning: There may or may not be observable signs that you are filled with the Holy Ghost, but you will know the difference within when you are. It is joyful and, at the same time, it can be an eccentric experience.

To be filled with the Holy Ghost means that you are momentarily in full submission to God. At that moment when you are being filled with the Holy Ghost, all manifestations of the flesh is suspended, and self is momentarily dead. You have no agenda of your own. Your attitudes, behaviors, and your desires are completely under the guidance of the Holy Spirit at that moment. Everything in you has surrendered unto God. You are now a living sacrifice. Your desires and wants are in the likeness of God's. Your thoughts are reflections of God's presence in the body of dust. You begin to see things as God sees them because you have been overtaken by Him. Your words and your prayers are like guided missiles. They will not come back to you, void, without doing what you have sent them to do. When overtaken by the Holy Ghost, the words you speak must do what you have sent them to do, because it is not you who speaks, but God through you, the body of dust. Your dusty flesh must die momentarily whenever the Holy Ghost takes over. That is why Jesus was able to do so many miracles. He was constantly overtaken and overfilled with the Holy Ghost without measure, and the demonic forces had no choice but to tremble and bow down, screaming in His presence.

Receiving the Baptism of the Holy Ghost!

A Christian can receive the Baptism of the Holy Ghost anywhere, anytime, if the soul is ready. You can receive the Baptism of the Holy Ghost in your prayer room, when reading your Bible, when singing spiritual songs, in your car on your way to work, or when you hear the Word of God preached. You may receive the Holy Ghost through the laying on of a minister's hand, by meditating on the goodness of God, etc. Being filled with the Holy Ghost follows the same principle as being saved. You must continue to be saved day by day. You are to be filled with the Holy Ghost. Becoming a Christian is not a destination but a beginning. It is a journey, continued. We must protect and maintain our Christianity; we must continue to be filled with the Holy Ghost, daily and until the arrival of our Lord.

My Personal Experience with the Baptism of the Holy Ghost

Though I prophesied for days after my encounter with Jesus Christ on July 27, 1974, I was not baptized with the Holy Ghost, not yet. It was on a Saturday afternoon when I met the Lord on my way back from visiting my parents. Yes, I was saved immediately after my conversion, and had a deposit of the Holy Ghost in me because no one can get saved with the word alone, without the word being escorted and inspired by the Holy Ghost. Faith comes by hearing, and hearing by the word of God. It is the word of God and the Holy Ghost that give birth to Salvation. Though I was saved and prophesying, I was not baptized in

-

the Holy Ghost, and not until 1982 on the concrete roof of a two-story building apartment.

On top of that building, I was praying all night and fell asleep. In my sleep, I started speaking in tongues until I woke up, and it lasted for about 10 seconds after I woke up. That was the first and the only time, I spoke in tongue. I was baptized in the Holy Ghost, and it was evidenced by speaking in tongue, but I do not have the gift of tongues. I was filled with the Holy Ghost, and the tongue only lasted a few seconds after I woke up. I have never spoken in tongue since then.

E. The main work of the Holy Ghost in the Believers

But ye shall receive power, after that the Holy Ghost is come upon you: and ye shall be witnesses unto me both in Jerusalem, and in all Judea, and in Samaria, and unto the uttermost part of the earth = (Acts 1: 8).

Simply put, the person of the Holy Ghost is the Christian's *Power House*. We need the Holy Ghost's power to witness effectively, overcome sin, love our enemies, live in victory in a world filled with evil, and maintain our joy in the face of life's struggles and inconsistencies.

F. Some of the gifts of the Holy Ghost

Now there are diversities of gifts, but the same Spirit. And there are differences of administrations but the same Lord. But there are diversities of operations, but it is the same God which worketh all in all. But the manifestation of the Spirit is given to every man to profit withal. For to one is given by the Spirit the word of wisdom; to another the word of knowledge by the same Spirit; to another faith by the same Spirit; to another the gifts of healing by the same Spirit; to another the working of miracles; to another prophesy, to another discerning of spirits; to another divers of tongues; to another the interpretations of tongues: But all these worketh that one and the selfsame Spirit, dividing to every man severally as he will. (1 Corinthians 12: 4—11).

3. The Lord's Supper

And as they were eating, Jesus took bread, and blessed it, and broke it, and gave it to the disciples, and said, Take, eat; this is my body. And he took the cup, and gave thanks, and gave it to them, saying, Drink ye all of it. For this is my blood of the New Testament, which is shed for many for the remission of sins.

(Matthew 26:26–28)

The Lord's Supper was observed by the apostles and the early churches, and it therefore becomes one of the requirements for the body of Christ. Paul was teaching the church in Corinthians how the Lord's Supper ought to be and ought not to be implemented (see 1 Corinthians 11:20–30).

Spiritual Exercises:

1. Explain why water baptism is a necessary step after one becomes a Christian.

2. Will a person go to hell if they accepted Christ but died before being baptized?

3. Why did Jesus go to John to be baptized?

4. Which scripture shows that Jesus Himself baptized some of His converts?

5. Is it a sin to baptize the believers' children?

6. Who is the person of the Holy Ghost?

7. What is the difference between the Holy Ghost and His gifts?

8. Name four groups of converts in the book of Acts who received the baptism of the Holy Ghost. Compare the four groups to the four regions that Jesus mentioned to the Apostles in Acts 1:8

9. What is the best way to measure if someone is filled with the Holy Ghost?

10. What are your gifts?

11. Compare what you do with your spiritual gifts to the parables of Christ in Matthew 25:14–29.

12.What is your conviction about participating in the Lord's Supper?

Special Assignment on Spiritual Gifts:

In addition to 1 Corinthians 12: 4-11, read Romans 12:6–8; Matthew 25:14–30; Ephesians 4:11–13; 1 Corinthians 7:7; 1 Timothy 4:14; and 2 Timothy 1:6. List all the gifts you come across in your reading and identify the gifts you think or know that you have and those you desire.

Chapter 16
THE CHILD MUST GROW

When you accepted Jesus Christ as your Lord and Savior, you were immediately born into the household of God. God becomes your heavenly Father, and Jesus becomes your brother, for He calls you brother. As a child, you must continue to grow into maturity in Christ. Can you imagine having a child who is not functioning age-appropriately? Can you imagine having a three-year-old child who is not able to hold his neck up without help or talk or sit by himself, or walk like many other children of his age? I have no doubt you would still love your child, because that is your child, your blood. But the question is, would you be happy with your child's situation? Would you be happy to continue to see your child day after day in this predicament? Many Christians have stagnated in their spiritual growth. Many of us have not advanced spiritually from where we were when we first got saved. Being spiritually stagnant is very unprofitable to God. It would be more profitable to Him if we died immediately after we are saved than to be crippled in our spiritual walk. Do you know that when you are crippled in the Spirit, you become a pawn in the hands of the devil? I mean a playground for the devil and his demons. Do you know that God allowed you and me to live longer on earth after being saved simply to become channels through whom He will save the unsaved and make the devil and his demons miserable? God wants to use us to war against the devil and demonic forces, but unfortunately, the opposite seems to be the reality in our days. Rather than us pitching war against the devil and his demonic forces, rather than chasing the devil and his demonic forces around the world or wherever they appear, many Christians are being chased around by these evil forces, either because of our ignorance, ungodly lifestyles, or lack of faith.

Without our constant growth in the Spiritual realm, we cannot be as useable as God desires. God is looking for useable vessels. God is looking for channels through which He will reach the wicked, sin-laden world. If you and I refuse to grow spiritually, and if our behaviors are not different from those in the world, how then shall we be able to convert the world? We are supposed to be the salt of the world. We are the light in a world full of darkness. Christianity is a life to live, not a destination (Matthew 5:13–16). As a collective body of Christ, our behavior and attitudes must reflect Christ, who dwells in us. The believers' attitudes don't just change overnight; we must work at it. We work at character building by simply living in obedience to God's Word. The Bible is the written Word of God, designed to help us accomplish God's will and purposes in life (2 Timothy 3:16). God's Word is the mirror in which you and I look at ourselves and our manner of life. The Bible is our guide in making life decisions when in doubt, confused, or facing life challenges beyond our human control.

Beginning from creation, God has interacted with His people in different ways and at different times. The Bible reveals the successes and failures of human beings, either as individuals or as a collective body. From Genesis to the book of Revelation, the Bible shows us how God dealt with His people, the nations of the world, and the devil himself. It reveals the past, confirms the present, and informs us of what will happen in the future. The children of God are not in the dark concerning God's plans for humanity. The Bible tells us about events that will be indicators that this world is coming to its end. It will be almost impossible for a born-again child of God to be profitable without the knowledge of how God dealt with people and nations before our time. Believers do not live by bread alone. It is our close fellowship with God in prayers, our obedience to His written Word, and the Holy Ghost that help us grow into spiritual maturity in the Lord. Our stagnation in the spiritual realm is neither profitable to us nor God.

Consider the following questions: Why did God call Abraham His friend? What made Noah find favor with God? Why was Moses chosen to deliver the children of Israel? Why was the devil fighting over the body of Moses? Why did the Angel Michael refrain from rebuking the devil directly but instead say to the devil, "God rebuke thee"? Why was Abram changed to Abraham, Sarai to Sarah? Why was Jacob changed to Israel? Who was Caleb? Why did the Israelites demand a king? Which of the judges were godly and which of them did evil in God's sight? What do you know about the pharaohs? Why did the Israelites spend forty years in the wilderness for a journey that should have taken them no longer than ninety days? Who were the three major kings in Israel? Which of them ruled well in God's sight? What were the sins of King Saul, the first king of Israel? What were the successes and failures of King David? What is significant about Solomon's reign? Why and how was Solomon's kingdom divided? What were the identities of the divided kingdoms by tribes? How is King David related to our Lord, Jesus Christ? Why did David call Jesus his Lord? Why do we call Jesus the Son of David, and the Lion of Judah? Who was Enoch? Who were Methuselah and Melchizedek? What do you know about Job's life, his trials, and his victory? What do you know about the city of Nineveh or the cities of Sodom and Gomorrah? What do you know about Nebuchadnezzar, the king of Babylon? Why did God call him "My servant"? (See Jeremiah 25:9; Jeremiah 27:6). Did he really become an animal? Where is the geographical location of Babylon today? Who were the three Hebrews that Nebuchadnezzar threw into the furnace? What happened to them in the furnace? Who was Daniel? Cyrus was a Gentile king; what did God say about him a hundred years before he was born? What does that mean to you? What was significant about the ministries of the prophets Isaiah, Jeremiah, and Daniel? What was significant about the life of Hosea, one of the minor prophets? Who was John the Baptist, and how did he live? Who were Ananias and Sapphira? Why did the Holy Ghost kill them? What did Saul, whose name was later changed to Paul, do to the early Christians? Who is Stephen in the New Testament, and how did he die? What do these people, and their lives, mean to you as a child of God? The lives of these individuals were recorded so that we may learn from their obedience and rebelliousness, their trials and tribulations, their successes and failures. God doesn't want us to fail. He wants you and me to be successful.

What is God looking for in His people? God is looking for obedience. Yes, obedience is the key. Our success in life depends largely on our obedience to God's Word. God wants us to live as born-again persons, not as the world lives. God still hates sin, my friends. He warned: "Behold, all souls are mine; as the soul of the father, so also the soul of the son is mine: the soul that sinned, it shall die" (Ezekiel 18:4). God never changes. God is the same yesterday, today, and forever (see Malachi 3:6; Hebrews 13:8). God still hates sin, all forms of evil, and ungodly behavior. God still hates envy, stealing, laziness, prostituting, killing of innocent lives, backbiting, idolatry, idle hands, slothfulness, gossiping, drunkenness, greediness, glutton, jealousness, wickedness, covetousness, malignity, evil eyes, maliciousness, pride, boasting, disobedience to parents, witchcraft, homosexuality, inventors of evils, all forms of lustfulness, pornography, and nature worshippers, just to mention few. The Scripture says that those who do any of those things are worthy of death. But on the contrary, God does honor those who honor Him. God honors those who live in obedience to His Word. Paul was asking the believers, "What shall we say then? Shall we continue in sin that grace may abound? God forbid . . ." (Romans 6:1–2).

In this chapter, we will examine briefly the lives of some of the people who have lived before us. We will glance at some of their successes and failures. I will select some events and their significances. The format in this chapter is like a four-step approach: first, I will throw out a question or questions; second, I will attempt to provide some answers based on my own knowledge of the Word of God; and third, you will discover for yourself the lessons you have learned. Finally, in the fourth step, you will come up with your own action plans as you see fit.

1. *Question: What was the main tool that the Serpent used to deceive Eve? (Genesis 3).*

Answer: The devil used lies. He still lies to us today; He is the father of liars. What lie has the devil told you lately?

What I learned . . .

My action plan . . .

2. *Question: Who is Cain? What did he do?*

    Answer: Cain was the first child. He was extremely jealous of his brother, Abel. Cain killed Abel and became the first murderer and the first fugitive. Even though God warned Cain before he committed the murder, Cain did it anyway. Cain killed his brother (Genesis chapter 4).

What I learned . . .

My action plan . . .

3. Question: *Who did Cain marry?*

Answer: Cain married one of his sisters. In that period of time, it wasn't considered a sin for someone to marry an immediate relative. God allowed that type of relationship then, but only temporarily, to populate the human race. Human beings are not derivatives of apes.

What I learned . . .

My action plan . . .

4. Question: *Who was the first person to marry two wives?*

Answer: Lamech was the first man to marry two wives, making him the first polygamist. Lamech was one of the great- great- grandchildren of Cain. Lamech broke the divine order of one man/one woman. Lamech killed a young man "to his hurt," as he said, possibly due to jealousy. Lamech became the second murderer (Genesis 4: 19–23).

What I learned . . .

My action plan . . .

5. Question: *Who is Enoch?*

Answer: Enoch was one of the great, great-grandchildren of Adam through Seth (Genesis 5: 3). He walked with God, and God took him alive (Genesis 5: 22–24). Enoch did not see death. Enoch's translation is a type of Christians' coming Rapture, the taking-away of believers at the appearance of Christ in the sky (2 Thessalonians 4: 16–17) before the great tribulation.

What I learned . . .

My action plan . . .

6. Question: *Who was the oldest person in the Bible?*

Answer: Methuselah, the son of Enoch, was the oldest person recorded. He was the grandfather of Noah, Methuselah lived 969 years before he died (Genesis 5: 27). How long can we possibly live today and why? (Read the entire chapter of Genesis 5).

What I learned . . .

My action plan . . .

7. *Question: Who were the "sons of God" according to Genesis 6: 4 that married the daughters of men, giving birth to giants?*

Answer: The "sons of God" in Genesis 6: 4 are the fallen angels who went into the daughters of men (in the manner of men), and produced giants, the superhumans of those days. The table below describes the current two prevailing views.[4]

Sons of God: View One	Sons of God: View Two
WERE SIMPLY CARNAL, MEN FROM THE LINE OF SETH	WERE ACTUALLY FALLEN ANGELS
• THIS THE MOST NATURAL WAY TO INTERPRET THE PASSAGE	• THE HEBREW LANGUAGE SEEMS TO FAVOR IT
• BECAUSE OF THE STATEMENT MADE IN MATT. 22: 30 ABOUT ANGELS	1. HEB. PHRASE BENELOHIM (SONS OF GOD) ALWAYS REFERS TO ANGEL IN THE O.T. SEE JOB 1: 6; 2:1; 38:7; DANIEL 3: 25
• BECAUSE OF THE STATEMENT IN 1 COR. 15:38-40 ABOUT ANGELS	2. HEB. WORD NEPHILIM (TRANSLATED "GIANTS" IN 6:4) SHOULD BE RENDERED, "FALLEN ONES"
• BECAUSE THE REGULAR HEBREW WORD FOR ANGEL IS MALEK, AND IS NOT USED BY MOSES HERE	
• BECAUSE OF THE LAW OF BIOGENESIS. SEE GEN. 1: 11, "AFTER HIS KIND"	• BECAUSE OF ANCIENT PAGAN LEGENDS OF INDIVIDUALS WHO WERE HALF MEN, HALF GOD (EXAMPLE GILGAMESH) MOST LEGENDS USUALLY BASED ON SOME TRUTH
• BECAUSE IT WOULD COMPROMISE THE CONCEPT OF THE VIRGIN BIRTH	

Sons of God: View One	Sons of God: View Two
WERE SIMPLY CARNAL, MEN FROM THE LINE OF SETH	WERE ACTUALLY FALLEN ANGELS
	• BECAUSE MOST JEWISH SCHOLARS HAVE HELD THIS • BECAUSE THE EARLY CHURCH HELD IT. BECAUSE OF THE PASSAGE IN 1 PETER 3: 18–20 • BECAUSE THERE EXISTS TWO KINDS OF FALLEN ANGELS CHAINED 2 PETER 2:4; JUDE 1: 5–7 • UNCHAINED. SEE EPH. 6: 12; Lk. 8: 27 MARK 1: 23 • BECAUSE ONLY 8 HUMAN BEINGS WERE SAVED FROM THE GREATEST FLOOD

These sons of gods were the fallen angels. They were demonic spirits that took on human flesh to corrupt the human race (Genesis 6). That is one of the reasons why God destroyed that world. God preserved Noah and his family, eight souls in total. The eight souls that God preserved populated the present world. What happened in the days of Noah is happening today. There are demonic operations everywhere in the world today—read Jesus' parable in Matthew 13:24–42.

What I learned . . . My action plan . . .

8. *Question: What is significant about Noah's ark?*

Answer: Noah's ark is a symbol of Jesus Christ, our Savior. When the people in Noah's days rebelled against God (Genesis 6) and would not repent, God destroyed their world with a flood and saved Noah, his three children, and their wives— eight souls in total (Genesis 7: 13). The flood lasted 371 days. The ark was 450 ft. long, 75 ft. wide and 45 ft. high. After the flood, God made a covenant with Noah that He would not destroy the world with flood anymore (Genesis 9:11–17). God will destroy the present world with fire (2 Peter 3: 6–7), as He did to the cities of Sodom and Gomorrah (Genesis 19: 24). Are you saved and protected in Jesus Christ? This world will be judged sooner or later (Psalm 9: 17). Only in Jesus Christ do we have the Real Boat of our Salvation. In this Pure Lamb of God, the believers are saved.

What I learned . . . My action plan . . .

9. *Question: Who were the three children of Noah and their contributions to the world?*

Answer: Ham, Japheth, and Shem were Noah's three children (Genesis 5:32). Ham's descendants demonstrated technology or

technical proficiency, a necessity for physical wellness. Japheth's descendants demonstrated the application of science or philosophy, a necessity for mental wellness. Shem's descendants have the oracles of God, a necessity for spiritual wellness.

What I learned . . . My action plan . . .

10. Question: What is significant about the tower of Babel?

    Answer: God instructed the people to scatter all over the face of the earth and populate it but the people refused to scatter as instructed. Instead, they colluded with one another to build a tower that would reach the stars in rebellion against God's command. God took away their one means of communication by giving them many languages so that they could not understand one another. Babel means confusion or chaos.It was the beginning of different languages and, as some interpret, the origin of racial divisions (Genesis 11).

What I learned . . . My action plan . . .

11. Questions: Who is Abraham and what is significant about him? There are many, but here are few of them:

    Answer a: Abraham as a friend of God: Abraham was formerly known as Abram. God changed his name to Abraham, meaning the father of nations (Genesis 17: 5). God called him His friend (James 2: 23). Abraham is also known as the father of faith. At age 75, Abraham answered God's calling to leave his father's house for a land that God would show him. Abraham trusted and obeyed God without doubting, for he had faith in God (Hebrews 11: 8). Without faith, it is impossible to please God (read the whole chapter of Hebrews 11). God promised Abraham earthly and spiritual

    Blessings, and that Abraham's descendants would be as numerous as the stars and difficult to count, and that through Abraham's Seed, the whole human race would be blessed (read Genesis chapter 12).

    Answer b: Abraham as a warrior: When Abraham heard that his nephew, Lot, had been taken captive, Abraham went with his servants and fought against the cities and the kings that held his nephew and family captive. He delivered his nephew with a great victory over the enemy. On his way back from the slaughter, Melchizedek, the King of Salem and a type of Christ, met him with bread and wine. He blessed Abraham, and Abraham gave Him a tenth of all the spoils of war (Genesis 14: 18–20). *The bread and the wine symbolized the holy communion, the bread and wine that Jesus shared with His disciples a few days before His crucifixion (Luke 22:17-20).*

The offering of the tenth of the spoils of war to Melchizedek was the origin of tithing.

Answer c: Abraham as an intercessor: Three angels visited with Abraham on their way to destroy the cities of Sodom and Gomorrah. Lot, Abraham's nephew, lived in Sodom. Abraham made a long and persistent intercession for Sodom and Gomorrah, but the sins of the two cities were so great that God decided to burn them down. God would have preserved the cities if He was able to find ten God-fearing people there. God saved Lot and his household, except his wife who chose to look back against the angels' instructions. Lot's wife became a pillar of salt (Genesis 19: 26).

Answer d: Abraham as a human being with all human frailties: Abraham's focus on God's promises shifted momentarily as he embraced his wife's suggestion regarding Hagar—"And Sarai said unto Abram, Behold now, the Lord hath restrained me from bearing: I pray thee, go in into my maid; it may be that I may obtain children by her. And Abram hearkened to the voice of Sarai...And he went in unto Hagar..." (Genesis 16:1–4). Through Hagar, Abram had his first, but illegitimate, child. The name of the child was Ishmael, described as a wild child according to Scripture, and considered the father of the Islamic world—see Genesis chapters 16 and 21. It is also helpful to read Galatians 4:22–31 to understand the resentment the and enmity between Jews and Muslims, as well as the origins of conflicts in the Middle East. The physical war in the Middle East is a spiritual war in disguise. Should we, then, blame Abraham the father of faith, for all this mess? God forbid. God allows things to happen for a reason or reasons. Consider the following scriptures:

Now, Sarai, Abram's wife bare him no children: and she had a handmaid, an Egyptian, whose name was Hagar. And Sarai said unto

Abram, behold now, the Lord hath restrained me from bearing: I pray thee, go in unto my maid, it may be that I may obtain children by her. And Abram hearkened to the voice of Sarai. And Sarai Abram's wife took Hagar her maid the Egyptian, after Abram had dwelt ten years in the land of Canaan, and gave her to her husband Abram to be his wife. And he went in unto Hagar, and she conceived: and when she saw that she had conceived, her mistress was despised in her eyes . . . And the angel of the lord said unto her, Behold, thou art with a child, and shall bear a son, and shall call his name Ishmael; because the Lord hath heard thy affliction. And he will be a wild man, and his hand will be against every man, and every man's hand against him, and he shall dwell in the presence of his brethren . . . Abram was fourscore and six years old, when Hagar bare Ishmael to Abram. (Genesis 16:1–16).

Now there is a conflict when Isaac, the promised child, is born:

And Abraham was an hundred years old, when his son Isaac was born unto him . . . And Sarah saw the son of Hagar the Egyptian, which she had born unto Abraham, mocking. Wherefore she said unto Abraham, cast out this bondwoman and her son: for the son of this bondwoman shall not be heir with my son, even with Isaac. And the thing was very grievous in Abraham's sight because of his son. And God said unto Abraham, let it not be grievous in thy sight because of the lad, and because of thy bondwoman: in all that Sarah hath said unto thee, hearken unto her voice; for in Isaac shall thy seed be called. And also of the son of the bondwoman will I make a nation, because he is thy seed. (Genesis 21: 5–13).

Now compare the accounts of Paul, the apostle of Christ, in the New Testament:

For it is written, that Abraham had two sons, one by a bondwoman, the other by a freewoman. But he who was of the bondwoman was born after the flesh: but he of the freewoman was by the promise. Which things are an allegory for these are the two covenants; the one from the mount Sinai, which gendered to bondage, which is Agar. For this Agar is mount Sinai in Arabia, and answered to Jerusalem, which now is, and is in bondage with her children. But Jerusalem which is above is free, which is the mother of us all . . . Now we, brethren, as Isaac was, are the children of promise. But as then he that was born after the flesh persecuted him that was born after the Spirit, even so it is now. Nevertheless, what saith the scripture? Cast out the bondwoman and her son: for the son of the bondwoman shall not be heir with the son of the freewoman. (Galatians 4: 22-30).

There will not be a genuine peace in the Middle East, no matter how much the rest of the world tries to ensure it, not until the arrival of Christ, who is the *Prince of Peace* (Isaiah 9:6).

Remember that God changed Abram's name to Abraham, which means "the father of nations." He also changed his wife Sarai's name to Sarah, which means "princess." God sealed His covenant with Abraham with the circumcision of Abraham's flesh, the custom that must be observed by Abraham's descendants until the arrival of Christ. *Christians' circumcision is of the heart, in the Spirit, not of the flesh* (Romans 2:25–29). The covenant that God made with Abraham was transferred to his descendants, first *to Isaac* and *then to Jacob, and finally to the children of Jacob, known as the twelve tribes of Israel.*

What I learned . . . My action plan . . .

<u>*About Isaac:*</u> Isaac was a promised child (Genesis 18), and a type of Christ. God instructed Abraham to offer Isaac, his legitimate and promised child as a sacrifice. Abraham obeyed God without questioning. He took Isaac and attempted to offer him to God as God instructed, *but*, instead of killing Isaac, God supplied Abraham with a substitute—see Genesis 22. Isaac is the father of Jacob and Esau.

<u>About Jacob:</u> *Jacob means "deceiver."* Jacob deceived many people, including his own twin brother, Esau and his uncle Laban. Jacob himself was also deceived. *His name was changed to Israel* after his all-night encounter with the Angel of God. Jacob is the father of the twelve tribes of Israel, including Judah. Jacob's beloved son was *Joseph,* who in many ways was a type of our Lord Jesus Christ. You are encouraged to read the book of Genesis, chapters 37 through 50, to learn more about Joseph's life and death: *his gift as a dreamer*, how his dream got him in trouble with his brethren, how he was *sold into slavery*, how he was accused of indecency with king's wife, *his imprisonment,* why he found favor, and how he became *the second in command to King Pharaoh, how he saved the Egyptians, his brothers, and his father* from the seven- year famine. Joseph died in Egypt at 110 years of age.

12. Question: Who was Job? When did he live, and what is significant about him?

Answer: Job was a human being like you and me.The exact time that Job lived is uncertain, but it is more likely that he lived before or during the time of the patriarchs, before the Exodus. Job feared God and appeared righteous in his own ways, but he failed to realize that all human righteousness is as filthy rags before God.

It is true that God referred to Job as an upright individual when introducing him to the devil. Being upright in God's sight does not necessarily mean righteousness. There is only one righteous person who ever lived, and His name is Jesus Christ, our Lord.

There are many significant landmarks in Job's life and trials. He was introduced to the devil in a manner similar to how Jesus was led by the Spirit into the wilderness to be tempted by the devil. God likes to showcase His obedient children - Job 1:8. The devil questioned Job's love and fear for God and asked God to allow him to torture Job to see if he would still maintain his fear of, and love for God – (Job 1:9-11). God granted the devil's request, allowing him to torture Job, but with limitations - Job 1:12-22. He could steal from Job, harm his body (John 10: 10), but he was not allowed to take his life - Job 2:1-10. Job suffered the loss of his material wealth, all of his children, his health, and public acclaim. His wife scolded him and encouraged him to curse God and die. His three friends—Eliphaz, Bildad, and Zophar—accused Job of ungodliness, telling him that he was suffering because of his own sins. But with all the rejections, the accusations, and the misguided advise from his wife, the Bible records that Job did not sin.

Job wanted to understand why a righteous man like him could be suffering like he was. Job wished he could see God to present his case before Him. Elihu, one of Job's friends, seemed to have a momentary glimpse into God's mind. He told Job to abandon his arrogance and self-righteousness. He told Job to recognize the Glory and Greatness of God. In the end, God revealed Himself to Job with a series of profound and existential questions.

Job was convinced, recognized his foolishness, and humbled himself before the Almighty. God extended Job's life and doubled his blessings. The end of Job's life was far greater and better than his life before the trials. The devil is a loser. Read the entire book of Job and count your blessings.

What I learned . . . My action plan . . .

This concludes my brief summary of the book of Genesis. Genesis means "the beginning." What we have covered so far are just a few of many lessons in the book of Genesis. You are encouraged to continue studying. The chapters following are designed to assist you in this pursuit.

Spiritual Exercises:

1. *Did you learn anything new about how God operates in this chapter?*

2. *Did you learn anything surprising about God's people in this chapter?*

3. *Did you learn anything that may help perfect your walk with God?*

Note: We need to continue to grow in the Lord, submitting ourselves unto God day by day. resist the devil, and he will flee from us according to James 4:7.

Rabiu Elijah Omolaja

Chapter 17
LIVING IN PEACE AND VICTORY
IN THE WORLD FILLED WITH EVIL

This chapter is dedicated to Christians who are struggling with life challenges, whether it is poor health, lack of finances, conflicts in relationship, or any other of life's less desirable situations. We need to know that God takes no pleasure in our pain and suffering, and nor is He the author of them. There are three possible factors in human experience God, the devil, and, of course, the person himself/herself. We know that God's thoughts towards us are not evil but good. We also know that the devil is the main enemy that humans have, according to Scripture. The devil is a thief; he comes to steal, kill, and destroy (John 10:10). The main factor that you and I don't always recognize is the part or parts that we are playing or not playing that may be nurturing the presenting problem(s). If you continue to feed your problems the devil's food, they will continue to thrive. Many of us have chosen the nurturing and preservation of our problems as a career, either consciously or unconsciously. Helping individuals overcome these self-defeating behaviors is the focus of this chapter.

Many Christians will continue to suffer pain and defeat at the hands of the enemy because they fail to recognize the main source of their problems, ignore their own self-defeating behaviors, or are simply ignorant of the power of the cross within them. Without knowledge, people perish. The Bible says, "Ye shall know the truth, and the truth shall make you free" (John 8:32). You may ask: What is the truth then that I may be free? This is the truth, and the truth is this: the devil is the source of all humans' woes either directly or indirectly. All of humanity's problems started after the transgression of Adam and Eve in the Garden of Eden, but thanks to God Almighty, for in Christ, we have overcome.

We need to recognize that our belief system is a formidable force. Your belief system has the potential to invite the devil into your life, and it is also capable of locking the devil out, depending on what you believe. God has given us authority over the devil and demonic forces. It is no longer God's responsibility to lock the devil out of people's lives. Christians are responsible for locking the devil out of their lives through the confession of their faith in the works of Jesus Christ. Many of us are doing this successfully, while others are indifferent. God wants His children to learn to learn how to effectively deal with the devil. Christians must be prepared to confront the devil whenever and wherever he manifests. We should learn not to take *"no"* for an answer when dealing with the devil. Believers have overcome the devil through the death and resurrection of Christ, and the devil knows. He knows that he has no authority or exclusive power over us, the children of God. However, if you and I chose to sell out to the devil, he will enslave us as he did with Adam and Eve and the children of Israel. Adam and Eve and along with children of Israel choose to sell out to the devil. The devil is a crook, a shameless creature. He is a taker, a thief, and will take anything you hand over to him. If you give your life to the devil, he will take it. He steals from the old and the young, from the rich and the poor. The devil preys on people's ignorance and weaknesses. Christians need to know that we are of God, and God is for us. If God be for us, who then shall be against us? (see Psalm 118:6; Romans 8:31; and 1 Peter 3:13). The Scripture commands us to submit ourselves therefore to God, to resist the devil, and he will flee from us (James 4:7). We must stop collaborating with the devil by our faulty belief system and the evil choices we are making. Our ungodly behavior, our rebelliousness, worldliness, lustfulness, bad company, and ignorance consequently crack the wall of protection that God has erected around us. Our disobedience to God's Word gives the enemy express access into our lives. Christians don't need to be chased around by demonic forces. Believers must hold their ground. We must keep the devil on the run as Christ and the apostles did. Our God, our Lord, never changes (Malachi 3:6). He is the same yesterday, today, and forever. If God has chased the devil out of his closet through Christ and the apostles, He can do the same thing through us. We are of God, and Greater is He that is in us than he that is in the world (see 1 John 4:4). If God is for us, who can be against us? – (Romans 8:31).

Doing Periodic Personal Life Inventory

Do you know that there are four categories of people and belief systems in the world? There are *1)* people who believe that they are not responsible for their problems and should not be held responsible for finding the solution to them; *2)* there are people who believe that they may be responsible for their problems but are not responsible for finding the solution to them; *3)* there are people who believe that they are responsible for their problems and are also responsible for finding the solution to them; and *4)* there are people who believe that though they may not be responsible for their problems, they are still responsible to find the solution to them. Questions: What do you believe about the situations with which you are struggling? Who are you blaming for your life's situations and challenges? Who are you holding responsible to find the solution to your problems? What are your attitudes toward life challenges in general?

It is important that we learn, and be willing, to do what I call Periodic Personal Life Inventory (PPLI). When was the last time you questioned yourself about the reasons behind some of the decisions you have made? Do you know why you do some of the things that you do? Do you understand that there are forces behind all of the decisions you are making? Do you realize that some of the choices you made in the past are having some effects on your life today? Is it possible that you could be your own demons, your own enemy? Christians need to STOP the BLAME GAME. We need to stop blaming the innocent. Stop blaming your spouse. Stop blaming your parents. Stop blaming your doctors. Stop blaming the government. Don't blame your pastor, and don't blame God. You cannot blame the devil either. Blaming the devil will not solve the problem, nor will it do you any good. The devil is getting used to us blaming him for our problems. Now, you may be silently asking: "Who, then, is to blame? Should I begin to blame myself?" The answer is no. You don't need to blame yourself either. What I hope that you will begin to do is first, realize the part or parts that you might have played that caused, or maybe maintaining, your problems. The second thing I want you to do is to confess your misdeeds and repent (Proverbs 28:13; 1 John 1:9). You need to know that the solutions to your life's problems are right at your fingertips, within you not in me. You have the solution in you if you are a Christian and firmly believe in the Scripture. Jesus Christ is the Answer to all of humanity's problems, whatever they may be, and He is not limited to any specific method. Our Lord can use anything and anybody to meet our needs if we believe. Jesus is the absolute authority in all things.

Finding Solutions to Human Problems

The solution to life problems begins with our obedience to God's Word. We must learn to live totally in Christ and for Christ. We must learn to fight the good fight of faith, doing what is right by our Spirit, our soul, and our physical body. Living daily in God's will and in obedience to God's Word will reinforce the wall of protection that God has erected around us. It will keep the enemy out of our lives, draw us closer to our blessings, create a transformation within through the help of the Holy Ghost, keep us in tune with God, ensure the protection and victory we already have in Christ, and help us to overcome the enemy and all his darts.

Human beings are made of spiritual and natural substances, according to Genesis 2:7. For us to live in victory, in peace, and in good health, we must learn to live in obedience to both. Christians must learn to obey the *Spiritual* and *Natural principles*. It doesn't matter how much of a Christian one thinks he is; it doesn't matter how spiritual you think you are; if you choose to live in contempt of either of these two basic principles, you will suffer repeated defeat. Human beings cannot afford to live in disobedience to the *Spiritual principles, nor can we afford to disregard natural principles.* Good health, victory, joy, and other fulfillments of life are largely depend on our spiritual life and how we naturally treat our bodies. If you choose to jump out of a flying aircraft without a parachute, you will get hurt on landing.

Spiritual Principles

1. We must love God, ourselves, and one another. Nothing is greater than loving.

LOVE is God's Nature. Loving is a spiritual weapon against the forces of darkness.

Loving God, ourselves, and others is a solid foundation upon which life's victories and success are built. Success here does not necessarily mean having money. Human success is not measured by material wealth. Let us hear what the Scripture says about love:

Thou shall love the Lord thy God with all thy heart, and with all thy soul, and with all thy mind. This is the first and great commandment. And the second is like unto it.

Thou shall love thy neighbor as thyself. On these commandments hang all the law and the prophets. (Matthew 22: 37–40).

a. *Loving God:*

Loving God is a commandment. Once we have accepted God's Love, Jesus Christ, into our lives, we must learn to live in obedience to the One who saved our souls. Jesus instruct His followers saying: "If ye love me, keep my commandments" (John 14:15). God loves us, and He desires our love. We must learn to love God with our soul, and our mind, as He desires. You and I have nothing to lose by loving God but have plenty to gain. Our God is loveable, and we cannot out love Him. He always loves us more and without measure.

b. *Loving Self:*

Loving self is also a commandment. You owe it to yourself to love yourself regardless of what you think about yourself, your situations, your past and present mistakes. You must admire yourself regardless of how ugly you think you look. You may be asking: "But why?" It is because you are made in God's image. It is confusing to want others to love us and treat us with care but then to treat ourselves with contempt, negligence, carelessness, etc. Frankly, how could you expect another person to love you when you "yourself" are having difficulty loving you? When you don't love yourself, you are living in contempt against the very foundation upon which you are built. Each of us must learn to love who we are because we are created in the image of God. We must also love others, for they, too, are created in the image of God. If you hate who you are, as an image of God, you will hate God, who created you and, consequently, you will hate those who brought you into the world, your parents. If you have self-hatred, you project hate onto others, because you can only give what you have.

Self-Hatred Is the Origin of All Crimes

Do you know why there are so many crimes in the world today? People who commit heinous crimes are mostly those individuals who look in the mirror and hate what they see. Most criminals have no respect for their own existence and therefore have no respect for others. Most criminals have no value for their own lives and therefore have no value for others. These monsters are thrilled to rape, steal, and maim. They kill the innocents, then turn around callously to take their own life. Do you know why the government cannot stop crimes in the world? It is simple. Crimes are spiritual problems, and only God has a permanent solution to spiritual problems.

The government may incarcerate the channels of the crimes committed—the offenders or persons used in the crimes—but it cannot incarcerate the demonic spirits behind the crimes. The moment the agent of the crime or the offender is incarcerated, the spirit behind the crime jumps out of them into someone else at large, someone else who is free in the world. That is why some inmates find repentance in prison cells. They found repentance behind the prison cells because the spirits behind the crimes they committed have abandoned them temporarily. Once these individuals are released, the same spirits are right there at their prison gates, waiting to jump back in the individuals upon release. Unless these individuals find genuine repentance in prison cells, they will be repeat offenders upon release. The devil and his demonic forces don't give up on us easily. The devil and his demons mean serious business, and if we only knew their desperation, we would do what the Apostle Paul suggested in his letter to the church of Ephesians (read Ephesians 6:10–17). Yes, we must stay armored all times. The devil and his demons believe that human bodies are their homes.

Let us read what the Lord says:

When the unclean spirit is gone out of a man, he walketh through dry places, seeking rest, and finds none. Then saith, I will return into my house from whence I came out; and when he comes, he finds it empty, swept and garnished. Then goes he, and taketh with himself, seven other spirits more wicked than himself, and they enter in and dwell there: and the last state of that man is worse than the first..." (Matthew 12:43–45)

c. Loving Others:

Loving others is a commandment. God loves, while the devil hates. God is Love, and when we love one another, we reflect God's presence in us. When we hate one another, we fulfill the deeds of the enemy, the devil. We either belong to God or the devil. There is no in-between.

Beloved, let us love one another: for love is of God, and everyone that loves is born of God, and knows God. He that loves not, knows not God; for God is Love. (1 John 4: 7–8)

Jesus told His disciples:

But I say unto you, love your enemies, bless them that curse you, do good to them that hate you, and pray for them which despitefully use you, and persecute you: That ye may be the children of your Father which is in heaven: for he maketh his sun to rise on the evil and on the good, and sends his rain on the just and on the unjust. - (Matthew 5: 44–45)

Paul wrote:

Owe no man anything, but to love one another: for he that loveth another hath fulfilled the law. For this, Thou shalt not commit adultery, thou shalt not kill, thou shalt not steal, Thou shalt not bear false witness, Thou shalt not covet; and if there be any other commandment, it is briefly comprehended in this saying, namely, Thou shalt love thy neighbor as thyself. Love worketh no ill to his neighbor: therefore love is the fulfilling of the law. (Romans 13: 810).

Special Assignment on Love:

No one can fully teach another person how to love except the Love Himself. God is Love. I encourage you to read 1 Corinthians 13:1–13. As you read this chapter, I want you to replace the word "Charity" with "Love" because that is what it means in the context. Read this chapter repeatedly until it becomes a part of you. I hope that the exercise will help you better understand what it really means to love yourself and others. We must continue to learn from God's Word through the Holy Spirit until our Savior comes.

2. *We must learn to forgive ourselves and those that have offended us.*

God wants you to be able to forgive yourself and be willing to forgive those who offend you (Matthew 6:14–15; Ephesians 4:32). It will take self-love to be able to forgive yourself for past mistakes. It will take genuine love to be able to forgive those who have offended us. But if that is what God wants us to do, then that is what we must do. God doesn't want us to be overcome by evil; but rather, He wants us to overcome evil with good. Yes, we have made some poor, thoughtless, irresponsible decisions in the past, and perhaps some of those decisions may haunt us for the rest of our lives, but still, we must be willing to forgive ourselves. It may be true also that some of us are hurting not because of our own doing but because of some decisions that other people have made in our lives, either directly or indirectly. Nevertheless, God requires that we forgive these individuals. God knows it may be difficult for us to want to pray for our enemies. It may be difficult to want to offer one's enemy a drink when he is thirsty or food when he is hungry, but if that is what God wants us to do, then that is what we must do. We must always remember that God knows what is best for us, and He will never ask us to do what He has not equipped us to do. As the enemies of the gospel were stoning Stephen to death, Stephen was praying, asking God to forgive his killers (read Acts 7:59–60). Jesus set the same example for us as He was dying on the Cross (Luke 23:33–34).

a. Forgiving self

The first step in forgiving yourself is to confess all your past mistakes to God, and to yourself. Confess as many as you can remember, trusting God to do what He has promised. The moment you confess your sins to God, He forgives you, as promised. That is one of the things that Jesus Christ is doing right now, up there at the right hand of God in Heaven. Jesus is sitting at the right hand of God interceding for us, according to Romans 8:34. Our main problem is that we find it difficult to forgive ourselves. It is not God that is not willing to forgive us, but rather, it is you and I that think we are too bad to be forgiven. If you know you have committed any sins, if you know where you have gone astray, why not go ahead and confess your sins to God and to yourself right now? What are you waiting for? God is listening, and He is faithful and just to forgive you and to cleanse you of all unrighteousness, as He has promised.

If we confess our sins, he is faithful and just to forgive us our sins, and to cleanse us from all unrighteousness. (1 John 1: 9)

He that covered his sins shall not prosper but whoso confessed and forsakes them shall have mercy.

(Proverbs 28: 13)

If my people, which are called by my name, shall humble themselves, and pray, and seek my face, and turn from their wicked ways, then will I hear from heaven, and will forgive their sin, and will heal their land.

(2Chronicles 7: 14)

b. Forgiving others

When you love someone, your love for them often overshadows their faults. God loves the world. It was God's Love that moved Him to send His only begotten Son into the world (John 3:16) to die for the sins He never committed so that those who believe in Him shall not perish but have everlasting life. It was Christ's love that moved Him to accept the painful death on the cross for the redemption of His friends' souls.

Jesus said: "Greater love hath no man than this, that a man lay down his life for his friends" (John 15:13).

It takes a divine love to forgive others. Similarly, it will take mental pain and anguish of the soul to hold grudges against offenders.

Did you know that refusing to forgive those who have offended you may hinder your prayers and impair your emotional, mental, and physical wellness? Do you know that holding bitterness and grudges will hurt you more than the person you refused to forgive and holding a grudge against? Do you know that you cannot hold someone down without staying down with him? Booker T. Washington said you can't, and I, too, tend to agree. Not forgiving your enemy builds up resentment and anger in the inside. Did you know that anger is like an acid? Yes, it is. Acid has the potential to destroy the object which it is poured on and harm the container in which it is kept. Let us read what the word of God says about forgiveness and anger:

For if ye forgive men their trespasses, your heavenly Father will also forgive you: But, if ye forgive not men their trespasses, neither will your Father forgive your trespasses.

(Matthew 6: 14–15)

Be ye angry, and sin not: let not the sun go down upon your wrath: Neither give place to the devil.

(Ephesians 4: 26–27)

3. *We must learn to give thanks to God in all things, thanking one another*

"It is a good thing to give thanks unto the Lord . . ." (Psalm 92:1). A sense of gratitude is very important in our walks with God. Learning to thank God for his many blessings is wisdom. When we thank God for how good He is being to us, we are blessing Him in our own way. We can bless God with the fruit of our lips.

The Psalmist wrote:

Bless the Lord, O my soul: and all that is within me, Bless His holy name. Bless the Lord, O my soul, and forget not all his benefits: Who forgives all thy iniquities; who health all thy diseases: Who redeemed thy life from destruction; who crowned thee with loving kindness and tender mercies.

(Psalm 103: 1–4)

a. Giving thanks to God always

We need to learn to always be thankful to the Lord. We should thank God in all things and for all things. We should thank God for His goodness (Psalm 100: 4; Psalm 95:2; and Psalm 92:1). We ought to thank Him for our salvation (Psalm 107:1–2), for the victory He gave us in Christ (1 Corinthians 15:57). Let us thank Him always (Ephesians 5:20), and in prayers (Philippians 4:6).

Giving thanks to God for all occasions and life experiences can unlock the doors of many more blessings that God has in store for us. When praise goes up, blessings come down.

Consider this passage:

And it came to pass, as he went to Jerusalem, that he passed through the midst of Samaria and Galilee. And as he entered into a certain village, there met him ten men that were lepers, which stood afar off: And they lifted up their voice, and said, Jesus, Master, have mercy on us. And when he saw them, he said unto them. Go shew yourselves to the priests. And as they went they were cleansed. And one of them, when he saw that he was healed, turned back, and with a loud voice glorified God. And fell on his face at his feet, giving him thanks: and he was a Samaritan. And Jesus answering said, Were there not ten cleansed? But where are the nine?

(Luke 17: 11–17)

There are many lessons to learn here, but my focus for now is on this one leper, the one leper who came back to give thanks. Jesus asked him, "Where are the nine?" Many of us are like the nine lepers who didn't return. These nine individuals thought they were entitled to their healing. They saw no need to turn around, wasting their time to come back to give thanks to their Healer. These nine lepers represent the thoughtless and ungrateful nature of many of us. These are spiritually blind, selfish individuals. Did you know that God doesn't have to do anything for us? Did you know that Jesus didn't have to heal the lepers? He chose to. Listen to what Jesus told this one leper in verse 19: "And he said unto him, Arise, go thy way: thy faith hath made thee whole."

This leper was already cleansed, and completely healed the first time. There was no more rottenness, no more discoloration of the skin, no more open sores, which were the most common marks of leprosy on this man. There were no blemishes, but Jesus still told him ". . . go thy way: thy faith hath made thee whole." What did Jesus mean by that statement? It seems to me that Jesus was saying to this former leper something like this: "I know that you have been healed of the leprosy that plagued your body. I know that the soreness is gone, the rottenness is gone, the bad smell is gone, and the discoloration of the skin is gone, but you are still missing some fingers and some toes, which are a common loss among people plagued with leprosy. Guess what, my friend? I will do something more amazing for you, right now, because of your gratitude attitude. I will do something that goes beyond your imagination. I will make you whole again because you came back to show me some appreciation. This is what I will do for you: I am replacing the fingers and the toes that you are still missing—with new and better. Your toes and your fingers that were missing I have now replaced. That is what you get for coming back to give thanks. This is what you get for your gratitude attitude."

Jesus told the man, "Thy faith in me hath made you whole." We Christians need to learn to be thankful unto God even for every little thing we take for granted, for every need that is met, and for those that are yet to be met.

Be careful about nothing; but in everything by prayer and supplication with thanksgiving let your request be made known unto God.

(Philippians 4: 6)

b. *Thanking one another*

We need to learn to thank and appreciate one another. Too often we take each other's goodness for granted. If someone is being good to you, it should be natural to have the courtesy to thank them for their kindness. We need to learn to show gratitude rather than feeling entitled. One of the reasons some of us don't say "thank you" to one another is because we think that we are entitled to other peoples' kindness. We assume others are obligated to be nice, and that they owe us. My friend, you are not entitled to anything. People choose to be good to you because they want to be good, not because they have to. Even though God commanded us to love and be good to one another, remember that people still have choices. Christians are encouraged to be as good as God is, but they are not compelled. Human beings have the choice to be good or not. We need to learn to appreciate one another. Even when people are not so good to you, try to show them some appreciation anyway. It feels good to be nice to one another. As it was once said, "Most of us may never do great things in life, but we can do small things in a great way" (Anonymous). A sense of self-appreciation and the appreciation of others is a necessary virtue to have. To be kind to one another is a necessary virtue for Christians.

4. *We must learn to praise God at all times*

There are hundreds of Scripture references about "praise" or "praising God." If you to look up the word "praise" in Bible references, indexes, or a concordance. You will find that there are many ways to praise God. How I praise Him may differ from how you choose to praise Him, but to praise is still the same as long as it comes from the heart. You can praise God by lifting up your heart, your hand, by dancing, by singing spiritual songs, shouting halleluiah or glory, making joyful noise unto the Lord (Psalm 63:5), with gladness (2 Chronicles 29:30), with thankfulness (Psalm 147:7), continually (Psalm 71:6), unconditionally, more and more (Psalm 71:14), day by day (2 Chronicles 30:21), and for as long as we live (Psalm 104:33).

Worshiping God is what we are created to do. It is also what the angels are created to do. That is what the angels are doing now in Heaven, and that is what you and I will be doing when we get there. Praising God is a central part of our worship. We are to praise God for

His Excellency (Psalm 148:13), for His Greatness (Psalm 145:3), for His Holiness (Exodus 15:11), because of His Goodness (Psalm 107:8, 15, 21, 31), for His Mercy (2 Chronicles 20:21), because of His Loving Kindness (Psalm 138:2), for His Creations (read Genesis chapters 1 and 2; Psalm 146 to Psalm 150). We must praise God for our salvation. God didn't have to save any of us, but He did it anyway.

5. *We must learn to pray continually.*

Prayer is the soul of a person talking to God. Peter told his audience, " . . . we will give ourselves continually to prayer, and to the ministry of the word" (Acts 6:4). Peter_followed through on this commitment (see Acts 3:1 and Acts 10:9). Every person God has used had some form of discipline in the art of prayer. Moses prayed. The Old Testament prophets and prophetesses were mostly prayer warriors. Elijah prayed. All God's people must learn and graduate in the art of prayer. No one can teach you how to pray to God but the Spirit of Christ, the Holy Ghost. The more you spend time with God in prayer, the more you will learn how to pray and the more you will love to pray. Daniel prayed three times a day (Daniel 6:10). David prayed three times a day (Psalm 55:17). Jesus prayed continually, and He recommended that we pray too (Matthew 14:23 and Luke 18:1). Paul recommended that we pray without ceasing (1 Thessalonians 5:17), anywhere, and at any time.

6. *We must continue to exercise unyielding faith in God's Word.*

Human beings often struggle to believe in what they cannot verify with their senses. We must continue to have faith in God's Word regardless of the opposition of our five senses. We must settle it in our minds that God means what He says in His Word, and He says what He means. God does not need to lie or sugar-coat like humans. We must learn to develop unyielding faith in God's Word. Without faith, it is impossible to please Him (Hebrews 11:6). When our reasoning is in conflict with the Word of God, you and I must train our minds, our thought process, to be obedient to the Word. Believers are not to lean on their own understanding but to lean on the word of God. That is what it means to be a living sacrifice for God (Romans 12:1–2).

Special Assignment on Faith:

There is much to say about faith, and I would like to get you more involved here. Consider reading Hebrews 11:1–40. You will be amazed by what faith can do through a child of God. I want you to meditate on the individuals mentioned in the chapter. Meditate on how these men and women of God were able to accomplish so much for God through faith. Remember that these individuals were ordinary people, just like you and me. The only difference is that they learned to live for God. They trusted God and His Word. We, too, can learn to do the same thing.

7. *We must learn to conquer ungodly thoughts.*

Question: How do Christians conquer the evil thoughts? By meditating on God's words. Paul, through the Spirit, instructed the children of God, saying:

And be not conformed to this world: but be ye transformed by the renewing of your mind, that ye may prove what is that good, and acceptable, and perfect, will of God. (Romans 12:2)

Finally, brethren, whatsoever things are true, whatsoever things are honest, whatsoever things are just, whatsoever things are pure, whatsoever things are lovely, whatsoever things are of good report, if there be any virtue, and if there be any praise, think on these things.

(Philippians 4:8)

Christians must learn to conquer evil thoughts continually by consistently bringing them into subjection, unto obedience to God's Word according to 2 Corinthians 10:5 and Romans 12:2. Joshua told the Israelites:

This book of the law shall not depart out of thy mouth; but thou shall meditate therein day and night, that thou mayest observe to do according to all that is written therein: for then thou shall make thy way prosperous, and then thou shall have good success.

(Joshua 1: 8)

David encouraged the children of Israel:

Blessed is the man that walketh not in the counsel of the ungodly, nor stands in the way of sinners, nor sits in the seat of the scornful. But his delight is in the law of the Lord; and in his law does he meditates day and night. And he shall be like a tree planted by the rivers of water, that bringeth forth his fruit in his season; his leaf also shall not wither; and whatsoever he doeth shall prosper.

(Psalms 1: 1–3)

Thy word have I hid in mine heart, that I might not sin against thee.

(Psalm 119: 11)

8. We must learn to conquer evil communication, abstain from evil behaviors.

The Scripture says that evil communication corrupts good manners (1 Corinthians 15:33) but I say unto you, my friend, that evil communication will corrupt your soul. Many Christians are careless with words. They don't pay attention to what they say or what they do. Christian's ought to monitor with diligence the words that are coming out of their mouths (Matthew 12:36). We must pay attention to the way and manner in which we conduct ourselves in this world. Jesus says:

Either make the tree good, and his fruit good; or else make the tree corrupt, and his fruit corrupt: for the tree is known by his fruit. O generation of vipers, how can ye, being evil, speak good things? For out of the abundance of the heart the mouth speaks. A good man out of the good treasure of the heart bringeth forth good things: and an evil man out of the evil treasure bringeth forth evil things. But I say unto you, that every idle word that men shall speak, they shall give account thereof in the day of judgment. For by thy words thou shall be justified, and by thy words thou shall be condemned.

(Matthews 12: 33-37)

Did you know that you can speak woes into your life? Did you know that you can speak peace and wellness into your life? The Bible says that out of the abundance of the heart, the mouth speaks (Matthew 12:34). Did you know that you can speak your own world into existence? The world was formed by the Word of God. You need to know that the words coming out of your mouth are formidable forces. The words we speak are like a powerful hammer with the capacity to break everything into pieces (Jeremiah 23:29). They are like a two-edged sword (Hebrews 4:12), with the ability to cut either way. Your words can lift you up or pull you down. They can create some hope or destroy it.

Even so the tongue is a little member, and boasteth great things . . . And the tongue is a fire, a world of iniquity: so is the tongue among our members, that it defileth the whole body, and setteth on fire the course of nature; and it is set on fire of hell . . . But the tongue can no man tame, it is an unruly evil, full of deadly poison. Therewith bless we God, even the Father; and therewith curse we men, which are made after the similitude of God. Out of the same mouth proceeded blessing and cursing. My brethren these things ought not so to be. Doth a fountain sends forth at the same place sweet water and bitter? Can the fig tree, my brethren, bear olive berries? either a vine, figs? So can no fountain both yield salt water and fresh.

(James 3: 5–12)

9. We must advance the Gospel and support it financially.

Christians have the responsibility to support the Gospel through prayer, witnessing, and substance. We must give money liberally to full-time ministries so they can take the Gospel to the rest of the world and to those in our community. Our giving must be done willingly in faith, not in grudge or as if under obligation. Anything you and I give grudgingly or as if under obligation is a sin. God wants a cheerful and willing giver. The Scripture says: "It is more blessed to give than to receive" (Acts 20:35). The wise men gave the new child— our Savior—gold, frankincense, and myrrh (Matthew 2:11). We may not be able to give to the ministry gold, myrrh, or frankincense, but we must be willing to give whatever we have to advance the Gospel of Jesus Christ, and we must be willing to help the poor among us. The wealth of the earth belongs to us all, including those in need, and the disadvantaged.

Give, and it shall be given unto you; good measure, pressed down, and shaken together, and running over, shall men give into your bosom. For with the same measure that ye mete withal it shall be measured to you again.

(Luke 6: 38)

Every man according as he purposed in his heart so let him give; not grudgingly, or of necessity: for God loveth a cheerful giver. And God can make all grace abound toward you; that ye always having all sufficiency in all things, may abound to every good work.

(2 Corinthians 9: 7–8)

Lay not up for yourselves treasures upon earth, wheremoth and rust doth corrupt, and where thieves break through and steal: But, lay up for yourselves treasures in heaven, where neither moth nor rust doth corrupt, and where thieves do not break through and steal. For where your treasure is, there will your heart be also.

(Matthew 6: 19–21)

10. We must abide by the laws of the land in obedience to God's Word.

It is a spiritual command to obey the laws of the land. We must obey the law of the land except when it is in conflict with God's Word. What does the Scripture say?

Let every soul be subject unto the higher powers. For there is no power but of God: the powers that be are ordained of God. Whosoever therefore resisteth the power, resisteth the ordinance of God: and they that resisteth shall receive to themselves damnation.

(Romans 13: 1–2)

Christians are commanded, according to Scripture, to obey the laws of the land. The only time you and I must resist the law of the land is when it is in conflict with God's Word, not when the law is in conflict with our own opinions. I may not agree with many laws and rules, but I am obeying them, and I should and will continue to do so as long as they don't hinder my relationship with God.

The rulers, the people in government, are called ministers:

Submit yourselves to every ordinance of men for the Lord's sake: whether it be to the king, as supreme; Or unto governors, as unto one that are sent by him for the punishment of evil doers, and for the praise of them that do well. For so is the will of God. . .

(1 Peter 2: 13–15)

For rulers are not a terror to good works, but to the evil. Wilt thou then not afraid of the power? Do that which is good, and thou shall have praise of the same. For he is the minister of God to thee for good. But, if thou do that which is evil, be afraid; for he bears not the sword in vain: for he is the minister of God, a revenger to execute wrath upon him that doeth evil. Wherefore ye must need be subject, not only for wrath, but also for conscience's sake. For, for this cause pay ye tribute also: for they are God's ministers, attending continually upon this very thing. Render therefore to all their dues: tribute to whom tribute is due; custom to whom custom; fear to whom fear; honor to whom honor."

(Romans 13: 3–7)

It is important that we pray for those in power, those who rule over us, if we want to live in peace. If we don't pray for them, if we don't present them to God in our prayers, they are human and may make unwise decisions that will affect all of us directly or indirectly, temporarily or for a longer time (read 1 Timothy 2:1– 5).

Natural Principles

1. We must learn to feed our brains and bodies with food needed to function naturally and effectively.

Just as the central processing unit (CPU) is to a computer, so is your brain to your body. Your ability to see, smell, hear, taste, or touch are a few of many indirect functions of your brain. Your brain supplies your five senses with the signals needed to retrieve information from your environment and the world around you. You would know little about the world if you couldn't see, hear, smell, taste, or touch. Your five senses collect empirical data from the environment and pass them to the brain. The brain takes the information received, filters it, and process it based on its capacity. Your brain's capacity to process information in a certain way depends on many factors, including your age, how you were raised, the child-parent relationship, and other environmental influences. The way we have structured our past experiences and the meanings we have attached to them consequently shape how our brains process the new information. In this chapter, my main focus is to help you enable your brain to do what God has designed it to do and to do it more efficiently. The human brain and the soul seem to depend largely on one another in this body of dust. The soul will not be completely free until it is taken out of this body of dust. Your brain is not your soul. Your brain is made of neurons or nerve cells. It is considered matter and is visible. Your soul is invisible. Your brain will eventually die, but souls never die.

a. Eating right, drinking right. Watching what you put in your mouth is crucial to your health.

The human brain is an entity made of particles called brain cells. Don't ask me how many brain cells are up there —I don't know. Brain researchers tell us we have trillions of cells up there, but that is speculative. No one knows exactly how many brain cells are up there except God, who designed it. A comprehensive study of the brain cells and their functions is beyond the scope of this chapter. My aim here is to capture your attention and make you more aware of the importance of how you are treating, or ought to treat, your brain. I want you to be more aware that whatever you are feeding your body, whatever you are putting in your mouth, has some crucial effects on your brain. You need to know that what you are feeding your body has the capacity to debilitate your brain or enhance its normal functioning.

Food, whether solid or liquid, is composed of some compound chemicals. Some foods are laden with chemicals that are beneficial to the brain, while others contain chemicals that are poisonous to the body and detrimental to the brain. The chemicals that your body absorbs from the foods you eat can alter or complement the chemical composition of your brain. A change in the chemical composition of your brain can make you a very different person, either permanently or depending on the extent of the damage inflicted by the chemicals absorbed. For example, if you get drunk on alcohol or high on drugs, chances are you will act like a fool momentarily. But if you have chosen alcoholism or drug addiction as a lifestyle, not only will you act like a fool momentarily, your liver may suffer permanent damage. Alcohol and drugs are not the foods that God prescribed for us to consume.

Let us hear what God's Word says:

And God said, "Behold, I have given you every herb bearing seeds, which is upon the face of all the earth, and every tree, in the which is the fruit of a tree yielding seed: to you it shall be for meat."

(Genesis 1: 29)

God gave Adam and Eve instructions to eat seeds, herbs, and fruits. Your whole body will get everything it deserves to function properly from this divinely instructed diet. This divinely approved diet was given before the fall of Adam and Eve in the Garden of Eden. After the fall, the dietary instructions didn't change, except that God added meat, flesh without the blood. The consumption of the flesh, meat without the blood, was approved after the flood of Noah.

Let us read what God said to Noah:

Every moving thing that liveth shall be meat for you; even as the green herb have I given you all things. But flesh with the life thereof, which is the blood thereof, shall ye not eat.

(Genesis 9: 3–4)

God created us and knows what is beneficial to our bodies. God wants us to eat natural foods. Many of our foods today are laden with different growth chemicals, preservatives, and additives that may do our bodies more harm than good. For example, chlorine is added into our pipe-water. It is added to help kill the bugs or bacteria that may harm us However,If chlorine is present in excessive amounts, our health may be at risk. Chlorine reacts with other substances in water and can form some cancer- causing compounds that promote free radicals. Some experts in this area suggest that free radicals are responsible for many of our illnesses. Do you see why many people turned to water purifiers to minimize or eliminate this problem? I don't know much about free radicals or how they operate, but let us read what one of the experts, Dr. Willix Jr., has to say:

Free radicals are like ravenous molecular sharks. These predators are so hungry they last only millionths of a second before they make a frenzied attack on a neighbor. A free radical is not a thing like viruses or bacteria. It's much smaller than that. It's a molecule. Viruses, bacteria, and all of the cells in your body are made up of molecules. The problem with a free radical is that it contains an oxygen atom that is missing an electron. A free radical can't rest until it replaces the missing electron, and generally the only place it can get an electron is by taking a bite out of another molecules. Your body is full of hundreds of billions of free radicals attacking your healthy cells.[5]

Free radicals are believed to be the major cause of many of our ailments. Although our bodies produce their own free radicals for certain purposes. Some additives enforce the formation of more radicals in our bodies. Don't ask me how many types of radicals there are, because I don't know. My main focus here is to help you avoid any intake that may promote free radicals and potentially harm your body in the long run. It's important to understand that there is a spirit behind every living thing, including bacteria, viruses, and even the free radicals. Depending on your eating habits, you can prevent or promote the presence of these unnecessary free radicals according to Dr. Willix Jr. He also wrote the following:

Cancer, stroke, and heart disease come in a bewildering variety of shapes. They seem to be caused by everything from smoking cigarettes to eating butter to pesticides. One type of cancer, like colon cancer, seems to have little to do with another type such as breast cancer. And both appear to have nothing in common with heart disease. Not until now, anyway! But now we know that all the diseases have the same underlying cause—free radicals. Do you know why radiation can cause cancer? Because radiation creates free radicals. Why does stress make us ill? It causes our bodies to form free radicals. Why is smoking harmful? It creates free radicals. Ditto for air pollution and some of the pesticides in our environment. Even the chlorine in our water can form cancer-causing compounds that promote free radical.[6]

It is recommended here that whatever you can do to help strengthen your immune system will help your body in the long run. Antioxidants are suggested as helpful supplements in rejuvenating the skin and strengthening the immune system. Vitamins such as A, C, and E, selenium, niacin, and zinc just to mention few, are also beneficial to our health. Other supplements including potassium and magnesium are helpful as well. Consult with your doctor. *b. Understand some of the negative effects of chemical compounds in cigarettes.*

Cigarette smoke contains chemical compounds that are known as cancer-causing agents carcinogens. The presence of these chemicals in the body may help explain why there are more cases of cancer-related illnesses, the diseases of the lung, heart conditions, circulatory problems, bronchitis, peptic ulcers, and other general poor health conditions among habitual smokers compared to nonsmokers. As a child, I watched my father smoke tobacco. I watched some City teenagers fallen in love with nicotine as well. So, in my late teens, I decided to try it myself. It started with just a puff, and the nicotine held me in bondage for seven long years. I broke the habit in the seventh year. If I can do it, you can do it too.

c. Understand some of the negative effects of chemical compounds in alcohol.

Alcohol is considered in this section as a depressant. There may be others who will disagree with this label. They may prefer to think of alcohol as a stimulant. Alcohol depresses the cerebral cortex. The cerebral cortex is part of the brain that controls behavior, memory, and reasoning. People act like fools when they are intoxicated with alcohol. The effects of alcohol can extend to the motor center. The motor center is the part of the brain that coordinates movements and reflexes. This is why people intoxicated with alcohol cannot maintain their balance. The effects of alcohol may extend to the midbrain. The mid-brain controls speech muscles and eye movements. Depending on the amount of alcohol consumed, frequency of use, duration of effects, the user's age, and the tolerance level, a severe consequence may occur, including inflation of the liver and hepatitis. "Cirrhosis of the liver—a fatty degeneration and hardening of the liver—is a disorder common among alcoholics."[7] Prolonged intoxication may lead to a coma, stroke, or premature death. Alcohol affects the whole person, including the central nervous system, peripheral nervous system, the overall brain functions, liver functions, the gastrointestinal tract, and muscles. Alcohol can affect memory, impair human judgment, promote aggression, alter the user's personality, and has caused many relationships to fail. What does the Scripture say about alcoholism?

Wine is a mocker, strong drink is raging and whosoever is deceived thereby is not wise.

(Proverbs 20: 1)

Who hath woe? Who hath sorrow? Who hath contentions? Who hath babbling? Who hath wounds without cause? Who hath redness of eyes? They that tarry long at the wine; they that go to seek mixed wine. Look not thou upon the wine when it is red, when it giveth its color in the cup, when it moves itself aright. At the last it bites like a serpent, and stings like an adder. Thine eyes shall behold strange women, and thine heart shall utter perverse things.

(Proverbs 23: 29–33)

And be not drunk with wine, wherein is excess; but be ye filled with the Spirit.

(Ephesians 5: 18)

d. Be vigilant about prescribed drugs

Let me make it clear that I am not suggesting that you don't need to take medications. Taking medications for any conditions you may have will not send you to Hell, nor does it make you any less of a Christian, but you need to know the limitations of your medications and the dangers that some of your medications may impose on your body or brain. For example, pain medication is not necessarily prescribed to cure you of your pain, but rather it was prescribed to provide you temporary relief. That is why you have to take them daily, or every four hours, or whatever frequency is suggested. Your pain medications are expected, at best, to disconnect the communication line between your brain and the area the pain is panging in your body. Most of our pain medications are narcotics, meaning they are mind-altering substances, and if they are taken for a prolonged period, they could cause severe damage to some of the internal organs. There are other medications we may take for conditions other than pain that may have similar effects on our bodies as well. Let us look at the way that some of these medications interact in our bodies.

If you have high blood pressure, the first thing the doctor will consider is putting you on a medication to help your blood vessels dilate more. Did you know that the medication that is prescribed to open up your blood vessels may also cause your heart to speed up more than normal? That is why the doctor must prescribe additional medication to slow down your heart. Any of these first two medications may consequently cause you to have water retention, a fluid build-up syndrome. If that occurs, your doctor will have to prescribe a water pill to help minimize or inhibit your water retention. The water pill that your doctor prescribed may cause dizziness, depression, or headache. These are considered normal side effects. you experience any of these side effects, your doctor may need to prescribe a new set of medications to manage those conditions as well. The medication prescribed for depression may likely cause your mouth to dry, affect your sex drive, and so on. Can you see now why and how some people may end up with a mini pharmacy in their homes due to a single condition that could have been managed or prevented simply by changing faulty beliefs and self-destructive lifestyles? Do you know that it is understanding who you are in Christ, aligning your belief system to conform to God's promises, and doing what is right for your body and Spirit are the only forces that can chase these spirits of infirmity, these filthy spirits, out of your body?

Do you know there are spirits behind high blood pressure, diabetes, cancer, and all of human infirmities? Do you know why psychiatrists cannot cure mental illnesses? It is because mental illnesses, whether they are genetically predisposed, results of one's lifestyle, or any other natural phenomenon, are the works of the enemy in disguise. God has not given us the spirit of fear but of power, and of love and of a sound mind (2 Timothy 1:7). The devil and his demonic forces will not honor, obey, nor listen to anything else but the faith dispensed in the name of Jesus Christ. The Scripture says that God has highly exalted Jesus Christ and has given Him a name, which is above every name, and that in His name (Jesus Christ) every knee shall bow (read Philippians 2:9–11).

2. *We must learn to control illnesses that are genetically predisposed.*

Just because your parents died of heart failure, diabetes, high blood pressure, or stress doesn't mean you have to experience the same fate. you can monitor and control your stress level? Do you know that you can monitor your blood pressure and the events that are likely to cause your blood pressure to rise? We can all work to stop, minimize, or prevent high blood pressure simply by watching what we eat, exercising, having good attitudes toward self, others, and life in general. We don't need to sit back and watch our lives fall apart in slow motion. We can come to our own rescue today. Changing your lifestyle and changing your eating habits will help your body and your brain in the long run. While some illnesses are inherited through our genes. They are genetically predisposed by our parents, *but* even though we are prone to have these illnesses, this does not necessarily mean that we must or have to nurture them. Yes, the tendency is there, but that doesn't necessarily mean that you and I are destined to have those conditions. We can minimize or prevent their manifestation and activation. Most of these genetically predisposed elements are activated or became inevitable because of our belief system and the choices we are making.

3. Other factors:

There are other factors that may compromise our health, particularly the proper functioning of our brain. Poor coping with stress, accidental or intentional trauma to the brain, high fever, meningitis, seizure episodes, birth defects, strokes, and any other organically based trauma to the brain are some of the other factors that may alter the normal functioning of the brain and its chemical composition. Except for stress, any of the possible factors listed in this section may even go as far as inflicting structural damage on the brain. In any instance where brain defects or abnormalities in functioning are due to structural damage, it will take a miracle to correct. No doctor can repair a structurally damaged brain but God, the Creator of the brain, can.

Note: While it is true that we may not be able to prevent the chemical imbalances caused by structural damage to the brain, we can prevent chemical imbalances that are behavior-induced.

Spiritual Exercises:

1. *If God is not the author of our problems, then who is?*

2. *Name three factors in human experience.*

3. *What are the three missions of the devil?*

4. *What factor do we often overlook when facing life challenges?*

5. *How does your belief system affect your attitude toward life challenges?*

6. *What did you learn about love from reading 1 Corinthians, chapter 13?*

7. *What did you learn about Faith in Hebrews chapter 11?*

8. *What did you learn about the roles of government in Romans chapter 13?*

9. *Your brain is to your body what the CPU is to a computer. Explain.*

10. *Why are what you eat and drink so important to your brain?*

11. *If medications are not designed to heal or cure illnesses, what are they designed to do?*

12. *What does it mean to resist the devil?*

13. *True or false? Some medications cause more medical problems than the symptoms they are meant to mask.*

14. *Why is it important to watch what you eat and drink?*

15. *Overall, what have you learned in this chapter?*

Chapter 18
WHAT A MIGHTY GOD? AND WHAT A MIGHTY CHRIST?

Our God is mighty, mighty in all His ways. He is ever-present, all powerful, and all knowing. This chapter is about some of the miracles that God performed, either directly or indirectly. There were miracles God performed to abase the proud. Some miracles He performed simply to honor those who honor Him. Some miracles God performed just to remind the world that He is still God and in charge, that with Him, nothing is impossible.

When Jesus was here in the flesh, He, too, did what He had seen His Father doing. He performed a host of miracles and commanded His disciples to do likewise. In fact, Jesus said that His followers will do more miracles than He did if they believe in Him and abide in Him as He abides in His Father (see John 14:11–12).

God never changed (Malachi 3:6). He is the same yesterday, today, and forever. God was all powerful yesterday, He is all powerful today, and He will be all powerful tomorrow. My friend, there are no situations that you and I are going through or are about to get into that are surprising or too much for God to handle. I hope that reading through the accounts of some of these miracles that God and His Son performed will help convey to you even more convincingly the powerful presence of God here on Earth. I hope that you will be convinced that God, who created the Heavens and the Earth, is still in charge and in control, and that with Him, nothing is impossible. God is still performing miracles today.

Some of the Miracles in the Old Testament

- *The Six Days of Creation (Genesis 1:1–31). The earth is not a result of a big bang. God created the Heaven and the earth.*

- *The emergence of humans. There are four different ways that human beings have come to be.*

1. *The formation of Adam—out of the dust and God's Breath (Genesis 1:26).*

2. *The formation of Eve—out of Adam's rib (Genesis 2:21–22).*

3. *The formation of you and me—by the unity of man's sperm and woman's egg, through pregnancy (Psalm 51:5).*

4. *The birth of Jesus Christ—by the Holy Ghost through pregnancy (Matthew 1:18).*

- *Enoch's translation (Genesis 5:24). Enoch's translation is a type of Christians' future Rapture. Enoch did not experience death because God took him alive. Christians, too, are waiting for their Rapture. At the sound of the trumpet, at the appearance of Jesus Christ in the sky, we will be taken upward to be with our Lord and Savior forever (read 1 Corinthians 15:52–55).*

- *The flood of Noah (Genesis 7:11–24). The world that exists now will be destroyed by fire (2 Peter 3:6–10).*

- *The confusion of tongues at Babel (Genesis 11:3–9). This is the beginning of different languages and races. Racism began in Babel. Different languages and racism are results of human disobedience. Babel means confusion. We were one body, one flesh, one language, one color, and one blood in the beginning. "And hath made of one blood all nations of men for to dwell on all the face of the earth, and hath determined the times before appointed, and the bound of their habitation" (Acts 17:26). Humans' disobedience at the Tower of Babel destroyed the human race unity.*

The destruction of Sodom and Gomorrah (Genesis 19:24). God destroyed the two sinful cities with brimstone and fire but saved Lot's household except one person, his wife, who chose to look back.

- *The miraculous destruction of Lot's wife (Genesis 19:26). Lot's wife looked back after the Angel of God delivered and instructed them not to. She looked back and became a pillar of salt.*

- *God gave an animal the capacity to speak in human language (Numbers 22:27–33). God is not limited. He can use anything, anytime, anywhere.*

- *God in the flaming bush (Exodus 3:2–4). The bush was burning, but the bush was not consumed. God spoke to Moses through the burning bush.*

- *Moses' rod turned serpent, his hand turned leprous (Exodus 4:2– 3; Exodus 4:6). God performed these two miracles to convince Moses, who was asking Him for signs.*

- *The ten terrible plagues against Egypt for Pharaoh's stubbornness (read Exodus chapters 7 through 14). Rivers turned into blood (Exodus 7:20–25); The land was filled with frogs (Exodus 8:1– 15); Lice covered the land (Exodus 8:16–1); Pharaoh's palace, houses, and cities were filled with flies (Exodus 8:20– 24); Murrain (Exodus 9:1–7). God sent a severe pestilence upon Egyptians cattle; God killed Pharaoh's oxen, horses, asses, cattle, all of his animals; Boils (Exodus 9:8–12). God gave Pharaoh boils, the soreness of the body; Hail (Exodus 9:18–24). God rained down terrible hail upon the children of disobedience; Locusts (Exodus 10:1–20). All Egyptians crops were destroyed by locusts; Darkness all over the land (Exodus 10:21–24); The death of the first-born (Exodus 12:29–30). All the firstborn in the land of Egypt were slain by the death angel.*

- *God's Presence in the pillar of cloud in the daytime and pillar of fire at night (Exodus 13:21–22; Exodus 14:19–20).*

- *God divided the Red Sea (Exodus 14:21–22). He is God Almighty. He made the Israelites to walk on the seabed with water erecting a water-hill on both sides.*

- *God fed the children of Israel with the manna that came from Heaven (Exodus 16:13–35). The children of Israel ate the manna in the wilderness for forty years according to verse 35.*

The Bible says they were fed with the food of angels. The manna was a type of Christ, the Bread of Life.

- *God gave the children of Israel water to drink out of the rock (Numbers 20:8–11). This rock and the water that came out of it were also types of Christ. Christ is our Rock. In Him is the Water of Life.*

- *The walls of Jericho collapsed without a touch (Joshua 6:6–20). The battle is of the Lord. God is a Warrior who needs no guns or bullets or human help to win.*

- *God allowed the moon and the sun to stand still for hours, reversing the course of nature momentarily through the request of Joshua (Joshua 10:12–14).*

- *Samson killed a lion with bare hands (Judges 14:5–6). Samson carried away the doors of the gates of a city with bare hands (Judges 16:3). God in us means power. God is the strength that we need for victory. In Him, we are undefeatable.*

- *The dragon house crumbled under the strength of one man (Judges 16:29–30).*

- *Elijah was fed by ravens (1 Kings 17:4–6). God will supply all our needs according to His riches. He owns all earthly and heavenly blessings. With Him there are no unmet needs. King David wrote: "Once I was young but now I am old but, I have never seen the righteous forsaken nor his seeds begging bread" (Psalms 37: 25).*

- *Elijah blessed a widow because of her generosity towards the prophet (1 Kings 17:12–16).*

- *Elijah raised the widow's son from the dead (1 Kings 17:17–23).*

- *Elijah's sacrifice, which he soaked with water to prove that His God is unlimited and superior to pagans' gods, was consumed by fire (1 Kings 18:38). Our God is the God that answers with Fire.*

- *Elijah prayed for rain when, at the time, there was no rain for three and half years and severe famine plagued the land. Elijah's request for rain was granted (1 Kings 18:41).*

- *Elijah divided River Jordan (2 Kings 2:8).*

- *Elijah was translated into Heaven in a chariot of fire (2 Kings 2:11). He saw no death.*

- *The Syrian army was defeated by unseen forces (2 Kings 6:16– 18). "As mountain surrounded Jerusalem so is God surrounding his people" (Psalm 125: 2).*

- *A dead man that was buried was raised from the dead when his body touched Elisha's bone in the grave (2 Kings 13:21). Elisha was a disciple of Prophet Elijah. He asked Elijah for a double portion of his power, and Elijah granted his request.*

- *A shadow reversed (2 Kings 20:11). God created nature and has exclusive authority over it.*

- *A Dragon crumbled before the Ark of Covenant (1 Samuel 5:1– 12). Idols are mute. They have eyes but cannot see, ears but cannot hear, legs but cannot walk, heads but without brains.*

- *God delivered three Hebrews out of the fiery furnace (Daniel 3:19–27). When we are going through persecutions or life struggles, God is right there with us, even though He is invisible. He is right there with us. God with us is far greater than the troubles and all the threats we are facing in the world (1 John 4:4).*

- *God delivered Daniel out of the lion's den (Daniel 6:16– 23). Our enemy—the devil—is like a roaring lion, but he has lost the power over the children of God. Jesus plucked out all of the enemy's teeth on the cross.*

- *Jonah was held for three days and three nights in a whale's belly (read Jonah chapters 1 and 2). This miracle is a type of Christ, who went to Hell for us. Jesus went to Hell for three days and three nights, but Glory to God, the Hell could not keep Him. My Lord rose the third day.*

Some of the Miracles Jesus Performed:

- *He cleansed a Leper (Matthew 8:2–3; Mark 1:40–43; Luke 5:12– 13).*

- *He raised the dead man (Luke 7:12–15).*

- *He healed Peter's mother-in-law of a fever (Matthew 8:14–15; Mark 1:30–31; Luke 4:38–39).*

- *He healed all the sick (Matthew 8:16–17; Mark 1:32–34; Luke 4:40–41).*

- *He stilled the storm (Matthew 8:23–26; Mark 4:35–39; Luke 8:22–24).*

- *He cast devils out of two men into the herd of swine (Matthew 8:28–32; Mark 5:1–13; Luke 8:26–34).*

- *He raised the ruler's daughter who was dead (Matthew 9: 18, 23– 33; Mark 5: 22–23, 39–42; Luke 8: 41–42, 51–56).*

- *He healed the woman who had the issue of blood for several years (Matthew 9:20–22; Mark 5:25–34; Luke 8:43–48).*

- *He healed the blind men (Matthew 9:28–30).*

- *He healed a man with a withered hand (Matthew 12:10–13; Mark 3:1–5; Luke 6: 6–8).*

- *He cured a devil-possessed blind and dumb man (Matthew 12:22; Luke 11:14).*

- *He fed the 5000 with a few fish and loaves of bread (Matthew 14:19–21; Mark 6:39–44; Luke 9:16–17; John 6:11–13).*

- *He walked on the sea (Matthew 14:25–27; Mark 6:47–50; John 6:19–20).*

- *He healed epileptic boy (Matthew 17:14–18; Mark 9:17–27; Luke 9:38–42).*

- *He obtained money out of a fish mouth to pay tax (Matthew 17:24–27).*

- *He healed a woman with infirmity (Luke 13:11–13).*

- *He healed the man with dropsy (Luke 14:1–4).*

- *He cleansed the ten lepers (Luke 17:11–14)*

- *He restored the servant's ear that was cut off by one of the disciples (Luke 22:50–51).*

- *He healed the man that was born blind (John 9:1–7).*

- *He raised Lazarus from the dead (John 11:43–44).*

- *Jesus Himself resurrected from the dead (Matthew 28; Mark 16; Luke 24; John 20).*

Note: Jesus said He is the Resurrection and the Life, and that he who believes in Him, though he may die, shall live (read John 11:25).

Spiritual Exercises:

1. *What do you think about God and miracles in general?*

2. *What do you think about the miracles performed by Christ?*

3. *Is God performing miracles through the body of Christ today?*

Chapter 19
SOME OF THE BIBLE PROPHECIES ABOUT JESUS CHRIST AND THEIR FULFILLMENTS

God spoke to our forefathers through the ministries of angels, prophets and prophetesses, visions, and dreams. God still speaks, but He is speaking to us today mostly through His written Word. How do we know that a prophet's message is from God? The message must be consistent, and in agreement with God's written Word. The message delivered by the prophet must come to pass. A prophetic message is God Himself speaking through a surrendered body of dust. We are channels through which God is reaching His people. The channels must be clean, able to receive and deliver the Word of God unhindered, purely, and incorruptibly.

Are you a prophet? You are like a pipeline, a spiritual pipeline receiving messages from God, and delivering them to His people. Imagine the pipe that delivers water to your house. If this pipe is leaking, it will not deliver with full capacity. If this pipe is rusted inside, the water it delivers into your house will be polluted with all kinds of substances. Can you imagine now how the lifestyle of a prophet can reinforce or contaminate God's messages? Are you called to be a prophet or prophetess? I encourage you to study the lives of the prophets and prophetesses who lived before you. You need to learn about what made them so usable and so effective in God's hands.

In this chapter, I want to share with you some of the prophecies in the Old Testament about our Savior, Jesus Christ, and their fulfillments in the New Testament. I want you to know or be reminded that prophecy, dreams, and visions are not given to confuse God's children; but rather they are given to enhance knowledge and understanding and to help us stay focused on God's plans for our lives, both now and in the future. The following are a few of the many prophecies about Jesus Christ—how He will be born, where He will be born, His Life, Ministry, Suffering, Death, and Resurrection. From the book of Genesis to Revelation, Jesus is revealed therein.

The Prophesy	The Subject	The Fulfillment
Genesis 3: 15	The Seed of a woman	Galatians 4: 4
Genesis 12: 3	The Son of Abraham	Matthew 1: 1; Galatians 3: 14
Genesis 17: 19	The Son of Isaac	Luke 3: 34
Numbers 24: 17	The Son of Jacob	Matthew 1: 1-2,17
Genesis 49: 10	The Son of Judah	Luke 3: 33
Isaiah 9: 6-7	The Heir to the Throne of David	Luke 1: 32-33
Psalm 45: 6	The Eternal	Hebrews 1: 8
Psalm 45: 7	The Anointed	Hebrews 1: 9
Micah 5: 2	He will be born in Bethlehem	Luke 2: 4-7

Isaiah 7: 14	He will be born of a virgin	Matthew 1: 23
Hosea 11: 1	He will be called out of Egypt	Matthew 2: 14-15
Jeremiah 31: 15	King Herod will kill all the newly born male children in his attempt to	Matthew 2: 16-18
Psalm 45: 6	The Eternal	Hebrews 1: 8
Psalm 45: 7	The Anointed	Hebrews 1: 9
Isaiah 40: 3-5	His Way will be prepared	Luke 3: 3-6
Malachi 3: 1	John the Baptist will be His forerunner	Luke 7: 24, 27
Malachi 4: 5-6	Elijah will come before His birth	Matthew 11: 13-14
Psalm 2: 7	He will be declared the Son of God	Matthew 3: 17
Psalm 78: 2	He will speak in Parables	Matthew 13: 3-51

Deuteronomy 18:15	He is the Prophet	Acts 3: 22-26
Isaiah 61: 1	He will minister to the brokenhearted	Luke 4: 18
Isaiah 53: 3	He will be rejected by His own people	John 1: 11
Psalm 110: 4	He is a Priest forever after the order of Melchizedek	Hebrews 5: 6
Zechariah 9: 9	He will ride on a colt	Mark 11: 7-10
Psalm 8: 2	He will be adored by infants, and hailed Hosanna	Matthew 21: 15-16
Isaiah 53: 1-3	Many will not believe Him	John 12: 37
Psalm 41: 9	He will be betrayed by a friend with a kiss	Luke 22: 47-48
Zechariah 11: 12	He will be betrayed, sold or traded for thirty pieces of silver	Matthew 26: 14-16

Psalm 35: 11	False witnesses	Mark 14: 56-59
Isaiah 50: 6	His accusers will smite Him, shame Him, spit on Him	Matthew 26: 67-68
Isaiah 53: 7	He will remain silent to His accusers	Mark 15: 3-5
Psalm 35: 19	He will be hated without a cause	John 19: 6, 15
Isaiah 53: 12	He will be numbered (crucified) with transgressors (thieves)	Mark 15: 27-28
Psalm 22: 7-8	He will be scorned and mocked	Luke 23: 35
Psalm 69: 9	He will be reproached	Romans 15: 3
Psalm 109: 4	He will pray for His enemies	Luke 23: 34
Psalm 22: 17-18	The soldiers will gamble for His garment	Matthew 27: 35-36
Psalm 22: 1	He will be forsaken by God	Matthew 27: 46

Psalm 34: 20	None of His bones will be broken	John 19: 32-33,36
Zechariah 12: 10	His side will be pierced	John 19: 34
Isaiah 53: 9	He will be buried with the rich	Matthew 27: 57-60
Psalm 16: 10	He will be resurrected	Matthew 28: 6; Mark 16: 6; Luke 24:6; Acts 2: 31-32
Psalm 110:1	He will ascend unto Heaven, and sit on the right hand of God	Mark 16: 19

Spiritual Exercises:

*** Write out twelve prophecies in the Old Testament about Jesus Christ and their fulfillment by Jesus Christ in the New Testament. Could you memorize these twenty-four references and share them with friends, relatives, and others? Thank you and God bless.

Rabiu Elijah Omolaja

Chapter 20
WHAT CAN WE LEARN FROM THE SEVEN CHURCHES OF ASIA?

"I John, who also am your brother, and companion in tribulation, and in the kingdom and patience of Jesus Christ, was in the isle called Patmos, for the word of God, and for the testimony of Jesus Christ. I was in the Spirit on the Lord's day, and heard behind me a great voice, as of a trumpet, saying 'I am Alpha and Omega, the first and the last: and, what thou sees, write in a book, and send it unto the seven churches which are in Asia; unto Ephe-sus, and unto Smyrna, and unto Per-ga-mos, and unto Thya-ti-ra, and unto Sar-dis, and unto Philadelphia, and unto La-od-i-ce-a."

(Revelation 1: 9–11)

Note: The seven messages to the angels of these seven churches in Asia are real messages. These messages apply to us also because the members of these congregations were Christians just like us. These messages are a divine mirror in which we view ourselves and by which we measure our own walk with Christ. I hope that by reading these messages, you will take your Christianity more seriously and follow the path that our Lord has set before us. John, the beloved apostle, is the author of the book. John was one of the members of the inner circle of Jesus Christ. History reveals that he, John, was under the persecution common to Christians at the time of his writing. He was forced to go into exile on the island called Patmos. On this island, he wrote the book of Revelation, also called Apocalypse, meaning "unveiling" or "to reveal." It is here revealed to John that Jesus is very concerned about the church, His body on earth. Jesus is concerned about how Christians are conducting themselves in a world filled with demonic activities.

1. *The Message to the angel of the Church in Ephesus:*

Unto the angel of the church of Ephesus write: These things saith he that holdeth the seven stars in His right hand, who walketh in the midst of the seven golden candlesticks; I know thy works, and thy labour, and thy patience, and how thou canst not bear them which are evil: and thou hast tried them which say they are apostles, and are not, and hast found them liars: And hast borne, and hast patience, and for my name's sake has labored, and has not fainted. Nevertheless I have somewhat against thee, because thou hast left thy first love. Remember therefore from whence thou art fallen, and repent, and do the first works; or else I will come upon thee quickly, and will remove thy candlestick out of his place, except thou repent. But this thou hast, that thou hatest the deeds of the Nicolaitanes, which I also hate. He that hath an ear, let him hear what the Spirit saith unto the churches; To him that overcometh will I give to eat of the tree of life, which is in the midst of the paradise of God.

(Revelation 2:1–7)

What are the rewards:

a. What are Jesus' commendations to this congregation?

b. What are the sins that Jesus found in this congregation?

c. What are Jesus' recommendations to this congregation?

d. What are the consequences for failure to obey Jesus' recommendations?

e. What are the rewards Jesus promised if they are obedient?

f. How can we apply this message to ourselves?

2. *The Message to the angel of the Church in Smyrna:*

And unto the angel of the church in Smyrna write; These things saith the first and the last, which was dead, and is alive; I know thy works, and tribulation, and poverty; but thou art rich, and I know the blasphemy of them which say they are Jews, and are not, but are the synagogue of Satan. Fear none of those things which thou shall suffer: behold, the devil shall cast some of you into prison, that ye may be tried;

and ye shall have tribulation ten days: be thou faithful unto death, and I will give thee a crown of life. He that hath an ear, let him hear what the Spirit saith unto the churches; He that overcometh shall not be hurt of the second death.

(Revelation 2:8–11)

Spiritual Exercises:

a. *What are Jesus' commendations to this congregation?*

b. *What are the sins that Jesus found in this congregation?*

c. *What are Jesus' recommendations to this congregation?*

d. *What are the consequences for failure to obey Jesus' recommendations?*

e. *What are the rewards Jesus promised if they are obedient?*

f. *How can we apply this message to ourselves?*

3. The Message to the angel of the Church in Pergamos:

And to the angel of the church in Pergamos write; These things saith he which hath the sharp sword with two edges; I know thy works, and where thou dwellest, even where Satan's seat is: and thou holdest fast my name, and hast not denied my faith, even in those days wherein Antipas was my faithful martyr, who was slain among you, where Satan dwelleth.

But I have a few things against thee, because thou hast there them that hold the doctrine of Balaam, who taught Balac to cast a stumbling block before the children of Israel, to eat things sacrificed unto idols, and to commit fornication. So hast thou also in them that hold the doctrine of the Nicolaitanes, which thing I hate. Repent; or else I will come unto thee quickly and will fight against them with the sword of my mouth. He that hath ear, let him hear what the Spirit saith unto the churches; To him that overcometh will I give to eat of the hidden manna, and will give him a white stone, and in the stone a new name written, which no man knoweth saving he that receiveth it.

(Revelation 2:12–17)

Spiritual Exercises:

a. *What are Jesus' commendations to this congregation?*

b. *What are the sins that Jesus found in this congregation?*

c. *What are Jesus' recommendations to this congregation?*

d. *What are the consequences for failure to obey Jesus' recommendations?*

e. *What are the rewards Jesus promised if they are obedient?*

f. *How can we apply this message to ourselves?*

Note: It is good to know that our enemy, the devil, is not omnipresent and he never will be. The devil cannot be everywhere at the same time, like our God. The devil is allowed to be present in a specific part of the world at a given time. His demonic spirits, however, may be everywhere, but the devil himself is not and cannot be. It seems the devil moves his headquarters around the world on Earth, periodically, as needed. The devil is restless. At the time the Apostle John was writing the book of Revelation, the devil's headquarters was in the city of Pergamos. The devil and his demonic forces wanted to kill the church at its birth, in its cradle, before it matured and began to spread all over the world. Thanks to God Almighty, the devil failed woefully. We need to take our salvation seriously. God still hates sin. The devil's mission is to continue to lure us to sin against God so we can share Hell with him. The devil will do everything within his power to accomplish this mission, but Greater is He that is in us than the devil and his demonic forces combined.

Know ye not that the unrighteous shall not inherit the kingdom of God? Be not deceived: neither fornicators, nor idolaters, nor adulterers, nor effeminate, nor abusers of themselves with mankind, Nor thieves, nor covetous, nor drunkards, nor revilers, nor extortioners, shall inherit the kingdom of God . . . All things are lawful unto me, but all things are not expedient: all things are lawful for me, but I will not be brought under the power of any. Meats for the belly, and the belly for meats: but God shall destroy both it and them. Now the body is not for fornication, but for the Lord; and the Lord for the body... Know ye not that your bodies are the members of Christ? Shall I then take the members of Christ, and make them the members of an harlot? God forbid. What? Know ye not that he which is joined to an harlot is one body? For two, saith he, shall be one flesh. But he that is joined to the Lord is one Spirit. Flee fornication . . .

(1 Corinthians 6: 9–18)

4. *The Message to the angel of the Church in Thyatira:*

And unto the angel of the church in Thyatira write: These things saith the Son of God, who has his eyes like unto a flame of fire, and his feet are like fine brass; I know thy works, and charity, and service, and faith, and thy patience, and thy works; and the last to be more than the first. Notwithstanding I have a few things against thee, because thou sufferest that woman Jezebel which calleth herself a prophetess, to teach and to seduce my servants to commit fornication, and to eat things sacrificed unto idols. And I gave her space to repent of her fornication; and she repented not. Behold, I will cast her into a bed, and them that commit adultery with her into great tribulation, except they repent of their deeds. And I will kill her children with death; and all the churches shall know that I am he which searcheth the reins and hearts: and I will give unto every one of you according to your works. But unto you I say, and unto the rest in Thyatira as many as have not this doctrine, and which have not known the depths of Satan, as they speak; I will put upon you none other burden. But that which ye have already hold fast till I come. And he that overcometh, and keepeth my works unto the end, to him will I give power over the nations: And he shall rule them with a rod of iron; as the vessels of a potter shall they be broken to shivers: even as I received of my Father. And I will give them the morning star. He that hath an ear, let him hear what the Spirit saith unto the churches.

(Revelation 2:18–29)

Spiritual Exercises:

a.   *What are Jesus' commendations to this congregation?*

b. *What are the sins that Jesus found in this congregation?*

c. *What are Jesus' recommendations to this congregation?*

d. *What are the consequences for failing to obey Jesus' recommendations?*

e. *What are the rewards Jesus promised if they are obedient?*

f. *How can we apply this message to ourselves?*

5. *The Message to the angel of the Church in Sardis:*

And unto the angel of the church in Sardis write: These things saith he that has the seven Spirits of God, and the seven stars; I know thy works, that thou hast a name that thou livest, and art dead. Be watchful, and strengthened the things which remain, that are ready to die, for I have not found thy works perfect before God. Remember therefore how thou hast received and heard, and hold fast, and repent. If therefore thou shalt not watch, I will come on thee as a thief, and thou shalt not know what hour I will come upon thee. Thou has a few names even in Sardis which have not defiled their garments; and they shall walk with me in white: for they are worthy. He that overcometh, the same shall be clothed in white rainment; and I will not blot out his name out of the book of life, but I will confess his name before my Father, and before his angels. He that hath an ear, let him hear what the Spirit saith unto the churches.

(Revelation 3:1–6)

Spiritual Exercises:

a. *What are Jesus' commendations to this congregation?*

b. *What are the sins that Jesus found in this congregation?*

c. *What are Jesus' recommendations to this congregation?*

d. *What are the consequences of failing to obey Jesus' recommendations?*

e. *What are the rewards Jesus promised if they are obedient?*

f.   *How can we apply this message to ourselves?*

6.   *The Message to the angel of the Church in Philadelphia:*

And to the angel of the church in Philadelphia write; These things saith he that is holy, he that is true, he that hath the key of David, he that openeth, and no man shutteth; and shutteth, and no man openeth; I know thy works: behold, I have set before thee an open door, and no man can shut it: for thou have a little strength, and hast kept my word, and hast not denied my name. Behold, I will make them of the synagogue of Satan, which say they are Jews, and are not, but do lie; behold, I will make them to come and worship before thy feet, and to know that I have loved thee. Because thou hast kept my word of patience, I also will keep thee from the hour of temptation, which shall come upon all the world, to try them that dwell upon the earth. Behold, I come quickly: hold that fast which thou hast, that no man takes thy crown. Him that overcometh will I make a pillar in the temple of my God, and he shall go no more out: and I will write upon him the name of my God, and the name of the city of my God, which is new Jerusalem, which cometh down out of heaven from my God: and I will write upon him my new name. He that hath an ear, let him hear what the Spirit saith unto the churches.

(Revelation 3:7–13)

Spiritual Exercises:

a.   *What are Jesus' commendations to this congregation?*

b.   *What are the sins that Jesus found in this congregation?*

c.   *What are Jesus' recommendations to this congregation?*

d.   *What are the consequences of failing to obey Jesus' recommendations?*

e.   *What are the rewards Jesus promised if they are obedient?*

f.   *How can we apply this message to ourselves?*

Note: There was no sin found in the churches of Smyrna and Philadelphia. Even though these two churches were facing the same temptations as the other five, both maintained a standard for Jesus

Christ. This is the desire of our Lord for every congregation, for each born-again believer, and for the collective body of Christ.

7. *The Message to the angel of the Church in Laodicea:*

And unto the angel of the church of the Laodiceans write; These things saith the Amen, the faithful and true witness, the beginning of the creation of God. I know thy works, that thou art neither cold or hot, I would that thou wert cold or hot. So then because thou art lukewarm, and neither cold nor hot: I will spue thee out of my mouth. Because thou sayest, I am rich, and increased with goods, and have need of nothing; and knowest not that thou art wretched, and miserable, and poor, and blind, and naked: I counsel thee to buy of me gold tried in the fire, that thou mayest be rich; and white raiment, that thou mayest be clothed, and that the shame of thy nakedness do not appear; and anoint thy eyes with eye salve, that thou mayest see. As many as I love, I rebuke and chasten: be zealous therefore, and repent. Behold, I stand at the door, and knock: if any man hear my voice, and open the door, I will come in to him, and I will sup with him, and he with me. To him that overcome will I grant to sit with me in my throne, even as I also overcame, and am set down with my Father in his throne. He that hath an ear, let him hear what the Spirit saith unto the churches.

(Revelation 3: 14–22)

Spiritual Exercises:

1. *What are Jesus' commendations to this congregation?*

2. *What are the sins that Jesus found in this congregation?*

3. *What are Jesus' recommendations to this congregation?*

4. *What are the consequences of failing to obey Jesus' recommendations?*

5. *What are the rewards Jesus promised if they are obedient?*

6. *How can we apply this message to ourselves?*

Chapter 21
THE STORY OF A PASTOR AND
HIS FAMOUS CONGREGATION

Allow me to share a preacher's account of his encounter with reality during one of his prayers regarding his congregation. This story was shared with us during a lecture at a Bible college in 1982. This is how the lecturer told it to us:

There was a pastor with a congregation of more than 5,000 members. This congregation appeared to be on fire for Christ to the outside world and was also rich in material things. One day, this pastor began to pray for a revelation about the status of his congregation. He prayed for many weeks, but he received no response from God. He prayed for months, and there was still no response. Then, he began to question his call into the ministry. His prayer changed from asking to begging God. He begged and begged God for a revelation, but nothing happened. Then he began to demand a revelation from God regarding the congregation He has given him to pastor. Finally, this pastor got God's attention. He went into a deep sleep. In his sleep, he saw a huge tree, full of fruits. The number of fruits on this tree was equivalent to the number of members of his congregation. They all looked the same and exceedingly appealing. Then, he heard a voice telling him, that "the fruits you see on this tree represent the members in your congregation." This pastor was extremely jubilant. He called for a party, and was doing an electric dance in his dream. Then he heard another voice telling him to start going around this fruit-bearing tree. The pastor obeyed with joy. As he was going around the tree as the voice commanded, on the seventh round, the voice asked him to look up and count the fruits. The pastor did as the voice commanded, but surprisingly, there were now only a few hundred fruits left on the tree. The pastor wanted to know what happened to the fruits. Then the voice told him to continue to go around the tree. On the second set of seven, on the seventh round, the voice told him to stop, look up, and count the fruits. There were only a few dozen of fruits left on the tree. Then, the voice told him to continue his rounds. On the third set of seven, and on the seventh round the voice asked him to stop, look up and count the fruits. At this time, there were only seven fruits left on the tree. Then, the pastor was puzzled, started sweating, and asked: "What does this mean?" God told him, "If I arrive today, at this moment, only seven of the members of your congregation will be worthy." This pastor was crying and crying in his sleep, thinking and introspecting, "Will I be one among those seven who are worthy or, will I not?

Christianity is "Life," an expression of Christ's Life on earth. Each believer is a member of the body of Christ. We are, and ought to be, the salt of the earth (Matthew 5:13) and the light of the world (Matthew 5:14–16). Christians must maintain the expression of Christly attitude at all times, even in the face of trials and tribulations (Matthew 5:10–12). If we fail to live for Him for better or for worse (Revelation 2:10), if we fail to bear our cross and follow Him as He has commanded us (Mark 10:21; Luke 9:23), we are not fit to wear the Crown. If we allow the cares of this world (1 John 2:16) to lure us away from following our Savior, we are not fit to reign with Him in His Kingdom. Only those who have become living sacrifices for the Lord will share in His Glory (Matthew 7:21– 23 and Revelation 3:21–22). Paul asked through the Holy Spirit, "What shall we say then? Shall we continue in sin, that grace may abound?" (Romans 6:1). "God forbid..." he replied in verse 2.

God Warns the Children of Israel:

God was very frank with the children of Israel. I want you to read Deuteronomy 28:1–68. This is a very powerful chapter and a strong warning against the children of Israel. God is not a man, that He should lie (Numbers 23:19). Moses, too, warned the children of Israel (Deuteronomy 31:27; Exodus 32:10; Deuteronomy 9:6–7, 13, 24). God hates disobedience. He hates rebelliousness. Rebelliousness is like witchcraft to God. God hates *stiff-necked* behaviors (Deuteronomy 10:16).

If my people, which are called by my name, shall humble themselves, and pray, and seek my face, and turn from their wicked ways; then will I hear from heaven, and will forgive their sin, and will heal their land.

(2 Chronicles 7: 14)

Jesus Himself Warned the Church:

Just as God was frank with the children of Israel, so also Jesus, in Matthew 7: 21–23, was frank with His followers. Throughout His ministry, described the criteria His followers must meet to inherit the Kingdom of Heaven. He told us how He wants us to live. As born-again believers, we must be willing to go theextra mile for our Lord. Jesus went to Hell for us so that we don't have to go there. He resurrected from the dead because death and Hell could not detain Him. At the resurrection, He said that all power in Heaven and on earth had been given to Him (Matthew 28:18). Christians may complain that the rose bushes have thorns, or we may choose to rejoice that the thorn bushes have roses.

A word to the pastors: Please don't give up and don't compromise the Word of God. Never take the Word of God lightly. Do your part as a minister and be a true representative of our Lord, Jesus Christ.

Paul wrote:

Take heed therefore unto yourselves, and to all the flock, over the which the Holy Ghost hath made you overseers, to feed the church of God, which he hath purchased with his own blood.

(Acts 20: 28)

Therefore, seeing we have this ministry, as we have received mercy, we faint not; but have renounced the hidden things of dishonesty, not walking in craftiness, nor handling the word of God deceitfully . . .

(2 Corinthians 4: 1–2)

Keep in mind that a three-member congregation that makes it to Heaven is better than five thousand members on their way to Hell. Don't sugarcoat the Word of God just to keep the building at full capacity or for financial gain. God owns the silver and the gold, the Heaven and the earth, and everything that is in and under them. He will provide. Remember that Judas Iscariot was one of the Twelve Apostles who followed the Lord, and perhaps the treasurer. He turned out to be the messenger of the devil, who betrayed the Lord with a kiss for thirty pieces of silver. Don't betray your Lord. There will always be someone in your congregation who, no matter how well you preach will not make it to Heaven. There will be some who heed your call, and if no one does, go forth alone, my friend. You can say this with me: as for me and my house, we will serve the Lord. Where He leads, we will follow. There will be no turning back. No turning back. There are no shortcuts to Heaven. Though, "It is easier to go down the hill, but the view is from the top" (Anonymous). At the mountaintop is where you and I belong. Remember that narrow is the way that leads to Heaven, and broad is the way that leads into Hell (Matthew 7:13–14). "Christianity does not remove you from the world and its problems; it makes you fit to live in it, triumphantly and usefully."[8]

Spiritual Exercises:

1. *What have you learned from this story?*

2. *If Jesus were to appear today, would you be ready?*

3. *What do you need to do today to get things right with God?*

Chapter 22
HUMANS: FROM ETERNITY
PAST TO ETERNITY FUTURE

You and I existed before our births (read Jeremiah 1:4–5). We were in existence with God before we appeared on the face of the earth. As humans, however, our lives did not begin until you and I were conceived in our mothers' wombs, at the moment when there was a unity between the sperm cells and the egg cells, when the two life substances joined together and became one. We are products of our parents' genetic properties. The abortionists are wrong in that many of them fail to recognize that human life on earth begins at conception. Though formless as it may appear, an embryo is a human being potentially and a human being in actuality. The argument about when a zygote becomes a human being is not my focus in this chapter. In this chapter, I want to take us on a journey through 1) before we were born, 2) our life on planet earth, and 3) beyond our deaths or the Rapture. I will share my understanding of human existence before being formed in our mothers' wombs according to Scripture. I will glimpse at our reign with Christ in the Millennium that is, before we start our eternal life with God according to the Scripture. Your life, according to God's Word, did not just start at conception, and it will not end after you are taken out of this body. It is important for us to know where we came from, how far we have come, and the direction we are heading.

As a child of God, you need to know where you fit today in God's program and where God wants to take you in the future. Christians must become more aware of the landmarks as we continue our journey with Christ. There are landmarks to look for and understand. What does it mean in God's program that the Israelites were becoming a nation? What is the significance of wars and rumors of wars, persecutions against the children of God, natural calamities, famine, earthquakes, ungodly behavior among the children of God, reckless lusts of the flesh, disobedience to parents, worldliness, unholiness, people without natural affection, and people having forms of godliness but denying the power thereof (2 Timothy 3:1–7). What are all these ongoing events indicating according to God's Word? Christians will not go through the great tribulation, but these occurrences are telling us that our Savior will not tarry. We are slowly but gradually getting closer to the return of our Lord.

The Eternity Past: Before the Heaven and the Earth were created

I want to start with these three questions:

Question one: "Where was God Himself before the creation?" Question two: "Where were you and I before we appeared on the planet earth?"

Question three: "What was God doing before He created the Heaven and the earth?"

Let us examine these three questions according to Scripture:

Question one: Where was God before the creation?

Answer: Before the creation, God was everywhere, according to the Scripture. He is everywhere now, or should I say that Heaven and earth cannot contain Him, according to the Scripture? (1 Kings 8: 27).

Question two: Where were you and I before we appeared on planet Earth?

Answer: Before we were born, you and I were wherever God was in eternity past. You and I were always with Him and in Him, according to the Scripture. Listen to what the Scripture says:

"...He hath chosen us in Him before the foundation of the world, that we should be holy and without blame before Him in love . . ." (Eph. 1: 4).

274

You and I existed with God from the beginning. He knew you and me by name before our parents decided to bring us into the world. He knew which of us would be born in or out of wedlock, nurtured by biological parents, or grow up in foster homes. And because He knew, glory to God! He has also given us all the strengths that we would need to endure it all. Even though God allowed these things to be, He did not necessarily approve of them. Our God is not the author of human pain and suffering, but He allowed them for some reasons we may never know or understand. Nonetheless, the life challenges and sufferings that failed to kill us made us strong, and in our weakness, God's strengths is made perfect. Scripture says that when our father and our mother forsake us, when everybody puts us down, the Lord our God will lift us up (Psalm 27:10; Isaiah 49:15).

God knows it all. He knows our trials and triumphs, our mountains and valleys, the number of hairs on our heads, the number of pores in our skin, the number of veins in our bodies, our strengths and weaknesses— God knows it all. He knows who will strive to obey or rebel against His authority. God knows all of our secrets. No one is smart enough in Heaven or on Earth to fool or surprise Him. God is omniscient, meaning that with Him there are no secrets or surprises.

Question Three: What was God doing before the creation of Heaven and earth?

Answer: 1. God was having fellowship with His Son (Proverbs 8: 22–30; John 17: 5, 24).

2. *God was creating the host of heavens (Job 38).*

3. *God was choosing the elect (Ephesians 1: 4 -5 and 2 Timothy 2: 9).*

4. *God was planning for the church (Ephesians 3: 9–11).*

5. *God was planning for a Kingdom (Matthew 25: 34).*

6. *God was planning for the Savior, for He knew that we would fall prey to the enemy and needed a Savior (1 Peter 1: 18–20; Revelation 13: 8).*

Many other things God may be doing that we have no accounts of (1 Corinthians 2: 9).

The Seven Dispensations

There are seven dispensations from the creation of Adam to the Rapture, the second coming of Christ. The Seven Dispensations are distinguished as follows: *1)* The Dispensation of Innocence, *2)* The Dispensation of Conscience, *3)* The Dispensation of Human Government, *4)* The Dispensation of Promise, *5)* The Dispensation of the Law, 6)The Dispensation of Grace, and *7)* The Rapture—the taking away of believers to be with Christ in the sky.

1. *The first Dispensation: Innocence*

The Main Event: This was a period when human beings were without sin. God was visiting and fellowshipping with Adam and his wife in the Garden of Eden in the cool of the day. There were no pains, no sweat, and no needs were going unmet. Adam and his wife were clothed in God's glory, happily married. The Dispensation of Innocence lasted from the creation of Adam until Adam and his wife ate of the fruit that God commanded them not to eat (Genesis chapters 1 and 2).

The Main Figures: Adam and Eve

The Applications: That was the best time ever for human beings on Earth. God was physically fellowshipping with Adam and Eve in the Garden of Eden. God's desire was, and still is, to fellowship with His children.

2. *The Second Dispensation: Conscience*

The Main Event: This is the reign of conscience. After the Fall— after Adam and his wife had eaten of the tree of the knowledge of good and evil—human beings became knowledgeable of sin. Adam and Eve became conscious of good and evil (read Genesis chapters 3 to 6). This dispensation lasted until God destroyed the world with the Flood.

The Main Figures: Adam, Eve, Abel, Cain, Seth, and their descendants

The Applications: The knowledge of good and evil is not the only problem in this dispensation. Adam and Eve lost the capacity to do only that which is good were more prone to do that which is evil—so also are their descendants.

3. *The Third Dispensation: Human Government*

The Main Event: This period began after the Flood of Noah. God had destroyed the human race with a flood but saved eight souls: Noah, Noah's wife, their three children, and their wives.

The Main Figures: Noah, Shem, Japheth, and Ham

The Applications: God doesn't take sin lightly. God is holy and hates sin. He warned the generation of Noah before He destroyed it with the Flood.

We know, according to Scripture, that this present world God will destroy with Fire (read 2 Peter 3:6–10). Another significant observation in this lesson is that God saved the household of Noah. That is exactly what God wants to do for your household and mine. He wants you, your spouse, and all of your children to be saved. That is why you shouldn't give up on them. Don't give up on any of your family members. It is God's desire to see them saved. Do your part and trust God in the process. You must continue to pray for your unsaved relatives if you care for them. Continue to trust God for their salvation and work with them until you see it happening. This dispensation started with Noah and continued until the call of Abraham (Genesis 12). Also, Noah's Ark is a type of Jesus Christ, our Savior. In Jesus Christ, we are protected against the just and terrible judgment of God that is coming upon the children of disobedience (2 Peter 3:6–10).

4. *The fourth Dispensation: Promise*

The Main Event: God established his covenant with Abram, stating that through him, the human race would be blessed, materially, and spiritually (Genesis 12:1–3). Abram is considered the father of faith and the father of nations. God's covenant with Abram (Genesis 15:1–18) was sealed with the *circumcision* of his and his descendants' foreskins (Genesis 17:10).

The Main Figures: Abraham, his wife Sarah, Hagar (their housemaid and the mother of Ishmael by Abram), Ishmael, Isaac, Esau, Jacob, and his children: the Twelve Tribes of Israel. Read the genealogy of Jesus Christ to see how it leads back to Abraham.

The Applications: God is faithful. What He promised, He will fulfill. The promise of the Seed that God made to Abram was fulfilled in His Son, Jesus Christ. There are more of God's promises to Abram that will be fulfilled in the future. After the Rapture has taken place, God will fulfill the rest of His promises to the house of Israel because of Abraham. The seven years of tribulation is the seventieth week of the seventy weeks spoken of by t h e Prophet Daniel in the Old Testament. The Bible is incredibly rich. May the Holy Ghost continue to illuminate our souls to understand God's plans and His purposes for humanity. The Dispensation of Promise lasted from the call of Abram in Genesis to the Exodus, when the children of Israel left the land of Pharaoh and the Law arrived. The Dispensation of Promise ended at the time when Moses received the Law on Mount Sinai.

5. *The fifth Dispensation: Law of Moses*

The Main Event: This dispensation started with the arrival of the Law on Mount Sinai and *ended* at the moment Jesus gave up the Ghost on the Cross. The Scripture says that the veil of the temple was torn in two, and dead bodies arose from their graves. Jesus atoned for humanity's sins once and for all. The Law of Moses *ended* with the death and resurrection of Jesus Christ, our Lord. Jesus entered the Holy of Holies in Heaven and ended the animal sacrifices for sins on Earth forever and ever.

Jesus, when he had cried again with a loud voice, yielded up the ghost. And behold, the veil of the temple was rent in twain from the top to the bottom; and the earth did quake, and the rocks rent; And the graves were open; and many bodies of the saints which slept arose, And came out of the graves after his resurrection, and went into the city, and appeared unto many.

(Matthew 27:50–53)

For Christ is not entered into the holy places made with hands, which are the figures of the true; but into heaven itself, now to appear in the presence of God for us. Nor yet that he should offer himself often, as the high priest entereth into the holy place every year with blood of others.

(Hebrews" 9: 24—25)

The Main Figures: Moses, Aaron, Pharaoh, and the children of Israel

Note: God was very clear to the children of Israel about how He wanted them to conduct themselves in a world filled with evil. Nevertheless, many of the children of Israel rebelled, and many died in the wilderness. Their journey to the Promised Land, which was supposed to have taken them no longer than three months, took more than forty years. For most of them, the journey was a painful experience, as it is with many of us.

The Applications: God is loving, holy, and just. The loving, holy, and just God will not compromise with evil. How is your walk with the Lord? Shall we continue in sin, that grace may abound? The Scripture says, "God forbid. How shall we..." (Romans 6:2).

6. *The sixth Dispensation: Grace—Jesus atoned for sin*

The Main Event: Jesus was born to die and to redeem the world from sin, according to God's Word from Genesis to the last book of the New Testament. The angels introduced Jesus at His conception (Luke 1:30–35) and at his birth (Luke 2:9–14). God Himself, introduced Jesus at His baptism. John was sent to precede Jesus and testified of Him as the Lamb of God "which taketh away the sin of the world" (John 1:29).

When Jesus began His ministry, He first presented His gospel of salvation to Israel, and then to the world. Many of His own did not believed him, according to the Scripture. Jesus was accused, tortured, belittled, ridiculed, and was hanged by the hands of those that He came to save. He died a painful death. He cried sorrowfully, asking God, "Eloi, Eloi . . . My God, my God, why hast thou forsaken me?" (Mark 15:34). Jesus died and went to Hell for three days for us. Glory to God, Hell could not contain Him. Jesus rose from the dead on the third day. He showed Himself to many for forty days (Acts 1:3), then ascended to Heaven, and He is now sitting at the right hand of God, interceding for us. Born of a woman, Jesus came as a servant, as a Son of Man, and also, as the *Son* of God. He is coming back as the *King* in charge, as the Lord God *Himself.* You better believe it. Your unbelief will not change the divine truth.

The Main Figures: John, the Angel Gabriel, Mary, Judas Iscariot, the rest of the apostles, Paul the latter apostle, the Pharisees, the Sadducees, the Priests, Jews, political leaders, the Roman rulers, the children of Israel, the early Christians, and the rest of the people in the world who were for or against Christ, our Lord. *Jesus Christ is the Main Figure in this dispensation.*

The Applications: Have you accepted the Gospel of Jesus Christ? There is no other name under Heaven among men by which you may be saved (read Acts 4:12 and 1 Timothy 2:5). This is where we are today in God's plan. We are in the Dispensation of Grace. Grace means Love. Grace means Mercy. Grace means Forgiveness. Grace means switching places with Jesus Christ, who took ownership of our sins and nailed them to the cross. Jesus went to Hell for us and gave us His Righteousness. Through His blood we are redeemed back unto God. In Christ, you and I have become God's property, separated from the world unto God.

7. *The seventh Dispensation: The Rapture*

The Main Event: Our Homecoming. This is the event that every born-again Christian has been waiting for. This event may take place before you finish reading this book. No one knows the exact time the Rapture will occur except God. Let us look at what the Scripture says about the Rapture:

But I would not have you to be ignorant, brethren, concerning them which are asleep, that ye sorrow not, even as others which have no hope. For if we believe that Jesus died and rose again, even so them also which sleep in Jesus will God bring with him. For this we say unto you by the word of the Lord, that we which are alive and remain unto the coming of the Lord shall not prevent them which are asleep. For the Lord himself shall descend from heaven with a shout, with the voice of archangel, and with the trump of God: and the dead in Christ shall rise first: Then we which are alive and remain shall be caught up together with them in the clouds, to meet the Lord in the air: and so shall we ever be with the Lord.

Wherefore comfort one another with these words. (1 Thessalonians 4: 13—18)

Behold . . . we shall not all asleep, but we shall all be changed. In a moment, in the twinkling of an eye, at the last trump: for the trumpet shall sound, and the dead shall be raised incorruptible, and we shall be changed. For this corruptible must put on incorruption, and this mortal must put on immortality. So when this corruptible shall have put on incorruption, and this mortal shall have put on immortality, then shall be brought to pass the saying that is written, Death is swallowed up in victory. O death, where is thy sting? O grave, where is thy victory?

(1 Corinthians 15: 51–55)

The Main Figures: Jesus Christ, His angels, and His church—the believers.

The Applications: Christians must prepare daily to meet their Lord.

Once you have believed in the Lord Jesus Christ, you need to start learning about Him. You must begin to study the Word, live by the Word and learn to trust in God, and not leaning on your own understanding. God is able to preserve your salvation in His Son to the end, according to the Scripture (Philippians 1:6). Jesus is coming back, as promised (John 14:1–3).

We will see Him as He is. He is the Lord of lords, the Judge of all.

He is coming back to reign and to judge the living and the dead.

For we must all appear before the judgment seat of Christ; that everyone may receive the things done in his body, according to that he hath done, whether it be good or bad.

(2 Corinthians 5: 10)

Every man's work shall be made manifest: for the day shall declare it, because it shall be revealed by fire; and the fire shall try every man's work of what sort it is. If any man's work abide which he hath built there upon, he shall receive a reward. If any man's work shall be burned, he shall suffer lost: but he himself shall be saved; yet so as by fire. (1 Corinthians 3: 13—15)

We need to know that Hell was made for the Devil and his angels; Hell was not made for human beings. God doesn't want any of us in Hell. - Matthew 25:41. If we end up in Hell, it is not God's fault; it is simply because we chose to go there by the choices we are making. Going to Hell is a choice. God doesn't want us in Hellfire.

For God so loved the world that He gave His Only Begotten Son, that whosoever believes in Him shall not perish but have eternal life – John 3:16

Jesus is coming as a thief in the night. Will you be ready when He comes for His own? Will He find you ready? We must be saved and stay saved each day. Our salvation is now, today —not yesterday or tomorrow. We need to make sure we are always saved, right now, at this moment, every second. Jesus is coming at any time to take us home. Rapture is the next thing on God's agenda, and it can take place before you finish reading this page. We are going home to be with the Lord. Do you believe in Rapture? It is real and coming soon. If you don't believe in Rapture, you need to read the words of Jesus Christ before He left the earth in the gospel of John.

Let not your heart be troubled: ye believe in God, believe also in me. In my Father's house are many mansions: if it were not so, I would have told you. I go to prepare a place for you. And if I go and prepare a place for you, I will come again and receive you unto myself; that where I am, there ye may be also. - John 14: 1- 3.

Consider the Parable of the 10 Virgins: Jesus cannot lie:

Then shall the kingdom of heaven be likened unto ten virgins, which took their lamps, and went forth to meet the bridegroom. And five of them were wise, and five were foolish. They that were foolish took their lamps and took no oil with them: But the wise took oil in their vessels with their lamps. While the bridegroom tarried, they all slumbered and slept. And at midnight there was a cry made, Behold, the bridegroom cometh; go ye out to meet him. Then all those virgins arose and trimmed their lamps. And the foolish said unto the wise, give us of your oil; for our lamps are gone out. But the wise answered, saying, Not so; let there be not enough for us and you: but go ye rather to them that sell, and buy for yourselves. And while they went to buy, the bridegroom came; and they that were ready went in with him to the marriage: and the door was shut. Afterward came also the other virgins, saying, Lord, Lord, open to us. But he answered and said, Verily I say unto you, I know you not. Watch therefore, for ye know neither the day nor the hour wherein the Son of man cometh - Matthew 25: 1-13.

Don't Be a Foolish Virgin

Now that we have established that the Rapture is real, you need to be ready at all times; don't be a foolish virgin. I want you to consider this scenario: you are a believer living obediently and applying the words of God to your everyday life. But one day, you just wanted to please your flesh for a change, just one time, thinking that all you have to do is repent quickly when you are done doing the ungodly. Let us say your fleshly desire is to rob a bank, or steal from your spouse, or kill somebody, or it is just a desire for sexual immorality- adultery or fornication- and you acted on your desire. But, as you are in the middle of the action, as you get the action going, all of a sudden, the trumpet sounds, Then, here He is: Jesus appears in the sky, coming for His own with His holy angels. But you are in the act of committing your desired sin, and you haven't had the chance to repent of your sin. Tell me, what will Jesus do with you?

God spoke to us in Ezekiel saying: Therefore, thou son of man, say unto the children of thy people, The righteousness of the righteous shall not deliver him in the day of his transgression: as for the wickedness of the wicked, he shall not fall thereby in the day that he turned from his wickedness; neither shall the righteous be able to live for his righteousness in the day that he sinned. When I shall say to the righteous, that he shall surely live; if he trusts to his own righteousness, and commit iniquity, all his righteousness's shall not be remembered; but for his iniquity that he hath committed, he shall die for it. Again, when I say unto the wicked, thou shalt surely die; if he turns from his sin and do that which is lawful and right; If the wicked restore the pledge, give again that he had robbed, walk in the statutes of life, without committing iniquity; he shall surely live, he shall not die. None of his sins that he hath committed shall be mentioned unto him: he hath done that which is lawful and right; he shall surely live. Ezekiel 33: 12-16.

In Matthew 7: 21-23, Jesus says this:

Not everyone that saith unto me, Lord, Lord, shall enter into the kingdom of heaven; but he that doeth the will of my Father which is in heaven. Many will say to me in that day, Lord, Lord, have we not prophesied in thy name? and in thy name have cast out devils? and in thy name done many wonderful works? And then will I profess unto them, I never knew you: depart from me, ye that work iniquity.

We must be saved and stay saved day by day. Our salvation is now, today, not yesterday or tomorrow. We need to make sure we are saved today, right now, at this moment, and every second. Jesus is coming at any time, like a thief in the night, to take us home. Do not be a foolish virgin.

The Eternity Future

At The Rapture, Christians will begin a new life. We will be living with our Lord and Savior. The Rapture is the beginning of our "Eternity Future." When living with Christ, Christians will taste the goods of Heaven, while the people we will leave behind on earth during the great tribulation, will experience the horror of Hell for seven terrible years.

People will be in so much pain that they will seek death, but death will flee from them. Read the book of Revelation, chapters 6 through 20. Somewhere in the middle of these seven terrible years, two witnesses will appear on earth. The two witnesses will appeal to the nation of Israel one more time. The Scripture says that 144,000 of the children of Israel, from all the twelve tribes, will be sealed for God (Revelation 7:2–8) to fulfill His promise to Abraham. These 144,000 souls will refuse the mark (666) of the beast, and God will preserve them for Himself because of His promise. Shortly after the selection of these 144,000 souls, the beast will war against the two witnesses, according to the Scripture. The two witnesses will be killed, and their bodies will remain in the street for three and a half days, according to the Scripture (Revelation 11:3–12). After the end of the three and a half days, a voice will come from Heaven, and these two witnesses will rise to their feet and ascend into Heaven, according to the Scripture. All eyes will behold them as they ascend unto Heaven, according to the Scripture. Glory and honor to our God. He is the God Almighty, unto whom every knee shall bow. What He preserves, no one can destroy; what He destroys, no one can preserve. Father, I thank You for loving me, and I thank you for helping me to accept Your Love.

Spiritual Exercises:

1. *Where were you and I in the Eternity Past according to the Scripture?* _____

2. *How many dispensations are described in this book?* _____

3. *What is the significance of each of the 7 dispensations to you?* _____

4. *What is The Rapture, and what does it mean to a Christian?*

   _____

5. *Describe briefly what would be the conditions on the earth after the Rapture.* _____

6. *There were 10 virgins. How many of them were foolish?*

   _____

7. *Are you a ready virgin, waiting eagerly for the Lord? Yes/No*

   _____

The voice of wisdom

I love them that love me, and those that seek me early shall find me. Riches and honor are with me, durable riches and righteousness. My fruit is better than gold, yea, than fine gold; and my revenue than choice silver. I lead in the way of righteousness, in the midst of the paths of judgment: That I may cause those that love me to inherit substance; and I will fill their treasures. The Lord possessed me in the beginning of his way, before his works of old. I was set up from everlasting, from the beginning, or ever the earth was. When there were no depths, I was brought forth; when there were no fountains abounding with water. Before the mountains were settled, before the hill was I brought forth: While as yet he had not made the earth, nor the fields, nor the highest part of the dust of the world. When he prepared the heavens, I was there: when he set a compass upon the face of the depth: When he established the clouds above: when he strengthened the fountains of the deep: When he gave to the sea his decree, that the water should not pass his commandment: when he appointed the foundations of the earth: Then, I was by him, as one brought up with him: and I was daily his delight, rejoicing always before him; rejoicing in his habitable part of his earth; and my delights were with the son of men. Now therefore hearken unto me, O ye children: for blessed are they that keep my ways. Hear instructions, and be wise, and refuse it not. Blessed is the man that heareth me, watching daily at my gates, waiting at the posts of my doors. For whoso findeth me findeth life and shall obtain favour of the Lord.

But he that sinneth against me wronged his own soul: all they that hate me love death.

(Proverbs 8: 17–36)

Summary

I hope I have testified to the goodness of God and His mercy towards me. I strongly believe that what He has done for me, He wants to do the same or more for you. As He has delivered me from all my afflictions, He wants to deliver you from yours as well, according to 1 Corinthians 10: 13; Psalm 34: 19; Jeremiah 29: 11. These are God's promises to you and me, and there are many more.

I hope that this book has stimulated your soul enough that you will now begin to take a second look at your own existence and become more aware of God's presence and involvement in your life. It is my hope that reading this book will help increase your faith and trust in the Lord. Jesus redeemed my soul on July 27, 1974, and my life is no longer the same (2 Corinthians 5:17). Jesus took me out of a thick darkness and brought me into a marvelous light. He is the Author and the Finisher of my faith. Jesus took ownership of my sins. He took my imperfections in exchange for His perfections. In Him, I am made perfect. Yes, Jesus is alive, and He lives in me. (Revelation 1:18). I pray that God will keep you and preserve you until the end in Jesus' name. If you feel blessed by reading this book, please be sure to recommend it to others. Let us be a witness for Him who hath died and washed away our sins. He made us as white as snow. Though He was dead, He is alive forevermore. He rose from the dead, ascended into Heaven, and He is coming back according to the Scripture (Acts 1:9–11). Jesus Christ is coming back to take us home, with Him. Heaven is our Home. Home Sweet Home. Our mansions are waiting for us (John 14: 2-3) in Heaven, where there would be no more pain, and no more hunger. It is a place of peace and everlasting joy.

Father God, I thank you for loving me, and for sending Your Son, Jesus Christ, to die for my sins. I know that without You, I am nothing; I have nothing, and I can do nothing. Unto You, O Lord, I surrender. Thy Will O Lord! Amen.

Bibliography

"The New Open Bible, Study Edition." The Scarlet Thread of Redemption. Thomas Nelson: 1992.

"The New Webster Quotation Dictionary." Templeton, Lexicon Publications: 1987.

Willmington, Dr. H.L. "A Pictorial Journey through the Old Testament." Liberty Home Bible Institute: 1979.

Turner, Rex Allwin. "Sermons and Addresses on the Fundamentals of Faith." Rex A. Turner: 1972.

Corey, Gerald. "Theory and Practice of Counseling and Psychotherapy." 4th Edition. Brooks/Cole Publishing Company: 1991.

La Place, Ph. D., John. "Health." 4th Edition. Prentice Hall Inc. Englewood New Cliffs, Jersey: 1984.

Willix, Jr., M.D., Robert D. "3 Minutes a Day to a 120 Year Lifespan." 1994.

Endnotes

1. *Turner, pg. 40, 1972.*

2. *The New Open Bible, Study Edition, 1990. "The Scarlet Thread of Redemption."*

3. *Corey, pg. 176, 1991*

4. *Wilmington, H.L. Liberty Home Bible Institute, 1979.*

5. *Willix, Pgs. 16–17, 1994.*

6. *Willix, Pg. 17, 1994.*

7. *La Place, pg. 304, 1984*

8. *Templeton, Charles. Webster Quotation Dictionary Pg. 45, 1987*